# A Practical Handbook of
# LANGUAGE TEACHING

## David Cross
Ecole Normale Supérieure, Abidjan

Edited by C. Vaughan James

ENGLISH LANGUAGE TEACHING

## Prentice Hall
New York  London  Toronto  Sydney  Tokyo  Singapore

Published 1992 by
Prentice Hall International (UK) Limited
Campus 400, Maylands Avenue
Hemel Hempstead
Hertfordshire HP2 7EZ
A division of
Simon & Schuster International Group

First published 1991 by Cassell Publishers Limited

Typeset by Fakenham Photosetting Ltd,
Fakenham, Norfolk

Printed and bound in Great Britain by
Redwood Books, Trowbridge, Wiltshire

British Library Cataloguing in Publication Data

A catalogue record for this book is available
from The British Library

ISBN 0-13-380957-9

2  3  4  5  6     98  97  96  95  94

# Contents

requiring some preparation (the magnet board, the felt board, wall posters, the portable blackboard, the whiteboard, worksheets)

tasks); guided writing (examples of guided writing tasks); writing
from maps, graphs and statistical data, pen friends

Language, communication and meaning; discussions and debate
(organising discussion groups, using discussion cues, project
presentations, topic talks); drama activities (role adoption, prescribed
role play, free role play, free role play from a text); the
communicative approach and the information gap (the nature of
information gap materials, adapting the communicative approach for
large classes, information gap activities)

# Acknowledgements

I would like to begin by thanking the Overseas Development Administration and the British Council for the opportunity to take part in two teacher education projects, in collaboration with the respective Ministries of Education. The book is very much the outcome of that experience. Of seminal importance was the curriculum development work conducted at the Centre for Developing English Language Teaching, Ain Shams University, Cairo. Dr Abdil Messih Daoud, Director of the Centre, led the project on behalf of the Egyptian authorities. The British Council role was managed by Dr Roger Bowers.

The structuring of the book, and the lesson models, closely reflect the training and teaching curricula and materials which were evolved during an Advanced Trainer Program at Ohio University, Athens, Ohio, USA, where I worked with trainers from many different parts of the world, analysing training needs for teacher education in their respective countries. I extend my thanks to my faculty colleagues there, as well as to the course participants.

I also thank Dr Amon Tchy and my fellow members of the TEFL department at the Ecole Normale Supérieure d'Abidjan. The institution provides initial training programmes and full time upgrading courses for experienced teachers. I regularly observe ENS trainees and colleagues applying the techniques and using material of a similar nature to those shown here during training and teaching practices, often with classes of up to 100 students. In finalising this book, I frequently had them and their classroom conditions in mind. I would particularly like to put on record my debt to two close friends who gave me advice and encouragement, as well as a great deal of their own time. Art Fell read all the chapters in their pilot versions, making me clarify issues and state them more simply. The reworked chapters then went to Alan Moore, a British Council English Language Teaching Officer with a lifetime's experience of teaching, training and materials development in many countries of the world. As well as reading critically, Alan identified several additional areas of need.

Special thanks go to my family. Daughters Lorraine and Sandra did all the graphics and my wife Marianne typed and retyped several early versions of the book, which is really a family effort.

Finally, I am grateful to my editor, Vaughan James, who encouraged me over several years in the writing and helped in finalising the form of presentation. Without him, the book would never have seen the light of day.

The efforts of all these colleagues and friends were invaluable in effecting improvements to the book, but opinions expressed and any defects in the final version are my own.

DAVID CROSS, ECOLE NORMALE SUPERIEURE D'ABIDJAN 1991

# Introduction

Experience as a teacher, trainer and trainer educator in different parts of the world has made me aware of the need for a comprehensive training manual which can be used in a self-access mode. The majority of language teachers have experienced little or no structured, practical initial training. Opportunities to take part in systematic in-service training programmes are rare, almost universally. Where there is a provision, teachers are often unable to attend regularly, for a host of social and financial reasons.

The aim of this handbook is to meet the needs of teachers and trainees, as well as those of their advisers, by combining the essentials of successful classroom management and teaching in a single, easily read volume. Thoughtful study, perhaps coupled with discussion with colleagues, should enable readers to learn to teach or to improve their teaching, quite independently. The emphasis throughout is on practicality. Activities based on the use of sophisticated equipment, or which are suited only to privileged settings, are not included. Theoretical issues do not receive undue emphasis, but readers are made aware of the rationale underlying any technique or approach.

There are no right answers in pedagogy, so there is no attempt to work towards a standardised teaching style wedded to a theory of learning or of linguistics. Questions arise, even with the most basic issues of teaching, to which solutions will depend on a host of factors. An idiosyncratic and eclectic approach, though, is only possible when practitioners have a wide range of techniques and strategies at their command. This book provides a repertoire of specific skills from which readers can fashion an approach appropriate to their own personality, local restraints and the preferred learning style of their students.

The four parts of the book cover the necessary component skills and knowledge areas in a roughly hierarchical way, with the most essential coming first. Although most examples are from the teaching of English as a foreign language (TEFL), everything is applicable also to the teaching of other modern languages.

*Part One* comprises six chapters and covers the most fundamental instructional skills and procedures. *Part Two* deals with a range of lesson types which incorporate all the skills demonstrated in the first part of the book. By the end of these eleven chapters, readers should be able to plan lessons and exploit the textbook in a lively way, encouraging spontaneity and natural language use. They will have learned to plan and execute four basic but flexible lesson types, focusing on listening, reading, role play and speaking, with writing in a supportive role.

The next two sections deal with valuable but less essential teaching skills, activities and strategies. In *Part Three* there are chapters which cover testing, teaching pronunciation, and using games, songs and rhymes. Additionally,

1

readers are shown how to extend and optimise learning time by the use of effective homework and revision. *Part Four* moves from basic pedagogy into a more communicative style of teaching. Although the skills of reading, listening, speaking and writing receive separate attention, the teaching is integrated, with the focus largely on authentic uses of language. Communicative language teaching is not easy for teachers who work with large classes, often with three students crammed onto one heavy bench. Even so, it *can* be introduced, though with modifications of materials and organisation.

Where tutors or trainers are available, the book can be used for both pre-service and in-service training. The first two parts form a self-contained initial-training programme. Because of the self-access style, much more ground can be covered than is the case with the usual filter-down approach to training. If the book is used in this way, the trainees should read a chapter at home, then meet for follow-up discussions and workshop activities. At these meetings, they would practise the techniques and activities in peer-teaching and micro-teaching situations. They would also produce materials and modify the worked examples to match their own textbook and classroom context. Each chapter carries enough substance for several practical training sessions of this sort. Ideally, trainees would observe each other applying the techniques in real classroom conditions during any subsequent or parallel teaching practice. Classroom observation instruments are easily devised to offer a checklist of the skills covered; the lesson planning chapter will be especially useful at this time.

The remainder of the book might be used as a manual for in-service courses, where teachers have already followed a comprehensive and practical pre-service programme. If so, training should be handled in the same way, with teachers reading and coming to training sessions primed for discussion and workshops. The order in which the later chapters are treated is less important, though several are clearly interdependent. Again, one chapter carries the substance of several two-hour training sessions. As a whole, the volume provides a coherent curriculum for teaching and training and continuing education for several years.

# Part One

# BASIC LANGUAGE TEACHING SKILLS

1 Presenting and practising vocabulary

2 Presenting and practising structures

3 Presenting and practising grammar points

4 Conducting meaningful drills

5 Managing pair and group work

6 Oral work: elicitation techniques

# 1 Presenting and practising vocabulary

## ■ THE IMPORTANCE OF VOCABULARY TEACHING

A good store of words is crucial for understanding and communication. A major aim of most teaching programmes is to help students to gain a large vocabulary of useful words. In every lesson, you have to introduce new words and practise them, making clear the meanings and the ways in which each can be used. In the pages that follow you will learn how to introduce vocabulary, how to practise it in a variety of ways and how to revise it.

There are two main ways to present (introduce) vocabulary. You can either *show* the meaning in some way or you can **use language** that the students already know in order to make clear the meaning of the new lexical item.[1] There is a third way, too, but one that is little used. You can present meanings through *sounds*. This third way is also described, as it offers yet another approach to the problem of introducing difficult words. During most lessons, you will use both of the first two ways. There are several techniques that may be used, whether you are working linguistically or ostensively. Some words are very easy to present (nouns, verbs, adverbs and adjectives). Some are more difficult because they represent abstract notions. Yet other words have no independent meaning, and so they cannot be presented in the same ways. These are the *grammar* words – eg articles, conjunctions, auxiliaries and some prepositions, and so on. They will normally become part of a grammar presentation rather than being introduced as lexical items.

Words have **form**. The form is a word's **shape**, when written, and its **sound**, when spoken. Some teachers believe that learners should always **hear a new** word before they say it and **say** it before they **read** it. Not everyone agrees. Many are convinced that learning is assisted if the written form is presented at the same time as the sound form. You should experiment to find what is best for your own learners. Remember that what is right for young students may not be best for older ones.

## ■ MODES OF PRESENTATION

There are several ways of making clear the meaning of a word, and these may be used alone or in combination.

### Ostensive means

Ostensive means *by showing*. Obviously, you can hold up things or point to objects in the classroom (such as *pen, bag, tallest boy, brown bag, my book*). This approach is widely used with beginner classes, but its potential with mature learners should not be neglected. You need not limit ostensive techniques to only those things which can be found in the room. There are also ways to show the meaning of words and concepts from the world outside the school, as you will see now.

### Realia

We call objects **realia**, real things. Realia can often be brought to school: a piece of bread or fruit, a whistle, a stick, toys, eggs and so on are easily carried. They also create interest. Use your imagination too. *Puddles* are found in the street when it rains, but you can bring in a small bottle of water and create a puddle by pouring some water onto the floor. *Crashes* and *skids* can be represented by the use of model cars or planes.

### Pictures

Objects that are not easily carried or which are unavailable can be represented pictorially. You will be collecting useful pictures from magazines as a matter of course, but often you will not have the one you need, or the one you have may contain too many unnecessary details. For presentation purposes, simple pictures are better because the focus is clearer and the meaning is less ambiguous. Use the blackboard to make rapid sketches of simple things such as a tyre, a cabin or a cat. It takes more time to draw more complex items such as a telephone, a zebra, a skyscraper or the beach. These should be drawn at home on a **flashcard**, using a thick felt tip pen and a large sheet of paper. Abstract concepts such as *last week*, *tomorrow*, *late* or *early* can be conveyed by use of a cardboard clock and a calendar. Use your imagination and you will be surprised at what you can contrive visually to help the students to understand.

### Body

Your body and those of the students can be used to get meanings across. These are the techniques you will use:

i. facial expression, to show feelings (eg happy, smiling, hot, thirsty, angry, tired),
ii. gesture, using hands and arms to show a range of meanings (eg fast, small, curving, wide, rolling),
iii. mime and actions, to show many verbs and some adverbs (eg to stagger, to eat, to slip, to wake up, slowly, angrily).

## Verbal definition

There are several ways to define the meaning of a new word using **teacher talk**.[2] Obviously, a linguistic approach is not suited to beginner classes as they do not have a large enough vocabulary to understand your explanation. You can use any of the following means to help comprehension.

### Word sets

Word sets are groups or related words, such as *child, boy, girl, infant, youngster, teenager*. You can use the words in a set that the students already know in order to introduce new related words. A concept such as *clothing* can easily be conveyed by giving different examples of items of clothing. The same would apply to other general words of that sort (transport, furniture, vegetables). You can work in reverse to present a more specific word. For example, to present the word *canary*, you would start from the already known concept of *bird*.

### Synonyms

Synonyms are words that mean more or less the same thing. Take the word *coach*, for example. It is a *bus*, but one that makes long distance journeys. Similarly, a *shrub* is a small *bush*, *damp* means *humid*, and so on. Synonyms are best shown on the board using the mathematical sign for *equals*, as in the following example.[3]

```
fierce = savage    unhappy = sad
shore = beach      residence = home
```

### Antonyms

Antonyms are words that have an opposite meaning. For example, *poor* is the opposite of *rich* while *dirty* is the opposite of *clean*. The sign to indicate an opposite meaning is an equals sign crossed through, in this way:

```
hot ≠ cold         full ≠ empty
```

### Cognates

Cognates are words in the students' own language that have the same, or very similar, form as the English word. If the students' mother tongue or second language is related to English there will be many hundreds, perhaps thousands, of such words available and readily comprehensible. It would be illogical to ignore this rich and readily available language resource.

Some teachers are fearful of using cognates extensively because they have

7

heard of *faux amis*. These are words which resemble each other in the two languages but which do not share the same meaning. It would be wrong to exaggerate this danger. There are many times more cognates than there are faux amis. Any bilingual French and English speaker, for example, could list hundreds of cognates, but would have difficulty to think of even a few faux amis.

*Illustrative sentences*

You can contrive a sentence or a sequence of sentences to create a linguistic context in which the meaning of the one unknown word is *illustrated* (becomes clear). Most words that cannot be explained in the easier ways above can be presented in this way. In the two examples that follow one has a good illustrative setting, the other has not. Can you see why this is so?

**Example 1: Hates**
My father *hates* potatoes, but he loves rice. He likes carrots, beans and most other vegetables, but he refuses to eat potatoes. He *hates* them.

**Example 2: Traffic**
There is a lot of *traffic* in cities. *Traffic* is a nuisance. *Traffic* is dangerous too.

The meaning of *to hate* has been made clear in the first example by contrasting it with *to like*. The teacher ensured that the class did not equate the new verb with the weaker meaning, *to dislike*, by insisting on the man's *refusal* to eat potatoes.

The second example is a poor one, though. The meaning of *traffic* is not made clear – pollution, smoke, drug dealing, and so on, are also a dangerous nuisance. It would be better to say:

There are many cars, buses, taxis and motor-bikes in the city centre. There are many vehicles passing through the streets. The *traffic* is heavy in the city.

Of course, the illustrative sentences that you write on the board, to be copied by the class, need to be as short as possible. For the two words, above, you might write:

```
to hate:
    Students hate punishments.


traffic:
    Road traffic is light at night.
```

*Build on general knowledge*

Capitalise on what the learners know about the world. For example, they know the names of the major towns in their own country. Therefore the points of the compass might be introduced in this way:

> North, South, East, West (*drawing the 4 cardinal points on the blackboard*).
> Our capital city is in the *south* of the country. The town of A is in the *west*. B is in the centre and to the *north* of B we have the town C. In the *east* are the towns of D and E.

The names of local towns and villages will help learners understand the difference between *near* and *not far from*. The names of local streets will enable you to introduce *market place*, *roundabout* and *bus terminus*. You can make use, too, of the students' interests and their knowledge of music, sports, school affairs and personalities to introduce new words.

*Scales*

You can show the meaning of some types of words by sequencing them along a scale between two antonyms. For example, between the extremes of *horrible* and *wonderful* we might have *nasty*, *unpleasant*, *pleasant* and *nice*, in that order. Temperatures of bath water run along a scale from *cold* to *hot*, through *lukewarm*, *tepid*, *warm* and *scalding*. To introduce a new word into such a set, just indicate its place on the scale.

Imagine that you have to present the words *rarely* and *frequently*. Begin by putting the two antonyms *never* and *always* on the blackboard. Then you can elicit other adverbs of frequency that the students already know. The board might then look something like the following:

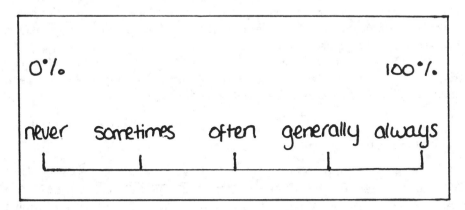

Next you elicit things that the students do, getting them to use those adverbs. Then you indicate a point between *never* and *sometimes* and say:

> I *rarely* lose my temper in class. Sometimes I'm angry but I *rarely* lose my temper (*putting a cross after never*).

> Is there anything that *you* rarely do? What about flying? Do you ever travel by air?

Having elicited activities that the students do, but only rarely, you indicate the space between *often* and generally, saying:

> However, I *frequently* have a lot of marking to do, so I *frequently* stay late at school (*putting a cross after generally*). Are there activities that you frequently do?

Having elicited things that the learners frequently do, you add the new words to the scale and have the whole scale copied. Practice or homework can in the form of having students write true sentences about themselves or friends, using the new adverbs.

### Translation

Translation can be used when no easy alternative suggests itself. Faced with a grammar word or a formulaic expression like *Have you by any chance . . . ?*, it is sometimes better to give the mother tongue equivalent, rather than to spend a great deal of time trying to define or show the meaning. The time saved can be used more profitably on other teaching points.

## Audio presentation

We come now to the third, very much under-used, way of signalling the meaning of a word. Many words are more easily presented by a tape recording than by the ways already described. The noises of an *argument*, a *jet plane*, a *locomotive*, a horse *galloping*, children *splashing* in water, a river *gurgling*, and so on, are easily obtained or created. The presentation procedure is simple. You just tell the class to listen to the sound of . . .

In an earlier example, the teacher took a great deal of trouble in contriving a linguistic context for the concept of *traffic*. Would it not have been easier and quicker to play traffic noises on a cassette recording?

## Running context

Whatever the mode of presentation, try to link all the new words in some way. This can be done after the presentation of the words as separate entities or during the entire presentation. In this way you make what is called a running context. This adds interest, as you tell what becomes a little story during or after the presentation stage. Supposing you were presenting *flood*, *thunder*, and *collapse*. The story of a storm with heavy rain which caused a house in your village to collapse, would create interest as the three new words are introduced. You would probably use a picture, or you might bring in a pack of playing cards and build a card house to demonstrate the meaning of *to collapse*. The important thing is to assist the process of memorisation by linking the lesson's new words in an interesting way if possible.

# ■ CHOOSING WHICH VOCABULARY TO PRESENT

You have to exercise judgement in deciding how many words to present in a lesson. There is no firm rule, but most teachers feel that 5 to 7 new words are enough for formal attention. The belief is that students can only internalise about half a dozen new words during a 40 minute lesson.[4]

The words that you select for presentation should be words of special value, but which are not guessable in the textual context. By words of special value, we do not just mean words like *postage stamp* or *soap*, useful though such words are. We are thinking more of a word's immediate value for use in the classroom, for activities and for talking about the students' own lives and interests. Underline all the unknown words in the day's text. Choose just a few of these for formal presentation.

Almost everyone agrees on one point when considering which lexical items to present. It would be wrong to present every single new word in the text. An important part of your task is to prepare students for the real world, where they will have to cope with spoken or written language containing words they do not know. Leave all guessable words unpresented.

Be critical of texts. Sometimes, there are words in reading passages which it would be a waste of time to teach because of their low value. In such cases it really is best not to lose time on them. Just throw in a quick explanation or translation of the word when you reach it in the text.

## Developing guesswork strategies

It is well worthwhile spending time on any sentence which has an unknown word in order to develop the students' guesswork strategies. Often they will be able to identify the grammatical category (even if they themselves do not know the terminology) as soon as they have developed a feel for English word order. If a word follows a determiner, it is probably a noun. If there is an unknown word between a determiner and a noun, it is probably an adjective. If the word follows an auxiliary, it may well be a verb. A word ending in *-ly* is probably an adverb, and so on. Provided they understand most of the words in the phrase, the whole thing becomes like an exercise in substitution, with the class calling possible words and finally choosing the most apt from the list that you have built up from their suggestions. Only then will you explain the exact meaning of the unknown word.

# ■ A STEP BY STEP PRESENTATION PROCEDURE

There are four steps to follow. You will bring in some or all of the ostensive and linguistic techniques described above as you make the series of five or six presentations.

*Step one: sound and the meaning*
Say the new word two or three times, pronouncing it clearly. Indicate the

meaning at the same time, ostensively or verbally. There is no point in making learners listen to strange noises which are meaningless.

### Step two: repetition

Get the class to repeat the new word a few times. Check the pronunciation carefully. If you are using a visual, keep it in front of them to ensure that they associate sound and meaning.

### Step three: written form

Write the new word on the blackboard and have the class read it aloud, without distorting the pronunciation. First, choose two or three individuals to say it, then get a chorus repetition so that everyone in the class has the opportunity to associate the written form with the pronunciation. In some countries, advisers insist that you also use phonetic script to indicate the pronunciation. If you are obliged to do this, do it with discretion. It is unnecessary, for example, to indicate the pronunciation of *cat* or *British*, as the spellings cannot cause confusion. On rare occasions you might need to write the phonetic script for the whole word, but often you will only want to draw attention to one syllable or phoneme, for example the *z* sound in *surprise*.

### Step four: illustrative sentence

Now put a short illustrative sentence on the board so that the meaning will be clear to anyone reading the notes afterwards. Your students will enjoy trying to compose good illustrative sentences themselves, but prepare your own short one in case their own are too wordy or not clear enough for the blackboard example. Do not take more than three or four suggestions before you choose one to be written on the board, otherwise you will never get beyond the Presentation Stage. If you have shown the meaning by use of a flashcard, stick the picture to the side of the board next to the illustrative sentence. Youngsters will enjoy drawing a similar one in their exercise books, at home.

That is the whole procedure. You will have to follow it for each word you present. Here, though, are a few more considerations.

## Practice

It is not enough just to present words and have them repeated. The students must *use* words if they are to internalise them. It is a simple matter to ask some **extension questions**. These are asked after the words have been presented and are all on the board, but before the text is seen. The idea is to make the students hear a word more frequently and to make them use it, as shown in the following examples. Here, the teacher wants to offer more exposure to the words *pet* and *crash*.

> TEACHER: What do we call a domestic animal? That's right, a pet. Alex, ask Rob if he has any pets. Who has a pet? Anyone? You do, John? What is it? What's his name? Tell us about your animals, Ella. What

sorts of animals do people keep in America? Which pets are best if you live in a city? What about farmers?

TEACHER: What happens when / drivers drive too fast / the roads are wet / drivers drink alcohol? Has anyone in this class ever been in a crash? What happened to that plane at X airport a few weeks ago?

More exposure to the new vocabulary will occur as the class works on the text. And of course, the words will be used again in the follow-up exploitation.

## The illustrative context

Many words, especially verbs, have different meanings in different contexts (eg the *head* of a river, a bed, an organisation, a flower). Unless you are working with advanced classes, give only the meaning of the word as it used in the passage. If the verb *to reach for* is in a text, it will only confuse the class if you talk about reaching home, reaching school, reaching out, and so on.

## ■ THE IMPORTANCE OF REVIEW

Review, also known as **revision**, assists the learning process, so it needs to be done regularly. Recycle any pictures that you used in introducing the vocabulary in the first place. Why not bring in the whole week's pictures at the end of a week or the beginning of the following week? The students can be challenged to remember the words that the pictures represent.

Another way to revise words is to get the class to write, from memory, some of the short illustrative sentences that they associate with the pictures. Walk around as they write, to ensure they are all trying. Nominate one of them to write on the board. The rest can compare this with their own versions. Having copied those illustrative sentences just a few days earlier, they are unlikely to make mistakes, so they get a sense of achievement. What does it matter if some of them cheat from their neighbours or simply copy from the blackboard? They will still be reviewing the words and illustrative contexts.

## ■ STUDENT EXERCISE BOOKS

The class normally copies any examples from the blackboard. For this reason, exercise books are called *copy books* in many countries. Often, all copying is done at the end of the lesson. However, it is a good idea to vary this occasionally and get the students to copy the example as you finish each word's presentation. This offers a brief change of activity and a break from the intense concentration needed during the presentation stage. It also gives you a moment to prepare materials for the presentation of the next word.

It is in the students' interest that they meet and use new words as often as possible if the words are to pass into their **active vocabulary**. Get them to keep their own separate vocabulary book, to write up at home from their copy book.

You may ask them to put all the new words into their alphabetical place in an *a* to *z* vocabulary book. A loose leaf folder is best for this. Alternatively you could decide that they should just copy **topic vocabulary** into their vocabulary book. In this case they would only copy those words which fitted into agreed topic areas (sport, weather, the family, transport, clothing, food and drink, the countryside, etc). This has the advantage of making the learners think again about all of the day's new words as certain words will go into more than one word set.[4]

## ■ DICTIONARIES

You need one or two dictionaries for professional use. Most useful of all is an elementary monolingual dictionary, written for very young native speakers. It almost always provides the illustrative sentence you need for a word, in simple language. If you can read phonetic script, a bilingual dictionary which shows the pronunciation as well as the meaning is another useful tool. If your students are in a position to buy a dictionary, a pocket bilingual dictionary is probably the most useful for them, as their main concern is with meaning.

## ■ CONCLUSION

Some words can be presented **ostensively**, using realia, visuals or the teacher's body. Other types of lexical item have to be presented **linguistically**, using explanation, definition, synonyms, antonyms, cognates, scales or translation.

The four steps of the presentation procedure are easy to carry out. Select vocabulary for formal attention on the criterion of usefulness and frequency. Less common or useful vocabulary can be glossed as it is met in the text. Try to fit new words into vocabulary networks that the students already have, on semantic grounds or by topic. Involve the students as much as possible. Give them the chance to try out new vocabulary items in sentences of their own making. Make the whole presentation stage enjoyable. Remember that words need revising if they are to be internalised. Work briskly with evident enthusiasm. In this way the class will acquire a big vocabulary and enjoy the process. A good vocabulary is more important than grammar or structure in comprehension and in communication.

## Notes

[1] A **lexical item** is a vocabulary item. Usually this is a word, but expressions are sometimes introduced as lexical items, rather than as structures or strings of separate words (eg *Good morning, I beg your pardon, Have a nice day, Enjoy you meal, My goodness!*).

[2] **Teacher talk** is the sort of language used in the classroom, a variety of talk that is different in many ways from natural speech. Teacher talk is one of a group of types of speech that are reduced grammatically in order to facilitate comprehension. The global term for these simplified speech forms is **caretaker talk** (or caretaker **speech**). We also

simplify speech when talking to small children (called **motherese**) and to foreigners (**foreigner talk**).

[3] All visuals are boxed in this book. Boxes in this chapter indicate the use of the blackboard, in other chapters boxes will depict wordcards, blackboard sketches, flashcards, wall posters, and other sorts of visual representation.

[4] Words that are internalised and can readily be produced are said to be in the student's **active vocabulary**. Words that they could not readily produce, but would understand, are said to be in their **receptive** (or *passive*) vocabulary.

# 2 Presenting and practising structures

## ■ TEACHING USEFUL STRUCTURES

The teaching of grammar is an enormous field to cover. Consequently, we have split it into two, beginning here with the teaching of structures. A structure is a **pattern** of words which make a meaningful utterance. The aim of teaching structures is to get students to internalise dozens of useful phrases, but with a sensitivity to the generative power of each one. The meaning is changed by a process of **substitution**, but the basic shape of the phrase remains the same.

The teaching of structures is probably the main aim of the textbook you are using, since most school textbooks were written in days when structures were the basis of the syllabus. Structures are seen as the building blocks of language, hence their name. Dialogues, especially, are often little more than a string of useful structures. Until comparatively recently, textbook structures were chosen largely on the criterion of simplicity. Simplicity was judged partly by length of utterance and partly by traditional grammatical progressions. The accompanying approved method stressed learning the structures by heart, with little attention to the communicative value of the utterances. Teachers who use these textbooks often retain the mechanical method of teaching those structures, and so we still hear unlikely exchanges of the following sort.

> TEACHER:   This is a table. Is it a table?
> STUDENTS: Yes, it is. It's a table.

A structural emphasis is still evident in the newer generation of textbooks. Nowadays, though, structures are chosen for their usefulness in communicative situations. The structures are taught as formulae, with no undue focus on the formal grammar rules which govern the patterns. The aim of this chapter is to make teachers aware of the communicative value of some of the structures they teach and to show how they can be practised in more meaningful ways.

To work with structures is quite easy. The word order is fixed, and we use what is known as a **slot and filler** technique to practise it. Take the utterance *Are you tired?*. If we regard *tired* as a slot, we can replace it by other adjectives to create *Are you bored/ hungry/ sad/ ill/?* and so on. The utterance *Are you playing chess this evening?* will generate a host of similar questions (*watching TV/ going to the cinema?* etc).

**Grammatically**, we describe that sentence as using the present continuous tense, with the interrogative form of the second person. As a **structure** we view

*[handwritten: What are the 3 elements of a structure?]*

it as *are you + the -ing verb form.* Looked at for its **communicative** (or **functional**) value, it is a way of enquiring about someone's future intentions.

### The presentation of a structure

As in the presentation of vocabulary, we show a structure's **form**, its **meaning** and also its **use**. We also use the same ostensive or verbal techniques to indicate meaning. Structures for beginner classes have invariably been chosen because meaning can be shown, rather than explained, but when more complex structures are introduced use must be made of verbal explanation, too. With careful planning and the creation of contexts which typify ways in which the structure is used, it is usually possible to stay in the target language.

*[handwritten margin: meaning ↓ show or explain]*

### A step by step procedure

*[handwritten: Begin w/ the context / sit. ⇒ elicit prior knowl.]*

If we look now at some step-by-step examples you will see that the procedure is not difficult.

#### Step one: presentation of form and meaning

Let us suppose that the structure in the text is *I've been learning English for two years.* You know that the utterance means that the process is still going on and that it began two years earlier, so you could saying something like this:

*[handwritten margin: contextualized ex.]*

> Two years ago, in 19––, I began to learn English. It is now 19––, so *I've been learning English for X years.*

*[handwritten margin: model ↓ use model]*

Repetition of the structure will follow, enough to familiarise the learners with the sound but not enough to bore them. Then you could show how the basic structure generates other utterances. Building on the model above, you might say when you started driving a car, when you began teaching, when you moved into your house. If possible be truthful, but above all be interesting and even amusing.

*[handwritten margin: generate other sent.]*

#### Step two: blackboard example

Now you can write the structure on the board, underlining the key features or highlighting them with coloured chalk. Most teachers would write all the words in the utterance, in the following way.

*[handwritten in box: I've been learning English for 2 years]*

*[handwritten margin: reduce utter. to essential components]*

Even better, you can show only the **bones** of the structure, so as not to obscure the form with unnecessary words. We might call this sort of representation a

*[handwritten: add unusual features (3rd p. sg)]*

17

**skeleton structure**, viewing the words that will be slotted in as the flesh of the utterance. Let us add the third person singular to our blackboard model. It will permit the class to talk about others as well as themselves. This change of person causes a grammatical change, but it does not change the word order (the structure). The addition of other persons to the model should only be done when the new utterances will be useful.[1] The skeleton of the structure above, but with the addition of the other persons of the verb, can be seen in the following example. The use of the skeleton structure has made the cue much easier for the class to generate new phrases.

> I (etc) 've
>
> S/he 's   been ...ing for { 1 hour
>                            { 2 weeks

*Step three: guided practice*

A substitution drill is the usual follow-up to this step. The teacher calls out the new elements or prompts them by means of visual aids. These might include pictures, flashcards, blackboard sketches or even easily read words on paper (wordcards). The students chant the resulting sentences, referring to the blackboard for support if necessary.

TEACHER:    Five years (showing picture of car).
STUDENTS:   I've been driving a car for 5 years.
TEACHER:    Many years (holding a maths book).
STUDENTS:   I've been learning maths for many years.
TEACHER:    My friend, 20 years (picture of a guitar).
STUDENTS:   My friend's been playing the guitar for 20 years.
TEACHER:    My parents, 30 years (picture of local town).
STUDENTS:   ...

In too many classrooms that is the end of the practice. Perhaps the students copy the structure or write a few sentences like those they have been chanting. But more could and should be done. If the practice stopped at that point the students have been cheated. The chief criticisms are that it was unrealistic and mechanical. It may even have been meaningless.

## Making practice meaningful

Those three steps can be kept. They will familiarise the students with the original structure, which you can now go on to use more communicatively. Bearing

18

in mind that the students understand more than they can actually say themselves, teachers can set out to offer a richer language environment. Teacher talk
can go beyond just the language requirements of the lesson's vocabulary and
structure. **Input** (listening and reading) is crucial to fluent production, so you
need not feel guilty about talking, provided that what you say is understandable
and interesting.[2] You can make student talk more meaningful, too, by involving
the learners in the *content* of what they say, leading them to use the structure in a
more natural way. The element of unpredictability adds interest and excitement.
To do this you can capitalise on their own experiences, in the following way.

TEACHER: OK. I've been learning English for 20 years. I began in 19.. (*write
the date on the board*) and I'm still learning. I learn something new
every day. So, I can say that I've been learning English for 20
years! What about you? (*pause*). Ahmed!

AHMED: I've been learning English for 3 years miss.

TEACHER: Right. You all began to learn English in 19... So, like Ahmed
you've been learning it for 3 years. Who can tell me about the
other subjects you are learning?

STUDENTS: I've been learning history for 8 years.

TEACHER: Eight years? Really?

STUDENT: Yes miss. I learn in primary school.

TEACHER: Oh yes, of course. You also learn*ed* history in the primary school.

Some errors may occur as you allow an element of free expression, but it would
be wrong to correct everything formally at this stage of less controlled practice.
The remodelling of an incorrect utterance, like the one given by the second
student, can be done in a subtle way that does not cause embarrassment. By
using the structure to talk about themselves, their family and friends, the
students are more likely to internalise it. The focus now is on **what** is being said,
rather than **how** it is said.

An optional final step is to check if the students can give the equivalent in
their mother tongue. It seems well worthwhile to elicit that one sentence in
order to ensure that everyone in the class thoroughly understands the structure.

Let us look at another structure and see how the teacher can involve the
students in what they are saying. The textbook structure of the day is *If I lost my
passport, I'd report it to the police.* As most students do not have a passport, this is
not a very intelligent thing for them to say, so the teacher changes the item for
the presentation and repetition, using *umbrella, ID card* and *watch* instead. The
structure that is put on the board is skeletal, to show the open nature of the
structure and the slots available for fillers.

If I ---, I'd ---

19

Using such a visual as a support, you can get the students to use the structure in more exciting ways:

TEACHER: Now. Imagine that you won ten thousand dollars in the lottery. What would you do? If *I* won the lottery, *I'd* buy a new car. Or perhaps I'd take my husband on a holiday. What about you? Put up your hands if you want to tell us what you would do. Yes, Koffi?

KOFFI: If I won the lottery, I'd buy a house for my mother and father.

TEACHER: You'd buy a house, eh? Hear that, class? He said that he'd buy a house for his parents. That's kind. And you, Remy?

REMY: Miss, if I won the lottery, I'd . . .

## FUNCTIONS

As we pointed out earlier, a major difference between textbooks of 25 years ago and those of today is that structures are chosen now on the criterion of **usefulness**. The focus is on **what you can do** with the structure. The use of a structure is called its **function**.

Think of things that you yourself **do** by means of English. If you put the suffix *ing* on the end of the things you do, you will have a list of functions. We use English for threatening, persuading, requesting and giving information, suggesting, expressing preferences, promising, asking permission, complaining, describing, and so on. There is a world of difference between knowing the verb *to complain* and actually being able to *make* a complaint.

Often a single function will have several forms. *Asking for directions* can be done in a variety of ways, depending on the context and the status of the speakers (eg Excuse me, could you tell me where . .? I say, any idea where . . .? Do you know where . .? Whereabouts is . . .? How do I get to . . .? etc). In the same way, a single structure may serve a different function if the context is changed. Take the utterance *This is my X*. In the arrivals hall of an airport and spoken to a porter this would serve the function of **giving an order** (to carry the case or bag). At a party the same expression would serve to **introduce** a member of one's family. In the classroom the structure is more often used to **identify** objects or to **claim ownership**.

Begin to look at the structures in your textbook in terms of their functional value in the real world. Try to imagine different interactive settings in which the utterances might be made. The useful ones are those you will exploit – the ones that enable the learners to do something with the language. Leave less useful structures for recognition and gradual assimilation through increasing familiarity.

## Creating a context or situation

Often, you can draw attention to the functional value of a structure you are about to teach by means of a context and situation, for which the students have to try to find an appropriate utterance. This creates a *need to know*, which is

valuable in gaining their attention. The new structure is only given *after* they
have made a few attempts to solve the communicative problem, in the following
way.

*See O'Neill egl in Situat*

> TEACHER: The other evening I was invited to a party. Unfortunately my
> friend had not been invited and I wanted her to go with me. So I
> telephoned the host. What do you think I said?
> STUDENT 1: Can my friend come too?
> STUDENT 2: My friend is here. She wants to come, please.
> TEACHER: No. Those are good suggestions, but I used a different form. What
> I said was this (*pause*) *Would you mind if I brought a friend ?*

*Sit.*

The teacher will get repetition. Next he or she will write a skeleton structure on
the board, drawing attention to the past form that follows the word *if*. The final
step is to get the students creating new requests for permission to do something.

## Identifying the structure

*Step*

Of course, the first essential in all of this is that you learn to identify useful
structures, which have a communicative value and which can generate many
useful utterances by a process of substitution. With very little practice, you will
find it easy to identify the bones of a useful structure (the part that does not
change when substitutions are made and to imagine realistic contexts in which
the structure might be used. You will also be able to contrive a label to identify
the function – the communicative value of the utterance. Try now. The phrases
that follow are typical of textbook language. Can you identify the **basic structure**
of each? Try also to identify the **function** of these structures and consider the
**substitutions** you might offer for practising the form. What **contexts** can you
think of to make practice more meaningful? It might be worthwhile to write
down your own responses, for comparison with the answers given below.

> – *descr.*
> 1 There's a lamp on the table.   – *invit.*
> 2 Would you like to go to the club this evening?
> 3 How many students are there in the classroom?
> 4 I'd rather stay at home this evening. – *prefer.*
> 5 Have you ever seen the Eiffel Tower?
> 6 I'd like to be a doctor when I grow up. – *[?]*
>   *expres. wish or hope*

*nos*

*Practice in Class!*
*declin. an invt.*

*Model answers*

Here are answers for that task, above. Remember that a structure sometimes
serves more than one function, depending on the context in which it is used, so
your own answers may well be worded differently from those given here.

21

1 *There's a lamp on the table.* This structure has the function of **describing**, or perhaps **giving information**. The basic structure is:

> There's a + noun + prep. + noun

We normally use such an utterance when the listener has not seen or cannot see what we are describing. There is an **information gap**. The listener has a reason for listening. In the classroom, we can establish such a reason by means of pictures. You could sketch half a dozen pictures and pin them on the board. In pairs the students can take turns in describing one picture while the partner tries to identify it from the description. The task can be made more complex, but linguistically simple nevertheless, by having several objects in each picture, often the same but in different positions (There's a pen on the table and a bag on the floor; There's a bag under the chair and a pen next to the bag, etc). Later, the students can be asked to use the structure to describe a room in their house.

2 *Would you like to go to the club this evening?* This structure has the function of **inviting** or **suggesting an activity**. The basic structure is:

> Would you like to + verb ?

Substitution practice can be prompted by means of flashcards to indicate what sort of invitation should be made (a TV set, a restaurant, a cinema, a football game). More meaningful practice requires that the responder be able to accept or decline, so you would also want to present and very quickly practise some useful responses of the following kind.

> Yes, I would, Good idea, Fine, By all means.
>
> No, I wouldn't, Not really, I don't think so.

Afterwards, the students can work in pairs, taking turns to suggest activities for the weekend or the holidays. The responder will be in a position to accept or decline the idea put forward.

3 *How many students are there in the classroom?* The function this time is **enquiring about numbers**. The sentence has the basic structure:

How __many__ X's __are__ there . . ?

This is another structure that is commonly introduced in the first few weeks of a language programme. In real life we would not ask such a question if we already knew the quantity. So, a realistic context can only be created by putting the students into a situation where they do not know the numbers involved. You could ask young learners to bring in some small objects the next day, in a box or bag. They would need to know the names of the objects, so get them to bring pens, erasers, pencils and so on. You can even add some new items whose names are useful, such as matches, elastic bands, needles, safety pins. You can imagine the pupils' enjoyment as they play their simple guessing game in pairs or even in small groups (by having alternate rows face the row behind). The **knower** asks a question, using the structure. The others just guess numbers, to which the replies will be *No, Nearly,* or *That's right*. These responses will be briefly practised and written on the blackboard. When the correct number is guessed, the winner takes over and produces a new box or bag of small items.

4 *I'd rather stay at home this evening.* The function here is twofold. First there is the **declining of an invitation**; and second there is the **making of a new suggestion**. The structure has the basic form of:

I'd __rather__ + verb.

Guided practice can be just as in 2, above, with a form of limited role play in pairs.

5 *Have you ever seen the Eiffel Tower?* The language function is **asking about someone's past experiences**. The structure has the basic form:

```
Have you ever + past participle ?
```

Mechanical practice can be from verbal prompts; *Rome* (been to), *plane* (travelled by, flown in, been in), the *President* (seen, met), *champagne* (drunk), and so on. As an alternative to oral stimuli, those single words can be clearly written on pieces of paper (**wordcards**) which are just held up silently. But of course, pictures of some sort are better. With pictures, the meaning is conveyed but the class has to find the words. The pictures can be in the form of flashcards or be cut from newspapers and magazines.

Later and more meaningful practice of this same structure has to be personalised. Perhaps you could ask the students to guess three surprising things that you yourself have done. The students can do the same in pairs, or in threes where benches are crowded.

6 *I'd like to be a doctor when I grow up.* The function is **expressing wishes or hopes**. The basic structure is:

```
I'd like to + verb.
```

Flashcards or pictures could be used to trigger substitutions such as *go to New York* (picture of skyscrapers), *meet so-and-so* (picture of a famous person), *have a big car*, *go for a picnic*, and similar types of activity. In fact the wordcards or pictures used in 5, above, can be used to practise this quite different structure.

Next, you can ask the students to suggest things they themselves might like to do. Here you get everyone's attention because of the magic of unpredictability. If you are lucky, they will offer some funny suggestions (blow up the school, give up smoking, and so on). To ensure the participation of all and to offer further practice, you might ask the students to write the two or three things they would most like to do. Walk around the class to check and assist. Some will need a word in English, others will want help with a spelling. Afterwards you make a public check by randomly choosing a few students to read out their first wish. Why not let the students put their names on the slips of paper and exchange them among themselves? This will give real reading and perhaps even lead to discussion and amusement.

# ■ CONCLUSION

Structures are the building blocks of language. If the students can handle a range of useful structures in a formulaic way, aware of the functional value of each and able to substitute the content to meet their communicative needs, then they are getting what they need. If the utterances practised have an obvious functional value, the students will perceive the language course as valid and relevant to their communicative needs.

Go through the textbook and underline all the structures that have a functional value. Imagine how each would be used in a realistic way. What would be the likely situations? What would be the most probable language contexts? Where can substitutions be made in the structure? What words will you prompt for substitutions practice? How can this practice be continued in a meaningful way, with the students providing their own fillers? Do not be limited by the content of the textbook. Be ready to supply useful words and additional structures that enable the learners to practise the key structure realistically. Even the least able can rote learn useful structures, so this sort of teaching is ideal for mixed ability classes.

## Notes

[1] The criterion for practising any structure is its usefulness. A formula such as *May I have ...?* is obviously worth knowing. However, transformations of the structure to create *May she have . . .?* or, even worse, *May you have . . .?* are not worth effecting. Structural transformations are dealt with in the next chapter.

[2] Some methodologists see the teacher's main role as provider of accurate and meaningful input. Student talk is less than perfect, they argue, so the more a class listens to the teacher, the better. This is directly opposed to the viewpoint expressed by those who see the teacher as a prompter of student talk. Avoid extremes in issues of this kind. Speak as much as you feel is necessary, but always ensuring comprehension and using natural speech forms.

# 3 Presenting and practising grammar points

## ■ WHAT IS GRAMMAR?

The body of rules which underlie a language is called its **grammar**. This grammar includes rules which govern the structure of words (suffixes and prefixes) and rules which govern the structure of words to form clauses and sentences that are acceptable to educated native speakers. Traditional descriptions of English grammar developed from the grammars of classical Greek and Latin.

Most teachers see grammar as a body of knowledge that they themselves need as professional linguists, knowledge they can use judiciously to help learners gain insights into the workings of the language. Fortunately, many grammatical niceties are systematic and so learnable. In the previous chapter we said that structures must be grammatical, that is, they must obey the rules of construction. Let us try to make clear the distinction between teaching a grammar structure as a formulaic and functional utterance and teaching a structure to bring out a grammar point.

### The difference between grammar and structure lessons

In Chapter Two we used the example *How many students are there in the classroom?* The function was enquiring about numbers, and in the practice which helped the learners use the structure meaningfully, they asked each other questions about hidden items. No mention was made of grammar. But there is an important grammar point embedded in that structure; it is countable versus uncountable. In presenting and practising that utterance as a useful **structure**, we used countable objects and avoided uncountables such as sugar, coffee, and sand.

In a **grammar** lesson the teacher will draw attention to that distinction. Practice of *How many?* (countables) will be contrasted with *How much?* (of uncountable items). The teacher's concern will not be with communication and mastery of a useful structure, rather it will be with understanding of the concept and mastery of that grammar point. There would be special attention to any clash between the mother tongue and the target language in terms of what is countable.[1]

We spoke, too, of the generative power of structure. Once the students have control of a skeleton structure, they can flesh it out to create dozens or even hundreds of utterances. Many grammar points offer similar generative potential. For example, it probably helps a learner of English to know that most plurals are formed simply by adding an *–s*, or that the insertion of *–'ll* between a pronoun and any basic verb form will produce a future tense in speech. On the

*general power*

*create more sent. based on Skeleton*

26

other hand, a great deal of the content of the grammar book is difficult and wholly inappropriate for the average learner. Much of it will only become truly comprehensible and applicable when the language is already fairly well mastered. Look back on your own learning. If difficulties have disappeared, is it a result of the study of the grammar, of simply the result of years of exposure and acquisition?[2]

# ■ METHODS OF TEACHING GRAMMAR

Some teachers see no need to teach and practise grammar at all. Some even regard structure practice and other forms of grammar teaching as harmful. Their view is that learners will pick up the regularities intuitively, provided they meet enough samples of natural language. The teacher's role, as they see it, is to provide a language-rich environment in which the learners meet comprehensible language as they engage in activities of various kinds. The learners are expected to pick up the language, just as they did their mother tongue. These teachers might occasionally draw attention to grammatical features of the language in a reading passage, but that is all. They would not wish to explain the grammar or to conduct even meaningful practice.[3] There is no firm research evidence to show that their way is any better or any worse than the methods below, so the non-teaching of grammar offers a valid third option to the two ways of teaching grammar that we shall look at now.

## The deductive method

The deductive method of teaching grammar is the academic and scholarly one which was devised in order to teach Latin and Greek. The approach is very simple. First, the teacher writes an example on the board or draws attention to example in the textbook. The underlying rule is explained, nearly always in the mother tongue and using the metalanguage of grammar. Finally, the students practise applying the rule, orally and in writing. Special attention is paid to areas of conflict between the grammar of the mother tongue and that of the target language. The whole approach is cognitive, with learners considering the rules and weighing their words before they speak or write. Little attention is paid to the value of the message.

Those steps are used by teachers who follow a grammar-translation method and by those who are working with a textbook which has a traditional grammar syllabus rather than a structural one. Varieties of grammar-focused approaches still flourish in certain educational circles, and they are successful when used with selected and motivated students. We must also remember that language examinations are mainly written, with accuracy as the criterion of success, so many teachers make increasing use of the deductive approach as examinations loom closer.

Although advocates of grammar-focused teaching have never claimed that their methods lead to oral fluency, their way of presenting grammar need not be rejected by those whose aims are more communicative or humanistic. A deductive approach will be useful to us all at times. This is especially true where we are confronted by a grammar rule which is complex but which we are expected to cover in the syllabus.

## The inductive method

To induce means to bring about, to cause something to happen. Teachers following the inductive approach **induce** the learners to realise grammar rules without any form of prior explanation. These teachers believe that the rules will become evident if learners are given enough appropriate examples. When teaching a grammar point, their first step is to demonstrate the meaning to the class. For example, they will hold up a book, saying *This is a book*. They will do the same showing other objects. Then they will hold up several books and say *These are books*. After giving several examples of the plural form they will contrast the two forms.

Their next step is to get the students to produce the two grammatical forms, working with the same set of objects. The teacher says nothing through this stage except to correct if necessary. Other objects the students can name will then be brought into the practice. With luck they will follow the models and produce grammatically correct utterances.

The grammar point is shown on the board only after extensive practice. Explanations are not always made, though they may be elicited from the students themselves. In such cases, the mother tongue might well be used. The model is copied and the class may be required to write sample sentences from the model.

## The eclectic way

*choose appropriate method*

With such conflicting views, what should the average teacher do about grammar? As in all choices of pedagogy, a middle path is probably best. Both methods above offer advantages. The deductive method is quick and easy for the teacher. Where a difficult grammar point has to be presented, and perhaps explained because the concept is not one that is in the mother tongue, this is probably the better way. Where time is short, it is useful, even for a simple grammar point. Many learners, especially older ones, prefer the deductive approach because they want to know how the language works.

The inductive method requires the students to identify the rule for themselves. It has the advantage of involving the students much more. The belief is that such learning will be more effective, though there is no certainty about this. This is probably the better approach for grammatical regularities which are easily perceived, understood, and applied.

Remember, there is also the option of not teaching grammar at all. Students can certainly pick up the usage over time. A compromise is to simply to draw the attention of the class to certain grammar points as they occur in a text but not to deliberately practise them. Eclectic teachers will use all three of these strategies at various times. This will make it easier to fit the lesson into the time available,

as well as enabling them to suit the differing needs and learning styles of the students.

## ■ EXAMPLES OF GRAMMAR TEACHING

Teachers should not expect miracles to result from grammar teaching of any kind. Even easy grammar points are only easy because they are easily explained. Internalisation may take years. With this warning ringing in our ears, we shall go on to explore ways in which grammar can be taught effectively and enjoyably, helping learners to produce correct forms in speech and writing. It will not be possible to give more than a few teaching examples, so we will look at a sample of grammar points which regularly receive attention in class. Most of the examples demonstrate the technique of contrasting related grammar points in order to facilitate comprehension and learning.

### Introducing tenses                              _see Azar's charts_

A visual representation can often be clearer than a verbal one to introduce a tense. This is especially true where the students do not have similar tense systems in their mother tongue. Time can be shown by a line across the board. An arrow pointing down indicates this moment, now. To the left of the arrow is past time, to the right is the future. A cross indicates a single event, a row of dots denotes an action that lasted or will last for a period of time. The uses of most tenses can be shown and contrasted pictorially on such a time line, as shown in the following examples.

1 *He used to smoke* (in the past, not any more).

$$\downarrow$$

. . . . . . . . . .

2 *She works in the market* (did in the past and will continue in the future).

$$\downarrow$$

. . . . . . . . . . . . . . . . . . . . . . . .

3 *He is having his supper* (eating now, having started a short while ago in the past, but this will not continue for any appreciable length of time).

$$\downarrow$$

. . .

4 *He got up at six o'clock* (in the past, a single event).

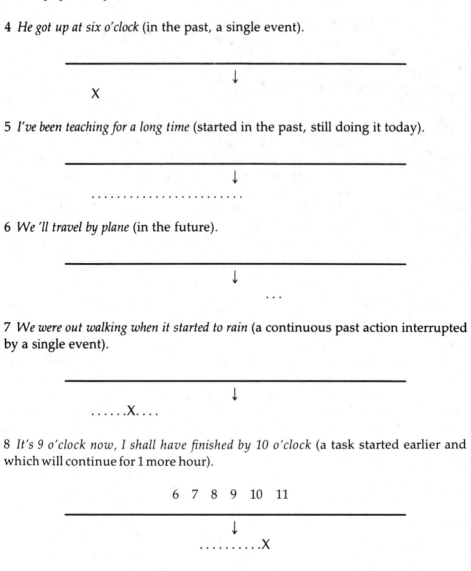

5 *I've been teaching for a long time* (started in the past, still doing it today).

6 *We'll travel by plane* (in the future).

7 *We were out walking when it started to rain* (a continuous past action interrupted by a single event).

8 *It's 9 o'clock now, I shall have finished by 10 o'clock* (a task started earlier and which will continue for 1 more hour).

This is by no means the full range of tenses, but once you have grasped the idea you will be able to use the technique to introduce others in the same way. You can also use a time scale to show concepts like *for 2 months, since April* and *from April to June*. This is done as in the following example.

Jan. Feb. March April May June July Aug. Sep. Oct. Nov. Dec.

## Practising tenses

It is helpful to learners to see the uses of tenses contrasted. For example, while either the present simple or the present continuous tense can be used to express a future intention (*Next week we go/are going to Australia*), there are some important differences between the two tenses. One difference is that we tend to use the continuous form to talk about actions that are going on now but will not continue for much longer, while the simple form is used to talk about actions that go on all or most of the time. *He's teaching* tells us that this act will stop eventually. *He teaches* implies a degree of permanence or repetition. So, where a class already knows the one form, such a contrast might well be made as the second is introduced.

### The present continuous tense

This tense is often the first one met in a language course. It can be presented and practised meaningfully by physical actions. In this way learners are provided with a comprehension aid as they become familiar with the sounds of English.[4] In the early stages, there is no need to force the class to speak at all, as in the following example.

> TEACHER: Go and touch the wall, then write your name on the blackboard *(student obeys)* Look. Ruth is walking towards the wall, she is touching it. Now she is writing her name on the board. Well done, Ruth. Who will be next?

Describing a scene is a natural use of the present continuous tense. So, pictures offer another good way to practise the tense. You can draw simple pictures yourself if the textbook does not have them. A magazine picture is often less suitable, as it may have too many unwanted details.

Practice can be made into a game. Make a set of half a dozen simple flashcard drawings of the verbs you are teaching (eg *they are playing tennis/watching TV/eating a sandwich*). Get the students to use the question forms in a guessing way. Write the structure on the blackboard to offer support (eg *Are they –ing?*). Then shuffle the six flashcards and hold one so they cannot see which you are holding. The students call out in turn until a winner is found as in the following example.

> STUDENT 1: Are they eating a sandwich?
> TEACHER: No. No, they're not eating anything.
> STUDENT 2: Are they listening to a record?
> TEACHER: No, they're not listening to music.
> STUDENT 3: Are they watching TV?
> TEACHER: Yes, that's right *(showing picture)*. They're watching TV.

Mime is another way to get students to use the continuous form. Get one student to the front and whisper a task (eg *Pretend you are opening a tin*). The others then guess what is being done (*Is she peeling a potato?*, *Is she knitting?*).

### The present simple tense

The present simple tense is often used with an adverb of frequency, so this is one possible way to present and practise it. This can be done using all or any of the adverbs along the scale from *never* to *always,* or by using adverbial phrases such as *on Sundays, every day, once a week, each summer, at 6 o'clock.* Teachers using an inductive approach might talk about their friends' routines as they build up a blackboard prompt. The resulting visual can support guided practice, as in the following example.

```
                    ROUTINES : SATURDAY
                         a.m.        p.m.       Evening.
      John                office      shops      squash
      Bill     + verb + s  shops      tennis     TV
      Carol                bed        housework  friend's
      Eve                  Mother's   Mother's   cinema
```

TEACHER:    Tell me about John's Saturday.
STUDENT 1:  He goes to work in the morning. In the afternoon he goes shopping and in the evening he plays squash.
TEACHER:    Fine. What about Eve?
STUDENT 2:  She goes to her mother's in the morning. She stays there for the afternoon / spends the day there.
TEACHER:    And Carol? What . . .

Such practice is controlled and unexciting. Everyone knows what will be said. However, the students do use a natural style of language. There is no attempt to force unnatural response patterns, where students repeat all of the information carried in the question, as in the following examples.

TEACHER:    What does John do on Saturday mornings?
STUDENTS: On Saturday mornings, John . . . (*instead of simply, he . . .*)
TEACHER:    Where does Eve spend Saturdays?
STUDENTS: Eve spends Saturdays at her mothers (*instead of just, at her mother's*).

*personalize*

Practice is more meaningful if it is based on the habitual actions of the students and their own families, rather than on the teacher's. This brings in the element of unpredictability that we seek. The students can be asked to make their own agendas for the weekend, following the blackboard example. Then they can change papers with their partners and write a few lines to describe their friend's weekend. The check is simple. As this is a grammar lesson (practising the formation of the third person singular of the present simple tense), the checks and corrections need only be concerned with the –s endings of each verb.

Therefore, it can be done orally. Just the verb forms (with the –s underlined) will be put on the board as they occur during the oral check, and the students will check their own or their partner's paper.

## Examples of grammar practice activities

Ensure that they understand the concept, especially where it is expressed differently, or not made at all, in their own mother tongue. Offer clear visuals to support practice. Make sure that the titles of the tables represent the use, the meaning, the communicative value of the grammar point. Teach only grammar points that are easily explained. Draw attention to a difficult grammar point that occurs in the text, but do not waste valuable time by making the learners grapple with niceties that they cannot possibly master. Linguistic competence is built up very slowly, over many years.

### Comparatives

If you are using the inductive method, you can offer examples, using short adjectives the students already know and adding the suffix –er. The exercise is easy, so you will soon be able to elicit other examples from them, perhaps by means of pictures. You should be careful to avoid irregular forms like better. After some oral work, your example will be put on the board and copied. It will look like the following table (notice the self-explanatory title).

> COMPARING 2 THINGS
>
> Buses are bigger than taxis.

Return to the oral work, but write the new comparatives on the board as they occur. Make the exchanges interesting but feed the students the adjectives to use as comparatives;

TEACHER: Do you think pop music is nice? Yes? And what about jazz? Yes, that's nice too? Which is nicer, jazz or pop? Alison, what's your opinion?

ALISON: I think jazz is nicer.

TEACHER: Nicer than pop, right? Who agrees? What about the volume? Is jazz loud?

STUDENTS: Yes, but pop is louder.

TEACHER: Who plays basketball? Is the ball big or small? Is it heavy or light? What about a football? Isn't that big too? Who can compare a football and a basketball?

Within a few minutes you will have a list of comparatives on the blackboard, all ending in *–er*. You can then wait for the class to notice that single consonants are doubled and that adjectives ending in *–y* change the *–y* to *–i* (*heavier*). This is the **inductive** approach. Or, you can draw attention to the spelling yourself (the **deductive** approach) as you are write the words on the blackboard. Afterwards, you can give the class a few additional *–y* adjectives to convert to comparatives as a short written activity.

The learners can be asked to compose a few sentences, using comparatives, for homework. To diminish the risk of errors (eg *beautifuller*), you can put a list of prescribed adjectives on the blackboard or ask the students to use only short ones (except *good*, *little* and *bad*) in their sentences.

In a later lesson students will meet longer adjectives, which use *more* to form the comparative. You may decide to save time by using the deductive approach, explaining the simple rule. Whatever approach is used, you will end up with a blackboard example something like the following.

COMPARING 2 THINGS (long adjectives.)
Girls are _more_ intelligent than boys.

Next you will want them to use comparatives in utterances of their own. This is where you will contrast the two types of comparison on the blackboard. You will need a table which will not invite errors but which will not restrict the students' natural inventiveness. The use of *etc* in a table invites thought and risk taking. The practice is guided but comparatively unpredictable, because the class can add other adjectives and choose the subjects of comparison. (See the table at the top of page 35).

### Superlatives

Because you can use the same approach to teach superlatives as was used to teach comparatives, let us just consider the use of pictures for controlled practice. To teach the vocabulary *prettiest*. *fattest, slimmest, cleverest, tallest*, and so on, you might use a picture like the one at the top of p. 36.

This same picture could also be used to introduce *best, worst, first, second, third, fourth* and so on.

### Modals

Modal auxiliaries express concepts such as ability (*can, could*), permission (*may, might, could, can*) obligation (*should, must*), possibility (*can, may, might, could*), prediction (*would, shall, will*), and so on. They do not vary their form in any way. The best way to present and practise them is by focusing on any differences. Depending on the approach, the blackboard cue would be made available either

```
COMPARING 2 PEOPLE OR THINGS

                    big (g)  ⎫
                    Slim (m) ⎪
                    rich     ⎬  + er
                    tall     ⎪
                    etc.     ⎭
     X is                              than Y
              ⎧  stupid
              ⎪  intelligent
     more   ⎨  handsome
              ⎪  attractive
              ⎩  etc.
```

before the oral presentation (deductive) or after it (inductive). The cue could be set out as in the following example:

```
              OBLIGATION
     Weak                    Strong
     Should                   must
```

The teacher would give several examples of each, to show the difference; for example:

I have a lot of marking to do. I *should* do it this evening, but there is a film I want to see on the TV.

My brother phoned to tell me that our mother is sick. I *must* visit her this weekend.

With the help of the visual cue, the students can go on to write a few statements about their own obligations. The act of writing helps learning as well as involving everyone. The teacher assists when needed. A quick oral check takes care of the marking, with a few students chosen at random to read out one of their sentences.

Next, the teacher can use either a deductive or an inductive method to draw attention to the fact that modals do not change when used in the third person and that there is no auxiliary in the question forms (eg *Must I go?*, but **not** *Do I must go?*). Because there is a contrast between modals and other verbs, clear visual support for these constructions will be needed during practice. A table like the following will enable the class to generate plenty of original sentences.

```
QUESTIONS  WITH  MUST & SHOULD.
must/should  +  subject  +  verb
   ( MUST           you        go ? )


   NEGATIVES  WITH  MUST & SHOULD.
subject  +  must/should  +  not + verb
  ( we          should          n't  go.)
```

Suppose you wanted to practise the modals of possibility and speculation (*might, may, could, must*). You will contrive a situation which makes clear the meanings but permits the students to be creative. You can use any of the persons of the verb, but the following example focuses on the third person pronouns.

```
              SPECULATION
              ( possibility.)


   They            ⎰ must
             +     ⎱ may      + have + past
   He              ⎰ might
         must = certainty
```

TEACHER:   This morning I went to that station to meet my friend. He was supposed to be coming to stay with me for a few days. He wrote and told me to meet the 6 o'clock train from X. I waited until everyone was off, but he wasn't on the train (*pointing at the structure on the board*). I wonder what happened?

STUDENT 1:  He must have missed the train.

TEACHER:    He did. You're right. But why, I wonder?

STUDENT 2:   He may have changed his mind.
TEACHER:    I don't think so, though he *may* have.
STUDENT 3:   He might have caught the next train.
TEACHER:    He didn't, I waited for that train, too.
STUDENT 4:   He might have decided to come by bus.
TEACHER:    I think you may be right. He *must* have decided to travel by bus.
            He must be on the way now.

*Transformation practice*
Teachers often need to practise changes of tense, question forms, negative forms
and so on, making **transformations.** The blackboard cues should be clear, not
cluttered with unnecessary words. Most students will internalise and work from
a skeleton layout like those used in Chapter 2 more easily than from a series of
exemplifying sentences. Signs are useful in transformation tables. They stand
for a category of word and allow the students greater freedom in practising the
changes of pattern, while involving them more actively. The students need to
know that WH signifies all of the possible questions like *When, Where, What,
Why, How often, How many, On which day, At what time,* and so on. They need to
know that *to + vb.* signifies the infinitive form, that *adj.* indicates an adjective
and so on. They will be taught that any bracketed item is optional, as in the
following examples. Although grammar terminology is not something that
learners need, a few basic linguistic expressions are very useful and save a lot of
wasted words.

QUESTIONS

Do

(WH)        (nt) + subject + verb

Does

e.g. Does / Doesn't Maggie like tennis?
Why do/don't you travel by train?

# ■ CONCLUSION

Undue stress on grammar can be boring and counterproductive to fluency and
communication. Teach only those rules which are simple and which do not have
too many exceptions. Grammar points which do not appear very useful are best

avoided. Just draw attention to their presence in the text and move on, having raised the students' awareness of the feature. If you do choose to teach a grammar point, use either the deductive or the inductive method, depending on the circumstances.

When you yourself are talking, do not be afraid to use grammar forms that the students have not met. Provided the context makes the meaning clear, you are giving them valuable exposure and real life practice in decoding utterances which contain forms they do not know.

Above all, do not imagine that because you have taught a rule it is now known and will be applied. It takes weeks and months of exposure to a grammatical form for internalisation to take place. It is the work of moments to teach a class that an apostrophe *s* is added to a proper noun to show ownership. It may be many years before the learners use it consistently in speech.

The metalanguage of grammar is for professionals, not learners. Teachers need to know terminology in order to find helpful pages in reference books, but school children do not need to know words like *auxiliary*, *preterite*, *reflexive pronoun* and *gerund* in order to speak fluently. Teachers who use unneccessary terminology will appear pedantic, and most of it will be utter nonsense to the students anyway. Titles on blackboard examples should be simple and meaningful, showing the communicative value of the grammar point whenever possible.

## Notes

[1] Although *information*, *news*, *advice* and *homework* are viewed as uncountable in English, they are countable in French. Other languages have no such grammatical distinction.

[2] For example, most learners of English are taught early on that the third person singular verb from in the present simple tense requires an –*s* suffix. Yet, the students will forget it time and time again, often for several years.

[3] The best known approach of this sort is the Natural Approach. There is no formal language syllabus. Nor do teachers actually teach, in the accepted sense of the word. They are there to provide a comprehensible language environment, much as parents do for infants. Through being immersed in the language and engaged in attention holding activities, the students, who do not in fact study, acquire the language without conscious effort.

[4] An action-based approach offers rich language input. Learners are immersed in language which they understand because of what they see, but are not made anxious by a need to respond orally. One influential way of teaching languages at the early stages is based entirely on commands, acted out silently by the students. The method is called Total Physical Response (TPR). The commands are combined into increasingly complex instructions. The mother tongue is avoided and the students say nothing for the first ten hours or so of instruction. If there is a misunderstanding the teacher demonstrates the required action. The approach mirrors that of the mother, who talks to the infant while making the meaning clear by means of accompanying actions. Practitioners of TPR claim that the **silent period** for the learners is beneficial in several ways. The atmosphere is relaxed as the learners are not forced to speak, the students have fun. They gain a better pronunciation and their listening competence is enhanced.

# 4 Conducting meaningful drills

## ■ USING DRILLS

The most common purpose of drills is to involve the whole class together in the practice of grammar patterns. We also use drills to get students to learn useful phrases by heart. For this we use a **repetition drill**. Repetition drills can be used to practise pronunciation, stress and intonation patterns, too. A **transformation drill** gives the class practice in making changes to grammar patterns. **Substitution drills** give students confidence in adapting the lines of a dialogue before they go into pair work practice. Other types of drill that we shall see are used too, but less frequently.

Drills are often criticised. They deserve this condemnation when they are done badly. They can easily become boring, mechanical and even meaningless. But, this need not be so, and drills are especially valuable when teaching large classes. At least half the utterances in a language lesson are probably made by the teacher. The fifty or more learners share the other half of the talking. Individuals can, and do, go through an entire lesson without an opportunity to open their mouths. By introducing an occasional choral drill, we ensure that everyone gets to speak. In addition, a drill allows the class to hear a structure many times, which assists internalisation.[1]

If you are in a society where it is normal for students to stand when they speak, it is preferable that they do not do so in a drill. It is an irksome interruption, especially if everyone stands for the full class chorus!

## ■ THE PRINCIPLES OF A DRILL

1 The learners must know what they are saying. Make the meaning evident as you present the utterance. This is a most important principle and it applies to every aspect of teaching.
2 Let the learners hear the pattern several times. They need to internalise the form before they are called upon to reproduce it.
3 Break down a long utterance into shorter parts.
4 Do not force individuals to speak until there has been some chorus repetition to build up familiarity and confidence.
5 Keep the drill brisk and short. 40–60 seconds is about right for each drill. Do not use more than six or so drills at one time.
6 Give clear gestures to show who is to speak, rather than using names.[2]

7 Show approval of well formed utterances, but leave verbal praise until afterwards.

## The repetition drill

Let us look at the principles above, and incorporate them into the steps of a fast moving repetition drill. First of all present the structure, as explained in Chapter 2, making certain that the class understands what they are about to say. The drill sequence can begin only when the phrase has been presented and understood. It is helpful to have the structure written on the board at this time.[3]

### Step one: attention
Gesture for silence by giving a *hush* sign and pointing to your ear. Ensure full attention.

### Step two: modelling
Give the model. Speak clearly but naturally. Use proper stress and intonation. Give the model 3 or 4 times with pauses so that the students can echo it mentally.

### Step three: full class choruses
Give the listen sign again and repeat the model once more. Immediately gesture for repetition. It is important that you give good gestures. Two hands beckoning is a clear signal for a repetition. This saves you having to interrupt with language other than that of the drill. Get 3 or 4 full class repetitions, until the students are confident and can speak at the same speed as in the model.

### Step four: half class repetition
Get half class repetitions, using an appropriate gesture. Stretch out one arm, dividing the classroom, while beckoning half the class with the other hand.

### Step five: small group repetition
By now the students should be confident. Move down to small group repetition. The signal is a circular wave of the hand in the direction of the group. Smile approvingly for good responses. If you identify a difficulty, remodel once or twice.

### Step six: individual repetition
At this point get some individual utterances. Point clearly, avoiding names. It does not matter if an occasional signal is misinterpreted and a different student responds or two people speak instead of one. Check the pronunciation, stress and intonation. Use that smile to reward and encourage. Remodel if help is needed, but keep the repetition following.

### Step seven: completion
Finally, get a couple more choruses or half choruses to involve everyone again.
That whole drill will take one minute at the most, during which time everyone

will have spoken at least half a dozen times. That is the end of the activity unless you are working on a dialogue, in which case you will have a few more sentences to drill in the same way. If the focus is on the functional value, you can move straight into meaningful practice, as described in Chapter 2.

# ■ CHAINING

Chaining is a technique by which the teacher adds new elements to gradually increase the length of the repeated phrase. The idea is to break down a difficult learning task into a series of easy steps. It is not possible for the average learner to keep more than 6 or 7 syllables in memory, even for a short time. If you doubt this, try calling back 9 or more digits after hearing them once only. Any utterance which is more than 7 syllables long should be split into chunks, to be chained together progressively.

## Forward chaining

The dangers of building up from the beginning of a phrase are that the intonation patterns may become distorted and the successive phrases can be meaningless, as in this example.

> TEACHER:  My uncle,
> STUDENTS:  My uncle.
> TEACHER:  My uncle always goes,
> STUDENTS:  My ...

And on until the whole phrase (My uncle/always goes/to the West Indies/for his holidays) has been completed and repeated. Consequently, the sentences to be repeated in this way must be chosen carefully (eg I'd be grateful/if you'd stay home tonight/and look after the baby).

## Back chaining

The reverse process, also known as the **backward build-up**, is less controversial. The chunks can almost always make sense in themselves if you work from the *end* and the intonation patterns remain the same. The bonus is that there is a strong finish to a long utterance because the end gets the most attention.

When selecting structures for repetition, count the syllables rather than the words. Where a phrase is too long, work out just where it can be cut to construct a *meaningful* backward build-up. Often only one cut will be needed, but long phrases may have to be cut into three or four segments. Let us look at an example of the backward build-up in action, using the 14-syllable phrase *Would you kindly direct me to the nearest police station?*

1 Model the whole sentence two or three times as the class remains silent.
2 *Police station?* (repeated 2 or 3 times)
3 *The nearest police station?* (ditto)

4 *Direct me to the nearest police station?* (ditto)
5 *Would you kindly direct me to the nearest police station?*

Continue with a regular repetition drill, with the whole phrase, following the six steps described earlier. Move from full class to half class chorus, to group, and then to individual repetitions.

## ■ OTHER KINDS OF DRILL

The repetition drill is the one most widely used by teachers. However, there are other types and we shall look at some now. We begin with the most commonly used variant of a repetition drill before moving to other sorts of drill.

### The substitution drill

As we saw in Chapter 2, most structures have points at which substitutions can be made. The original sentence frame can then generate many useful utterances, all in a formulaic way. This usually goes easily and quickly, once the main structure has been thoroughly drilled. The substitutions can be prompted by flashcards, to ensure that everything remains meaningful. Here is an example, practising the formula for making a polite request.

> TEACHER:    Would you please . . . (gesture to the door)
> STUDENTS: Would you please open the door?
> TEACHER:    (showing picture of a chair)
> STUDENTS: Would you please sit down?
>
> (and so on, with *clean the board/give me a pen*, etc.)

Structures often have several slots where substitutions can be made. In this case visual support will certainly be needed. After repetition of one or two sample sentences, you can invite the students to look at a table like the following as they compose new phrases. An *etcetera* sign leaves room for initiative.

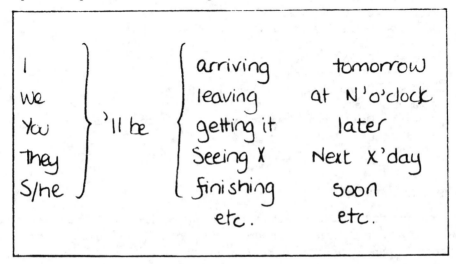

## The ripple drill

For variety, when introducing a short phrase, the teacher can use a **ripple drill**. The phrase ripples around the class from one student to another without teacher intervention. After the model has been heard, one student starts, passing the phrase along to a neighbour and so on until everyone has said it individually and publicly. In big classes this would take too much time, so the ripple drill is adapted. One student in every front bench starts, so there are several chains of repetitions as the phrase passed from the front to the back of the class down all the rows simultaneously.

## Chinese whispers

This is another variety of ripple drill, but it is done without public modelling by the teacher. Each row sends out one student from the front benches. The teacher whispers a short, simple phrase. They repeat it once or twice, quietly. Then they go back and pass it to their neighbour, who passes it to a student in the desk behind, who passes it to his or her neighbour, and so on. Because the people at the back could not hear the teacher model, what arrives is not always exactly what was sent; there is distortion as the message travels. This leads to laughter when the check is conducted, before everyone joins in a repetition of the original utterance as a follow-up. It can even become competitive, with each row trying to finish first.

## Incremental drill

With this type of drill, which is sometimes known as an **expansion** drill, the class has to decide where to add new words given by the teacher. Although it is challenging and almost gamelike, the process is cognitive; comprehension and grammatical sensitivity are required. So this type of drill is best done with quite advanced students. An example will make the technique clear.

| | |
|---|---|
| TEACHER: | Do you like cassettes? |
| STUDENTS: | Do you like cassettes? |
| TEACHER: | My |
| STUDENTS: | Do you like my cassettes? |
| TEACHER: | Of rock'n roll music. |
| STUDENTS: | Do you like my cassettes of rock'n roll music? |
| TEACHER: | Really. |
| STUDENTS: | Do you really like my cassettes of rock'n roll music? |
| TEACHER: | New |
| STUDENTS: | Do you . . . |

## The transformation drill

To transform a sentence is to **change its structure**. The transformations can be from affirmative to negative, to interrogative to passive, and so on. There can be changes of person, or of tense. Your own textbook will probably contain transformation exercises. These are intended to be done orally, but there is no reason why they should not be done as written exercises for variety.

The process can easily become mechanical, with no importance attached to meaning. Everyone's attention is on accuracy and the form of the new structure. This is certainly a danger to which teachers must be alert. Good presentation procedures, described in the preceding chapters, will usually ensure comprehension. If not, gloss the structures to be practised in the mother tongue.

When the drill is conducted orally, cues for transformation are often given verbally, but tense changes can be signalled by a backward or a forward gesture. Here is an example of a transformation drill.

| | |
|---|---|
| TEACHER: | I travel to work by bus. |
| STUDENTS: | I travel to work by bus. |
| TEACHER: | Dr Daoud. |
| STUDENTS: | Dr Daoud travels to work by bus. |
| TEACHER: | Question. |
| STUDENTS: | Does Dr Daoud travel to work by bus? |
| TEACHER: | Yesterday. |
| STUDENTS: | Did Dr Daoud travel to work by bus yesterday? |
| TEACHER: | Negative question. |
| STUDENTS: | Didn't Dr Daoud . . . |

If you must practise transformations formally, reduce the level of difficulty as much as possible. The aim is not to discourage students by expecting them to accomplish mental gymnastics. Focus on a single transformation rather than on a sequence of changes. Offer visual support, contrasting the patterns, so that errors are unlikely, as in the following blackboard prompt.

THEN AND NOW.

Q. What did your X use to do?

Then: My X used to (verb) . . . ,
Now: But he { doesn't (verb) any more.
              { verb +s now.

Practice, based on that table, can be done in a more meaningful way by having the learners ask each other questions in **public pairs**. One student stands and nominates another by name. This second student also stands. The first then asks a question and the designated partner answers truthfully. Having answered, he or she addresses a new question to another student. The language exchanges will sound like this:

STUDENT 1: Tell us about your big brother, Jacek.

JACEK: He used to be a good footballer, but now he doesn't play any more. Vladimir, tell us something about your uncle.

VLADIMIR: He used to drive a Skoda. Now he drives a Volkswagon. Izabella, ...

Most structure changes can be elicited naturally by the use of pictures. A wall picture, done at home and with a lot of detail, will elicit lots of sentences with the describing structures *there's a/an X* and *there's a X –ing* (There's a policeman near/opposite the shop/bank; there's a child playing/skipping/eating). The students can also compose questions about the picture.

The tenses are easily changed. After practice, yesterday's date or some other date in the past can be put on the board. Or, the pictures can simply be taken down. The students now have to transform the phrases they gave earlier to the past tense. With any future date, the future tenses can be elicited in a similar way (These activities are what Mr and Mrs X are *going to do* on holiday next year. Tell me about their plans).

Later the teacher can get even more transformations by asking, What are your own plans for the holidays? And what about your brother/father? And me? What do you think I am planning to do in the long holidays?

## Variational drills

Here is an example of a blackboard table designed to cue changes in order to drill a *grammar point*. Although the word order is not changed (pronoun + verb + complement) the meaning varies as the pronoun is changed. Grammar points of this sort often appear in textbooks in this form. The simple layout and the practice which flows easily because of the table can be deceptive. It may take months or years for the learners to gain mastery of grammar content such as this.

| I've | | my | |
| You've | found | your | watch |
| We've | | our | cash |
| They've | lost | their | bag |
| S/he's | | her/his | |

That table will generate many different sentences, all grammatically correct. In fact, there are almost 1000 different grammatical sentences hidden within it. After some oral practice, bringing in other verbs and nouns, why not ask the students to *write* 5 or so different sentences from the model? This writing will ensure that everyone is involved. Let them substitute other articles for those in the final column if they wish, it will be almost impossible for them to write ungrammatical or nonsensical phrases. After a few moments do a quick oral check. Ask individuals to read aloud one of their sentences, insisting that each be different from those heard before. In this way, everyone listens carefully, internalising the grammar forms. Sometimes a student can be challenged to translate what has just been said, as a check.

## ■ CONCLUSION

Repetition drills are easy to use and can be conducted at any phase of the lesson. It is vital that everyone understands what is being practised. Where possible, use visual prompts to convey the meaning. One or two briskly conducted repetition drills will ensure that everyone has been involved to some extent. Use chorus repetition if there are problems of pronunciation or intonation or when students stumble over an expression. Use a limited number of drills to build up confidence in saying the parts of a dialogue, to teach the words of a song or rhyme, or to give the learners the language they need to play a language game. A repetition drill is the easiest way to teach the students the classroom language they need to use with you. They can rote learn phrases like, Please Miss, may I leave the room? I don't understand, How do you say (mother tongue word or phrase) in English?

Transformation drills are difficult and learners need a lot of support if they are not to make mistakes and become discouraged. Only conduct a transformation drill when you are sure that it will go easily. Use the blackboard to offer support. If the learners have a good table on the board or in their books, mistakes are less likely. Remember that it is easier to *write* transformation drills than it is to *speak* them. Writing offers a change of pace and activity, as well as involving everyone.

Other types of drill offer variety to the learning situation, but do not overuse them. Practise your gestures in front of a mirror and develop a clear set of signals to use consistently. Prepare your cues carefully. Keep the drills short and fast moving. Conduct boldly, moving around the front part of the classroom. Look alert, smile and appear to enjoy yourself. If you seem to be having fun with drills, there is a good chance that the class will enjoy them too.

## Notes

[1] I write these lines moments after observing a class of eighty 16 year olds. The lesson was well conducted, with plenty of oral work. Even so, few of the students made more than two or three contributions: some said nothing. With large classes, chorus work becomes essential.

[2] A drill should be fast moving, with no interruptions. The use of a name, or an instruction, can be a distraction. Imagine that someone gives you a seven digit telephone number. It is in your short term memory. You can call it back or dial it instantly. If, though, the person adds something else (They should be home at about this time), you are distracted. In all probability you will want the number repeated before you dial. The same thing happens in drills. As long as the learners are hearing and saying the pattern, there is no difficulty. But, the moment you disturb the memory trace with a name, a command, criticism or praise, that short term memory trace can disappear. Names are fine at other times, but not during a drill.

[3] The moment at which you should permit the students to see the structure on the board is a decision that you must make for yourself. Orthodox belief is that they should not see it until after the drill. Today many teachers believe that learners are helped by being able to see the structure as they work. If you do write the structure on the blackboard, allow the students to glance at it as they listen to others, but get them to look at you as they speak. This stops them simply reading aloud.

# 5 Using pair and group work

## ■ ORGANISING PAIR WORK

In previous chapters, various activities were described as suitable for pair work, but no guidance was given for setting up the arrangement. The organisation of pair work or group work is a **management** task, but one which presents no real difficulties. However, in many societies a teacher-centred approach to education is the norm. To introduce a pedagogy which is in conflict with current educational practice may be difficult at first. And yet, if pedagogy is to be effective it should be in harmony with the aims and the nature of the subject. The aim of most language programmes is to equip the learners to interact with others, at ease and conversing reasonably fluently. Therefore, teachers must offer practice in speaking and communicating. To engage in interaction, the students need to talk to each other.

In teacher-centred classes, there just is not enough time for everyone to make a significant contribution. If we disregard the few chorus responses in a drill, the average student in a large class will probably only speak for a total of 10 or 15 seconds. Extra time for talking can only be gained if they all talk at the same time for parts of the lesson.[1]

You may imagine that to have all the students talking at the same time will be a noisy business. This is not the case. A repetition drill is far noisier than simultaneous pair work. When learners talk to an immediate neighbour they tend to speak quietly. The effect is of a continuous murmuring; it is good noise, a learning noise.

## The teacher's role during pair work

Teachers who have never before relinquished total control have to adopt new attitudes, thinking more about the *learning experience*. And their pedagogical role is quite different during these new lesson phases. During pair work the teacher has two roles. One is to act as a **monitor**, listening to a few of the pairs and noting any persistent errors. Pair work should not be interrupted unless absolutely necessary. Serious errors will receive attention another time, perhaps at the start of the next lesson. The second role is that of **resource person**, providing help, information and feedback upon request.

## Introducing pair work

When you use pair work for the first time, explain the reasons for using pairs to the students (the arguments above). You will probably have to use the students' mother tongue. Additionally, the students must understand the following rules.

- Pair work time is not to be used for chatting.
- When they finish the set task they can change roles and do the task again.
- If they have not quite finished when the activity is stopped, this is not serious. They will still have done a lot of talking.
- They can ask for help if they need it.
- There will be a check on their participation afterwards.
- If you work in a very crowded classroom some students will be three to a desk. Explain that the third student will monitor the language exchanges and take the place of one of the others when the practice has been done once. Any student sitting alone should automatically join another individual or a nearby pair as a third participant.

You should also demonstrate the gestures you will use to set up pair work. Get repetition of the words *pairs* and *pair work* so that students become familiar with the words. You might introduce *a pair of shoes/socks*, and so on, to give the sense of the word, but avoid single items, like pairs of trousers or spectacles. This will enable you to manage the organisation in English in the future.

## Steps in using pair work

*Step one: preparation*
Prepare carefully, by means of presentation and practice, so that everyone is confident in using the language. Leave any needed visual support on the blackboard.

*Step two: teacher–student model*
Call upon one student to stand. Take one part yourself and go through the whole task. Ensure they all know what they have to do.

*Step three: public pairs*
Designate two students who are sitting well apart; this makes them speak loudly enough for all to hear. Get them to repeat the task, as a second model. If necessary, get further public pair models.

*Step four: timing*
Tell the class how long the activity will last, typically only two or three minutes.

*Step five: private pairs*
Tell everyone to begin. This is sometimes called **simultaneous pair work**. While it is going on, go around the room to monitor and assist. There should be little need to interfere if the preparation has been thorough.

*Step six: public check:*
Stop the activity when you see that most of the class have completed the task.

Choose one pair at random to stand and do the task again, publicly. This will be easy and quick if they have indeed been practising. Choose a second and a third pair to do the same. This stops students chatting in their mother tongue during pair work. They work harder if they know they may be checked afterwards.

## Suitable activities for pair work

As you gain experience you will discover many opportunities for using simultaneous pair work. In the early stages of teaching it is best to use it for intensive practice purposes. In addition, some of the activities suggested later for group work may equally well be done in pairs. The practice activities described now are easy to use in pair work.

### 1 Dialogues
These are obvious targets. The two or three parts are first practised by means of a repetition drill. Then some substitutions are cued, so that the students know how to personalise details in the dialogue (eg using their own names and the name of their own school, the length of time they have been studying English, the times of lessons, and so on).

### 2 Substitution drills
When you have patterns of the sort described in previous chapters, the learners can alternately compose new sentences from a visual cue which leaves plenty of room for creativity. Imagine how many original substitutions could be made on the basis of the following.

When I'm
- alone
- on holiday
- at my friend's

I love to +vb.

(chat, watch videos, read magazines, etc.)

### 3 Grammar practice
In Chapter 3 we saw a blackboard table with a routine schedule. It was designed to practise the use of the third person singular in the Present Simple tense. It

was later used to get students talking about their own plans and their friends' plans for the following weekend. Blackboard prompts of that sort are ideal for grammar practice in pair work, following a short presentation and formal practice, as the following example shows.

```
1.                          2.              3.

Last month              1/we            went
On Saturday evening     My friends      saw
During the holidays     My brother      played
    etc.                    etc.          etc.
```

Here is another example of a blackboard cue for meaningful grammar practice in pairs. This one is used to contrast countables and uncountables. It is assumed that structures for making enquiries (*Have you got any . . .?, Is/Are there any . . .?,* etc.) have already been presented and practised before this pair work phase.

```
Flour           70c         Carrots         75c
Sugar           90c         Cassava         30c
Coffee        $1.90         Oil            $1.40
Tea           $1.25         Paraffin        20c
Soft Drinks     35c         Sardines        50c
(kilo, tin, bottle, litre, packet, etc.)
```

The students can be asked to add a few more items to their own list, writing them in their note books, but not showing their partner. This brings in a needed element of surprise. The pair work exchanges will be like the one below. The teacher will be monitoring the use of appropriate singular and plural forms, which are shown in brackets and by underlining:

STUDENT 1: Have you got any sardines? (*–s marker*)
STUDENT 2: Yes we have.
STUDENT 1: How much *are* they? (*plural verb form*)

STUDENT 2: Fifty cents a tin.
STUDENT 1: What about apples? (*–s marker*)
STUDENT 2: We haven't any. But, we do have mangoes.
STUDENT 1: No. No thanks. What about oil? (*no plural marker*)
STUDENT 2: Yes, we have palm oil.
STUDENT 1: How much *is* it? (*singular verb form*)
STUDENT 2: It's ...

## 4 Informal tests

Testing can be made instructive. By allowing students to collaborate on a short test you will encourage learning, as weaker students can be helped by their partners. Sometimes you can include a quick written test at the end of the lesson and mark it at once. An informal test need not be related to that day's lesson, it can focus on almost any aspect of language use. Get the class to turn direct speech to indirect speech, active to passive voice, statements to questions by adding question tags, and so on. The stimulus sentences can be written on the board and the check can be made orally, with adjacent pairs marking each other's work.

## 5 Describing pictures

In Chapter 3 the teacher used flashcards in a sort of guessing game, to get the students using the present continuous tense. Any picture can be the stimulus for a similar activity in pairs. Looking at the pictures that accompany the texts, students can take turns to compose true-false statements about the picture. The second of the pair only has to reply agree or disagree. Because they will have studied the text beforehand, there is little chance of error.

## 6 Providing titles

Before studying a text in class, ask the pairs to read it quickly and to compose and write down a new title for it. Allow a minute at the most and then make an oral check. This is an excellent activity, as the class is really reading for information and not just for practice. You will sometimes realise, as a result of a variety of sensitive answers, that the text has been adequately understood. If so, why bother to conduct any other form of follow-up? The reading that has gone on was very realistic and purposeful. Why spoil a good activity?

## 7 Question and answer work

The questions which follow the text can be done in pairs. The students can work orally, with the teacher making spot public checks afterwards. Alternatively, the answers can be written and neighbouring pairs can mark each others' work afterwards, under the teacher's direction.

## 8 Illustrative sentences

As the day's new vocabulary was introduced, short illustrative sentences were put on the board. If time remains at the end of the lesson, erase one or two of these sentences and ask the class to work in pairs to reproduce them. In this way you can check that the meaning and the possible uses of a new word have been understood.

# ■ ORGANISING GROUP WORK

Desks cannot be moved in many classrooms. The only way to make groups in these circumstances is to ask alternate rows to turn and face those in the desk behind. This creates groups of four to six, depending on the number of students on a bench. A class of 80 individuals is reduced to 15 to 20 groups. You now have some chance of providing individual attention.

It is usual to have one member of each group acting as a **leader** or **secretary**. This is the person who will come to you with any difficulties or with a final completed task. This makes class management much easier. You can appoint the leaders by choosing the most able linguists, or you can allow the groups to select their own. You may even insist that the job be rotated, so that everyone gets a chance to be the leader. Whatever you decide, be sure that the students know exactly who their group leader is. As a result, they can begin work at once without waiting for a nomination.

Setting up groups is done in much the same way as setting up pairs. The mother tongue may be useful the first time or two but the students soon learn to recognise instructions like, *First row, turn and face the second. Third row, turn and face the fourth, please. Now work in groups.*

## The role of the teacher in group work

The teacher is the manager of the activity and must plan it, organise it, start it, monitor it, time it and conclude it. During group work activities the teacher stays mainly at the front of the class, perhaps making a rapid check on a group or two to see that all is well. The leader-secretaries report to the teacher's table with assignments or with queries. Corrections are made on the spot and any new instructions issued to the leader. The corrected copy and instructions are carried back to the group by the leader.

The teacher is active; marking, remaining sensitive to the atmosphere and pace of the groups and noting persistent errors for remedial teaching. Should the task be seen to be going drastically wrong, the teacher will stop it and revert to some form of practice before starting group work again.

## Suitable group work tasks

Group activities tend to be freer and more interactive than pair work. Several types of activity are collaborative and easy to use, even by comparatively inexperienced teachers.

### 1 Games
Simple guessing games that practice Yes–No questions can be played in groups

after a demonstration at the front. Easy ones to use are *Who I am thinking of?*, *What's my profession?* and *Guess what I did* (last night/during the weekend).[2]

## 2 Question construction

After a text is read, each group can be asked to write a few questions that they could ask about the text. Afterwards, the leader of a group will nominate another group and ask a first question. The second group must try to answer grammatically as well as factually. Then this second group directs a different question at another designated group, and so on until each group has asked at least one question.

## 3 Guided practice

Let us suppose you have used a substitution drill to build up familiarity with a structure with a functional value. Further and more meaningful practice can often be made more gamelike and creative in group follow-up. Let us suppose that the structure is like this one, on the blackboard.

ADVICE

You should /shouldn't + verb.
(you should eat more fruit.)

The groups can be given some prompts which leave room for expression. In a well resourced classroom the teacher would write some problems on a work-sheet and each group would get one copy. (See the example at the top of p. 56.)

Naturally, the same activity can be done using the blackboard. However, it would be unwise to take the time to write so much. It would be better to write just ten or so single words to represent problems. For example;

WALLET   (I've lost my wallet./You should report it to the police.)

SHIRT   (my shirt is torn, dirty./You should get it repaired, washed.)

WATCH   (my watch is broken, has stopped./You should buy a new one.)

BAD MARKS   (I got bad marks for science./You should work harder.)

ACHE   (I've got a headache, toothache./You should see . . .)

The students themselves might suggest some real life problems that can be added to the list in the same one-word form. Members of the group take turns to speak. The first chooses a problem from the board or invents new one, and

---

WHAT WOULD YOU SAY?

A friend's car will not start.
An old relative falls and hurts herself
while out shopping.
A man is smoking and coughing.
A brother is offered promotion, with
lots of extra work.
A friend has cut her finger.

---

states it in his or her own terms. The others offer advice. Then a new problem is stated, and so on. The turn-taking continues throughout the activity, which might last for a maximum of three or four minutes.

STUDENT 1: I've got a headache today.
STUDENT 2: You should take an aspirin.
STUDENT 3: You shouldn't drink so much beer.
STUDENT 4: My umbrella has holes in it.
STUDENT 2: You should get a new one.
STUDENT 5: You should get it repaired.
STUDENT 6: I got bad marks for science.
STUDENT 7: You shouldn't . . .

Because the other group members cannot predict the exact nature of a problem or of the advice that will result, the utterances are interesting to everyone.

### 4 Dictation

Why should teachers always dictate a passage? It can easily be done by the group leaders. Of course, they will only be assigned short texts that have already been worked on in class. In this way, pronunciation is good and the success rate is high. The leader can be responsible for checking for errors, too, after each complete sentence. In this way, feedback is quick and when you call a stop, no-one is holding a page of uncorrected work.

### 5 Role play

This offers good follow-up to a lesson in which the class practised a structure with a functional value. The groups can be asked to compose a short scene in which someone makes a complaint, exchanges a bought item of clothing for another, requests information in a place of travel, and so on. Role play enables the group to create an entire playlet with several players. If the group writes out the scene, the secretaries can get the work checked as it is composed. Afterwards, some or all of the groups may wish to act out their little play in front of the class.

## 6 Guess ahead

Before more advanced students read a new text, the topic is announced. They are then asked to make group predictions of the content or vocabulary that might be in the text. In a text about *pollution*, we might predict that it will deal with the sea, the forests, the use of fossil fuels, smoke from car exhausts, and so on.

## 7 Speculative questions

After a text has been read, a question or set of related questions can be asked for which there are no factual answers in the passage (eg Why did Roberta act in this way?, What do you imagine her feelings were?, What sort of a childhood do you think she might have had?). The follow-up check is public; each group gives an agreed opinion.

## 8 Discussions

Discussion permits free expression of opinions, so its value in a language class is obvious. The teacher asks a topic question (What do you think about women as politicians? What should be done about all the beggars on the streets?) and allows a few minutes for the group members to express their views. Afterwards, one member of each group is asked to report on their findings. The reporter could be the group leader, but it is better to nominate reporters at random after the discussion. This ensures that everyone participates. Full class discussion or argument might well follow the reports. There is absolutely no need for the teacher to express an opinion, unless intolerant ideas are going unchallenged.

## 9 Essays

These are ideal for group work when class numbers are high, as a teacher cannot monitor and help 80 students, all of whom are writing something different. What is more, correcting 80 essays is irksome, to say the least! Some methodologists view unmonitored writing as harmful. They argue that learners should not write and internalise incorrect English. By establishing groups, the teacher of a large class is able to keep simultaneous control of all the creative writing that is going on.

You may be guiding the essay by means of questions on the board, by a wall picture or by word prompts. Perhaps the groups each have a letter to read and reply to. The leaders know that they alone can come to the teacher's table for help. They also know that they should come out and get the group's work checked every two or three sentences. In this way everyone contributes, everyone gets instant feedback on errors and everyone shares the success.

# ■ CONCLUSION

Teachers can multiply the opportunities for practice and for creative language use by introducing pair and group work. Equally important, changes of learning activities and of the patterns of interaction help to retain the students' concentration. They also come to realise that they have some autonomy and responsibility for their own progress.

The feedback from watching, listening and marking written work is invaluable in the insights it provides into learning processes. The monitoring teacher identifies problems that will need remedial teaching, or new language that needs to be presented. Teachers have to learn to be tolerant of errors that do not impede the message that is being conveyed. Students should be encouraged to be adventurous with words.

Perhaps most important of all, the students will come to view the teacher as someone who is sensitive to their learning, someone to whom they can go for advice. Relationships with students can be transformed for the better. In a resource person role, the teacher is viewed as being **an authority**, not simply as someone **in authority**.

## Notes

[1] Even with small classes, lack of talking time for individuals is a problem. Many teachers who read these pages will regularly take classes of 60. Some will have twice as many. Let us assume that in the traditional lesson the teacher does about half of the talking (in fact it is usually rather more). The one hour lesson is rarely more than 50 effective minutes in length, but let us suppose that all 60 minutes are used properly. Really, we should deduct time for thinking, hesitations and writing, but again we shall be generous and imagine that the whole lesson is oral and fast moving.

So, the teacher talks for 30 minutes. The class talks for 30 minutes. There are 60 individuals to share those 30 minutes. This means that on average each has *half a minute* of talking time. And they get that only under impossibly ideal conditions.

[2] Classroom games are dealt with in Chapter 12. If you are especially interested in using games, look at some now. Those given in the early pages of that chapter are very easy to introduce and are very motivating.

# 6 Oral work: elicitation techniques

## ■ ENCOURAGING STUDENTS TO TALK

Language teachers spend more time eliciting oral contributions from the class than do teachers of any other subject. Questions are the most widely used way of getting learners to speak, but they are not the only possible means. In this chapter we examine the many types of **elicit** that teachers can use to cue utterances from students. We also look at strategies for involving the whole class and for providing opportunities for learners to frame their own questions. We reflect on the nature of errors and the corrections that might be made at different points of the lesson.

What are your objectives in teaching the spoken language? Do you want students to speak *authentically*, or do you intend to impart a variety of speech that is only found in classrooms? Most readers will say that their aim is to equip the students for meaningful communication. If that is the case, it is hard to justify question and answer patterns like these;

TEACHER:    What's your name?
STUDENT:    My name is Saidah.
TEACHER:    Class! What is his name?
STUDENTS:  His name is Saidah.
TEACHER:    Good. Repeat class. His . . .

The teacher already knew the boy's name. Even if he or she didn't, there was no need to ask the class once it had been given. Other unauthentic features are the lack of contractions (*What is* should have been said as *What's*, etc) and the length of the responses. Proper answers would just be *Saidah*. If Saidah had been asked how much pocket money he got each week, nobody could have predicted the amount. This would be a **real question**. And if the answer were given in a natural way (*50 cents*) and not as a sentence, we would have something approaching genuine speech.

By requiring full sentences, we are making learners use English abnormally in order to display their ability to compose grammatically correct sentences. The criticisms may be unfair. Students and teachers alike know that belief and reality are sometimes suspended in language lessons and that teachers sometimes ask for information they already possess. Even so, the points are important. Good teachers can contrive ways to make students answer in ways that approximate to natural usage, even when they are talking at length. Throughout the chapter, and in fact this whole book, we shall be concerned with finding ways of practising language in ways that, wherever possible, are representative of authentic patterns of interaction.

# ■ THE RANGE OF QUESTION FORMS AND PROMPTS

As well as examining the range of question types, we look at **prompts**, which are better than questions for eliciting longer utterances. Some elicits obtain a one word response, others two or three words. Some have to be answered by a full sentence, but in a natural way. Some elicits oblige students to be creative, rather than simply to lift answers verbatim from the text. The fact that different response patterns are provoked by the different types of elicit is most important. Teachers who require a full sentence, whatever the type of question or cue, are ignorant of the possibilities offered by the range of quite different elicits.[1]

The question types and prompts that follow are in an approximate sequence of difficulty for the learners. The early ones require comprehension, but limited oral response. They are valuable for developing listening skills but they also reduce anxiety on the part of the learners, who do not need to compose lengthy answers. Later types require greater production and are useful for practising the language of the text. Questions which can only be answered in unpredictable ways are useful for fluency practice. We shall consider the uses and appropriacy of the various question forms as we work through the chapter.

## Short-answer elicits

### 1 Yes-No Questions

These are answered with a monosyllable, a nod, a shake of the head, or by raising a hand. They are ideal for beginners and for comprehension work with groups of all levels. Pictures can be exploited with yes-no questions to offer intensive listening practice. These questions are especially useful in mixed ability classes, where teachers need to involve less-able students. Do *not* expect yes-no questions to be answered with a tag when they are used in a quick fire way (Yes, he did/No he wouldn't, etc). Tags are extremely difficult for students, as well as unnecessary.[2] Yes-no questions always begin with an auxiliary. Here are some examples.

> Did Mr Green go to work by bus?
> Was there a queue at the ticket office?
> Was he there on time?
> Does he usually work on Saturday mornings?
> Do you come to school on Saturdays?

### 2 True-false statements

These function in much the same way as yes-no questions. They, too, are delivered fast and can be used to exploit the text or a picture. The students call out *true* or *false*, or just raise a hand to show agreement. The technique can also be used independently of the textbook. Nonsense statements can be used as a warm-up activity at the start of a lesson, in the following way.

Monkeys are very interesting insects.
Cows eat grass and give milk.
Most Chinese speak fluent Italian.
Before we send a letter we put a stamp on it.
Most of the students in this class are lazy.
English teachers are wonderful.
The cheapest cars are made by Mercedes Benz.

## 3 Choice-questions

The question includes the word *or*, giving an option. Because the answers are built into the questions, they are good for beginner classes. They are also useful in more advanced classes for going quickly through the main features of a text, but bringing in additional vocabulary in the process, as in the example that follows. Choice questions can also be used in conjunction with pictures. The answers should *never* be in full sentence form.

TEXT: Lee is a teenager, almost sixteen. He lives at home with his father, mother and twin sisters, aged twelve. He is a trainee salesman in a clothing store in downtown Hong Kong.

TEACHER:   Is Lee 15 or 16 years old?
STUDENTS: Fifteen.
TEACHER:   Is he the youngest or oldest of the children?
STUDENTS: The oldest.
TEACHER:   Does he work in a factory or a shop?
STUDENTS: A shop.
TEACHER:   Does he sell clothes or footwear?
STUDENTS: Clothes.
TEACHER:   Is the shop in the market place or the town centre?
STUDENTS: ...

## 4 WH short-answer questions

When we speak of WH-questions (pronounced *double you aitch*), we include all the following:

*Why, What, What for, When, Where, Who, Whose, How.*

Most are answered by a short phrase. Full and totally unnatural answers to WH-questions produce that strange variety of language called *classroom English*. Notice how all the answers in this example of the exploitation of a text respect the natural features of discourse.

TEXT: Mr Adler was driving, much too fast in view of the heavy rain, towards the airport. His wife was due there at 3.30 and he was rather late. She had been to Amsterdam to buy stones for the diamond company, for which she worked. Suddenly he saw the flashing light in his rear view mirror and heard a police siren. He immediately slowed down but it was too late. The ...

TEACHER: Where was Mr Adler going when the police stopped him?
STUDENTS: To the airport.
TEACHER: Who was he going to meet there?
STUDENTS: His wife.
TEACHER: Where was she coming from?
STUDENTS: Amsterdam.
TEACHER: Why had she gone there?
STUDENTS: To buy diamonds.
TEACHER: How was Mr Adler driving?
STUDENTS: Fast/too fast.
TEACHER: What did he ...

Once Mr Adler's name is given, the teacher refers to him as *he* in the next question. *Amsterdam* becomes *there*, and *his wife* becomes *she*. If WH question and answer routines are done like this, there are few mistakes and they offer good practice for engaging in genuine language exchanges at some later date.

## Using short-answer elicits with beginners

Short-answer WH-questions, with choice-questions and yes-no questions, can be combined for **personal questions** at very early levels. The students themselves need not say much, but communicative, natural exchanges take place, as in this example.

Who heard the Alpha Blondie concert? (*Hands go up*).
Did you enjoy it? (*chorus yes/no*)
What was his best song? (*titles are suggested*)
You didn't listen, Keita? (*no*)
You don't like him? (*yes/no*)
What do you prefer, African pop or American? (*one word*)
Which is best for dancing? (*one word*)
Do you prefer cassettes or discs, Joseph? (*one word*)
Cassettes, eh? What have you got? (*titles, names*)
What about the rest of you?

And so on.

## Longer-answer elicits

### 1 Inverted WH-questions

These incorporate the whole range of WH-question types. Teachers often neglect this sort of question. In a way, they resemble the prompts which we shall see later. Unlike the usual WH-questions, inverted questions *tend* to elicit a sentence length answer. However, the responses are fairly easy because the questions have a **subject + verb** word order, just like the answers. So, no mental juggling of word order is required on the part of the students, even though they sometimes need to provide a different verb in their answer. Some examples will make this clear.

TEXT: It was the 24th of December, Christmas eve. The children were singing carols round the Christmas tree, in the living room. Their father was playing the guitar as an accompaniment. That is how they all failed to hear the noise of a ladder being placed against the window of the parents' bedroom, at the back of the house, upstairs. Nor did they hear the intruder as he climbed the ladder and lifted the window. Once inside, the burglar moved around the room, putting ...

Tell me *what* the children were doing.
They were singing carols (round the tree).

Explain *how* the burglar got into the house.
He climbed a ladder.
He got in through a window.

Who knows *what* the burglar put the jewels into?
He put them into ...

## 2 WH longer-answer questions

Some WH-questions must be answered with a longer phrase, though not necessarily a full sentence. They are used in guided practice, when a text has been read and understood, probably after a series of short-answer questions have been used. Here are some examples of WH-questions that could not be answered with one word.

TEXT: The Jones family heard an almighty crash as they were having supper. They rushed out to see that a van and a car had collided, head on, at the traffic lights at the corner of their road. One of the vehicles must have jumped the lights. The van looked little damaged, but judging by the condition of the saloon car, the driver and passengers of that vehicle could be seriously injured. Mrs Jones told her husband to go and help while she phoned for help. She told the children to ...

Why did the Jones family go out of the house?
What had happened in the road outside?
How did this occur?
What about the passengers in the vehicles?
What did the Jones family do?
Who could tell me (why, when, how, what, who, where) ...?

*longer answer questions*

## 3 Speech prompts

Prompts are not questions at all, but they do get students talking, and at length. Yet many teachers fail to use them. Because they make greater linguistic demands on the students, they are best used after a text has been well exploited. However, the responses do not always require originality or creativity, in many cases they can be taken from the text. Prompts can be made into a proper question form by prefixing them with *Could you* ...?, or *Who can* ...?, and so on, but there is no need to do this.

Tell me about ... Say what happened after/before ...
Summarise the story in your own words.
Talk about ...
Try to explain ...
Describe ...

## 4 Inferential questions

Unlike the questions we have seen so far, these require a thoughtful and creative response. The students have to make inferences and compose original utterances. Most important, their answers cannot be predicted. Ten students might well have ten different reactions, so there is always a great deal of interest in the responses. These questions offer real fluency practice, vastly increasing the amount of communication taking place in the classroom. There are three types of inferential question. Let us look at each separately, though they need not be used separately in class.

**a) Hypothetical** (or *speculative*). The students make guesses about the topic, events and characters in the text.

What do you think might have been the reason for . .?
Why do you think they . .?
Can you think of any possible explanation for . .?
How do you explain . .?
What do you think should they have said/done?
What do you think happened before this/may happen next?
What if . .?

**b) Personal.** The students have to give their own opinions or reactions and imagine those of their family or friends.

In his place, what would you/your father have done?
Supposing you/your sister . .?
Can we justify . .?
How would X react if . . ?
What is your opinion about . .?
What is the attitude of your parents to . .?
Do you yourself believe . .?

**c) General questions.** These are of a more educational nature, to encourage students to relate an issue to the wider world.

Could something like that happen in this country?
How do other countries deal with problems of . .?
What other countries share similar advantages?
How was life different in the olden days?
Are women treated in this way in all societies?
Do attitudes like this exist in other societies?
Is this a universal condition?
What about our own police/government/etc?

Are conditions like that found . .?
What else do you know about . .?
In your geography/history lessons . .?

## 5 Tag questions

It may seem surprising that this type of question has been left to last. In most textbooks these question and answer forms receive early emphasis. They are introduced in year one and continue to cause difficulties for years afterwards. Some teachers add to the problem by converting what should be simple yes-no questions into tag questions, and insisting on full tag answers, as shown below.

TEACHER:    He's often late, isn't he?
STUDENTS:  Yes he is.
TEACHER:    He wasn't late yesterday, was he?
STUDENTS:  No he wasn't.
TEACHER:    He'll be on time tomorrow, won't he?
STUDENT:    Yes, he will.

These tag forms are extremely difficult to master. Native speakers only gain full control of this feature when they are of school age. The rules are easily explained but the use will not easily be mastered by learners, even after hours of drilling. Those hours can be spent more profitably in the learning of more useful language, leaving these complex forms to be acquired over several years from the *teacher*'s use of them. The language functions of expressing agreement or disagreement can be expressed in ways that are more typical of natural interaction, as well as being easier to learn (see note[2] again).

## Getting students to question each other

Students need to be able to phrase questions as well as to respond. There are several ways for teachers to develop this skill.

## 1 Cued questions

Simply tell the student what question to devise (*Pierre, ask Laurent what time he gets up; Dominique, ask Francoise about her family*). With good cues you can get students forming all of the question types described above.

## 2 Written questions

Everyone can be asked to write down a few questions on the text they have read. The follow-up can sometimes be conducted in simultaneous pair or group work, which gives everyone a lot more talking time.

## 3 Anticipatory questions

Students in more advanced classes can ask questions about a text they have not yet seen. If, for example, the text deals with the world's rain forests, the students can be told the topic and asked to anticipate the questions that should be answered when they read. If this is done in groups, the teacher can build up a selection of questions at the blackboard by asking each group to read out their best question, but one which is different from those already suggested. With a class of sixty, in groups, there will be a dozen or so original questions on the blackboard before the text is read. During follow-up the questions can be referred to, though answers will not have been provided in the text to every single one.

### 4 Warm-up

Get the class to use questions in a guesswork warm-up activity. You can put a student at the front or answer questions yourself, like this.

TEACHER: Guess where I went this weekend and what I did!
STUDENTS: Did you . . .?
TEACHER: Yes, you guessed right, Zosha, I did go to a restaurant, but what did I eat there?
STUDENTS: Did you . . .?

This could lead into simultaneous pair work, with students guessing each others' activities. Although the questions are limited to the yes-no type, there is a genuine exchange of message and an unpredictability that can be exciting.

## ■ MANAGING THE CLASS DURING QUESTION TIME

Teachers who nominate a student before phrasing a question risk having the majority opt out. Why should they bother to think if the question has already been assigned to someone? The same chance to drop out occurs in classes where students compete for the teacher's attention by calling *sir* or *miss*, or by snapping their fingers. It is easy to observe students in these lessons who win all the attention and those who make no attempt to work. Less obvious are those who cleverly snap their fingers at the teacher just at the moment another student is designated, to make it look as though they are participating. Inexperienced teachers in boisterous classrooms of this sort often think, wrongly, that their lesson is going well. By working almost exclusively with volunteer students, they are neglecting part of the class.

Another bad practice is to direct questions only at those students who will be able to answer quickly and correctly. Usually this is because the teacher wants a brisk lesson, with no awkward silence. This teacher, too, is ignoring the needs of many members of the class.

### Good nomination strategies

Stop all calling out and finger snapping. Every single student is there to participate. There is no opting out. Use all of these techniques to ensure that everybody makes some form of oral contribution during every lesson.

### 1 The surprise nomination

Name the student who is to answer, but only after a question has been put so that they all prepare a response. It is important to scatter the nominations, not neglecting the back and the corners of the classroom. If the pupil cannot answer, nominate another, but return with a different question.

### 2 The shotgun nomination

This is similar, but this time you walk up and down the aisles while talking, with the students looking as well as listening. After putting a question you *snap* your fingers at a designated student, who provides the answer. This keeps things moving very swiftly and the finger snaps keep everyone alert. You can point across intervening rows or spin around to *shoot* in any direction.

### 3 Chorus responses

After giving an elicit, you pause and then call out *Class?* This can only be done with short-answer question types.

### 4 Written answers

Tell the class to write down their answer, quickly, instead of answering orally. The check is random, but instead of expressing approval or disapproval, you ask *Is that correct?* This gives everyone the chance to contribute orally (even if it is only a *yes* or *no*), as well as in writing. There is no need to write the answers on the board or to check spellings. This is a strategy to involve everyone, not a writing test. You can treat a succession of questions in this way from time to time.

### 5 Written questions

Allow the class a few moments to look at the reading passage. Then tell them to work in pairs to write a couple of questions about it. Next, choose a few students to read one of their questions aloud. Before each is answered, get the others to say whether or not the question form is grammatical. If not, they themselves should make any needed corrections. Only then will you nominate the person who is to answer, and so on. Not everyone will have time to put one of their questions, but they will all have been involved. If you are lucky, the spread of questions will be wide enough to render further exploitation of the text unnecessary.

## ■ COPING WITH MIXED ABILITIES

The uses of the different types of question have been indicated. In a nutshell, those that require one word responses are used mainly for warm-up and for familiarisation with a text. Those which elicit an utterance of two or three words are suitable for assessing comprehension and the initial exploitation of the text. Questions which force a longer (but natural) utterance are useful later, for guided practice. Prompts and hypothetical questions are useful for initiating discussion, debate and communication.

However, the different question types do not have to be used only in those ways, logical though the progression is. In every class there are students who are less confident alongside star performers. The less able deserve the chance to contribute and earn praise. If they are neglected they will fall further behind. Yet, the more able must not become bored by remaining unchallenged. We can cope with this problem by judiciously sharing out the different question types and elicits, so that everyone contributes to the lesson.

## Keeping them all involved

It will be easier for you to be flexible in your question distribution if you group the questions by type when you are preparing the follow-up to the text. During exploitation, the easier question types can be directed at less able students while more able students can be required to produce longer answers. The most able can be required to change tenses and even create new language. Here is an example of this strategy in action. Let us suppose that this is part of a longer text.

TEXT: On Thursday evening, as usual, Jill finished her homework and then went to the club. There she met Alex, her best friend. They enjoyed a game of table tennis and some disco-dancing. Afterwards, they . . .

TEACHER:    What's the name of Jill's friend? (*nominates a weak student*)
STUDENT 1:  Alex.
TEACHER:    Where did Jill go on Thursday? (*choosing another weak student*)
STUDENT 2:  To club.
TEACHER:    And what happened before this? (*more able student*)
STUDENT 3:  She/Jill did her homework.
TEACHER:    What did the two girls do together? (*able student*)
STUDENT 4:  They played table tennis and danced.
TEACHER:    What day of the week was this? (*weak student*)
STUDENT 5:  Thursday (evening).
TEACHER:    Tell us about Jill's usual Thursday. (*able student*)
STUDENT 6:  She usually . . . . .
TEACHER:    And what do you think she might do next weekend? (*a very able student*).

# ■ ERRORS AND MISTAKES

We cannot discuss the answers provided by students without thinking for a moment about incorrect responses. Some teachers regard any deviation from accurate pronunciation and syntax as evidence of carelessness, but this is not always the case. Today, mistakes and errors are viewed as an inevitable and necessary part of the process of language development. What is more, they are of value because of the feedback and insights that a teacher can gain from them.

Teachers should be aware of a major distinction, between **errors** and **mistakes**. We can usually disregard **slips** (or **lapses**) which arise because of a moment's inattention. Because errors and mistakes require quite different reactions from a teacher, the distinction is an important one.

## The nature of errors

Errors are evidence of positive progress and the mastery of regular grammatical features. They occur when students use their intelligence in constructing novel utterances. Often they are applying a rule which, in this case, does not work, as *Over-generaliz*, in the following examples.

> I dislike to play football (by analogy from "I like to ...")
> I readed a book last night (past participle + ed)
> He musted to it (expectation of a past form for a modal)

A teacher who gets statements like those should jump for joy, though perhaps remodelling at the same time. Any one of those errors might have been made by a native speaker child.

Some errors are evidence of rule ignorance. Often they demonstrate thoughtfulness and an attempt to form a phrase on the basis of a mother tongue construction or feature. For example, French students may ask for *some informations* and a German may say that *it is dangerous in the river to swim*.

The real test of an error is whether or not the students can self correct. If they can, then it is a mistake, not an error. Errors are inevitable if you want to permit free expression and interaction strategies.

## The nature of mistakes

These are quite different. Here the learner *knows* the rule and can self correct. As yet the language point has not been internalised, so the learner cannot apply it consistently. It is now generally recognised that there is a **readiness** stage for all the features of grammar, in our mother tongue as well as in second and subsequent languages. Some grammatical features will be mastered very late indeed, regardless of an early place in the syllabus.[4]

## ■ DEALING WITH MISTAKES AND ERRORS

Rewards are more effective than punishment. Any good response deserves some sort of acknowledgement; a nod, a smile or a word of praise. Many good teachers convey approval by gesture and facial expression, rather than verbally. Even a partially correct answer may demonstrate involvement and effort. If possible, make some sort of natural response to *what* has been said. Never adopt a threatening or punishing attitude when a mistake is made. This will do more harm than good. Students will be afraid to speak, the atmosphere will be spoiled and they may well grow to dislike you and the language.

## ■ MISTAKES DURING PRACTICE

We begin by considering the treatment of mistakes during practice and while the text is being exploited. It must be understood that the strategies suggested now are suited mainly to *practice* activities. Later we shall consider the phase of the lesson in which teachers encourage free expression.

During formal practice the teacher and learners can usually predict the answers, and attention is being paid to accuracy of pronunciation and syntax, as well as to content. The nature of the correction will depend on the aim of the practice. If the question is designed to make the students produce a specific word and pronounce it correctly, then correction is due if it is mispronounced. If the aim is to practise a structure or grammar point and it is wrongly produced, then correction (and perhaps more presentation) is again expected. All the same, corrections should be made with discretion, sensitivity and appropriacy.

## Indicating the mistake

Many strategies can be used to indicate that something is wrong. Which is used will depend on the situation, the level of difficulty and the competence of the student who made the mistake. The teacher can do any of the following.

1 Nod in a quizzical way, indicating that the answer is partially correct but can be improved.
2 Look puzzled or give a shake of the head.
3 Give a non-verbal indication of the sort of error made. A gesture forward, downwards or backwards indicates a tense. A finger near thumb will show the absence of a short word. Three fingers show that the third person agreement of the verb has not been made. Finger counting gestures can indicate the third, fourth, fifth word, or wherever a fault is situated in the sentence.
4 Repeat the answer but stop at the point where the error occurred.
5 Repeat the incorrect phrase with a rising tone to show surprise.
6 Ignore the answer and repeat the question.
7 Pretend not to understand.
8 Indicate the nature of the error verbally (eg by saying *plural* or *pronunciation*).

## Obtaining corrections

The teacher has to decide who should make a correction. The decision will depend on the circumstances; pressure of time, the ability of an individual, the complexity of the answer, the nature of the mistake, and so on.

1 Make the correction yourself, then ask the question again so that the student can respond accurately.
2 Choose another student to answer, then go back to the first for a correct answer.
3 Nominate another student to answer and keep the lesson flowing by moving to a new question (perhaps an easy one to the original student).
4 Invite the whole class to call out the correct version (*Class?*).
5 Ask for volunteer to answer (*Who can help?*), returning to the first student afterwards for a repetition.
6 Invite the student to self correct.
7 Another alternative is to ignore mistakes altogether. Some teachers never

correct or require self correction. Nor is there any research evidence to show that corrections result in more fluent and accurate communicative ability. In fact, the weight of evidence is to the contrary – undue attention to form detracts from performance. Each teacher must come to an individual decision in respect of the treatment of mistakes. What works well in Madrid may not work in Tokyo.

## Avoiding practice mistakes

If too many mistakes occur during practice, this is indicative of poor teaching. The teacher has not made an effective presentation, or is asking **display questions** to force the students to compose complex answers. Never put students into a position where mistakes are likely during formal practice. Learning is no fun when students are constantly being stopped and corrected.

If attention is switched to comprehension and meaning, and if natural forms of answer are expected, fewer mistakes will occur during the exploitation of the text and guided practice. Make more use of short-answer question types. Mistakes will then be of fact, rather than of language. This will indicate the need for an explanation of a misunderstood point in the text. Such clarification might well be made by another student.

WH-questions which require a full phrase utterance are more liable to trigger an answer that is linguistically wrong. However, the information conveyed may be correct. If so, this should be acknowledged in some way. Often the student will be able to make a correction alone, especially if there is some visual support on the blackboard. However, if the student is clearly in difficulty, he or she must not be embarrassed in any way. If a second student gets into similar difficulties, things begin to disintegrate. In such cases it is best to get a volunteer to give a correct model.

## ■ ERRORS AND MISTAKES DURING A FREE EXPRESSION PHASE

The phase of a lesson in which students are given opportunities to be adventurous with language is often called the **production**, or the **performance** stage. During this phase, referential questions and prompts play a major part. Often the teacher can move to the side of the room and allow debate to continue under its own momentum.

## Monitoring errors

You have to accept that some errors are inevitable during any sort of communicative activity. However, as we saw earlier, errors are often indicative of progress or a rational attempt to compose new utterances which incorporate grammar points that have not yet been taught. To stop the class at such a time is pointless. Most errors are best ignored, provided communication is achieved. After all, the aim of this phase is to provide opportunities for self-expression, to move attention away from the formal properties of language. The teacher needs to interrupt only if there is a breakdown of communication. If any utterance is wholly ungrammatical it will not be understood anyway and so intervention and help become essential.

 You can make a note of persistent errors, though. They can be the subject of revision in a later lesson. You will also discover areas of language that the class needs to be taught formally, so that they can engage in debate more freely another time.

## Correcting mistakes

Of course there are mistakes, as well as errors, in discussion. The mistakes are of two main sorts. The first is of fact or content, in which case the message is distorted by the language is correct (eg *I had my supper at seven o'clock yesterday morning*). Probably the students themselves will pick this up (*Do you mean breakfast or do you mean yesterday evening?*). If not, you yourself should ask the student to make the meaning clearer.

The second sort of mistake is a linguistic one and often this is a momentary slip. A taught structure may be incorrectly formed or a grammar rule broken. If the discussion continues to flow, why interrupt and spoil it?

Of course, where an utterance is loaded with mistakes, then you must step in. Not to offer practice, though! Remember the focus now is on *what* is being expressed, not on *how* it is said. In such cases you might yourself rephrase the utterance, in one of the following ways:

> What she means . . .
> What he is trying to say is that . . .
> He wants to know . . .
> I think she means . . .
> Oh, I see what you mean. You want to say . . .
> That's a good point but difficult to express . . .
> Are you trying to say that . . ?
> Do you mean . . ?

Having helped to get the message across, you can again withdraw and continue to listen to the arguments while monitoring for deviant utterances that need to be dealt with at another time.

## ■ CONCLUSION

Language exchanges should approximate to real use. Teachers who want students to display their linguistic competence should use appropriate question types and prompts to elicit the desired forms. We have also distinguished between errors and mistakes. Mistakes and errors alike provide valuable insights into learning and information on the effectiveness and needs of the teaching programme.

Mistakes are inevitable, but if there are too many it is probably the result of insufficient practice or poor exploitation strategies. In no case should students be punished for mistakes. Teachers have an array of techniques and nomination strategies for getting any correction that needs to be made. Correction techniques should be helpful and supportive, not disparaging. Mistakes are less likely to be made during practice and exploitation if teachers use the full range of question types and encourage students to respond naturally.

Errors are more likely to arise during a free phase. They are often proof of intelligent attempts to construct novel utterances. Where there is no breakdown in communication, they are best ignored. Systematic errors indicate a need for presentation and practice, at a later time, of the needed grammar point or structure.

Less able students should not be excluded from any part of the lesson. Teachers have a range of strategies for involving every member of the class in oral work.

## Notes

[1] Responses can also be elicited by means of rising intonation, by a gesture, or even by looking quizzically at a student. And, teachers can pass on a question simply by naming another student after it has been answered once.

[2] In real life, tag answers are much less frequent than textbook writers would have us believe. What is more, the question form of the textbooks (*That was a terrible storm last night, wasn't it? It rained hard, didn't it?*) are often phrased and answered quite differently. Sometimes, *eh?* replaces the tag (*Lovely day, eh? Late again, eh?*). Frequently the whole utterance is reversed and delivered with a falling tone to sound like a statement rather than a question (*Wasn't that a terrible storm last night! My word, didn't it rain!*) In other cases tag questions are genuinely seeking information (marked by rising intonation) and the responses are quite unpredictable, as in these examples.

SPEAKER 1:       He's often late, is he? (*rising tone*)
AGREEMENT:       That's right. I don't know how he keeps his job./Too often, in
                 my opinion.
DISAGREEMENT:    No, not really./Sometimes, but not often.
SPEAKER 1:       He wasn't late yesterday, was he?
AGREEMENT:       I don't think he was, actually./That's correct./No, he was right
                 on time.
DISAGREEMENT:    In fact, he was./I'm afraid so./Just a little./A few minutes.
SPEAKER 1:       He won't be late this afternoon, will he?
AGREEMENT:       I shouldn't think so./I doubt it.
DISAGREEMENT:    It's quite possible, I imagine./It wouldn't surprise me one little
                 bit./You want to bet?/You must be kidding!/I wouldn't bet on
                 it!/That's a good one! You should be so lucky! Ha Ha! If he's
                 not, it'll be the first time in years. Wait and see.

[3] There is an important feature of pronunciation to note in WH-questions. The auxiliary that follows (was, has, does, are, and so on) is unstressed and the vowel sound becomes a schwa (like the short vowel sound in *the*). Usually there is a contraction as well. Properly pronounced, questions will sound like these examples (phonetic script is avoided).

Wher dzi work (Where does he work? 3 syllables, not 4)
Why di do that (Why did he do that? 4 syllables, not 5)
What si done (What has he done? 3 syllables, not 4)

[4] I recently conducted oral interviews with practising teachers of English. Several, in the excitement of self-expression, neglected to add the –s of the third person singular when talking about a friend or parent. They themselves teach it to first year students. They know the rule. They can even correct themselves. This is an example of a **mistake**, not an error. It is interesting that this simple feature is one that is developed comparatively late in the acquisition of English by native-speaker children.

# Part Two

# STANDARD LESSON TYPES

# 7 Exploiting the text

## THE NEED FOR VARIETY

All the strategies and skills presented in all the previous chapters are brought together now, as we consider ways to exploit texts in order to develop the students' listening, speaking and reading skills. In this chapter there are many suggestions for varying the approach to the reading passages in the text book. A worked example of the exploitation of a passage is included. Finally, there is advice on reading aloud for listening practice.

Textbook passages frequently need modification. Some are too complex, others lack interest. At times, teachers, have to rush to cover the text in the hour. On other days they strive to stretch an insufficiency of content over the lesson. As well as considering how to use passages of different lengths and levels of difficulty, we shall look at criteria for the selection of language for formal presentation.

Traditional guidelines for dealing with a text are now discredited, but we still see them applied, even so. Some teachers are careful not to introduce more than six or seven new words and one new grammar point or structure into any one lesson. Consequently, one potentially interesting passage is split into several parts and spread over several lessons. After presentation and practice the few lines are read aloud by a student. Exploitation is in the form of a question-answer session. The aim is to ensure that the learners get to know every word and the main grammar point.

Such treatment is predictable and boring, perhaps even harmful. There may be times when you want, or are obliged, to teach a lesson that has such a restricted focus, but to do this every time would be wrong.

## EVALUATING A TEXT

The text is a major resource, permitting you to vary the learning activities from lesson to lesson. There are four main factors to consider when deciding how to treat a passage.

### Linguistic complexity

It a text is full of difficulties but contains useful new vocabulary, a few lines of it will easily provide the substance of the whole lesson. A complex passage may well be split into two or more parts. If, on the other hand, it is fairly easy to understand, it might be dealt with in a few moments. Why waste a whole lesson on one passage when two could be covered? The complexity of the text will also lead the teacher to decide if it is to be read or if it is to be heard. A simple text is more suitable for listening comprehension than one which is loaded with unusual vocabulary or which is made up of long sentences.

## Length

Do not feel obliged to split long passages into several parts. In general, the longer the text the better it is for a reading lesson. Do not attempt to restrict the text length to half a dozen new words – the students do *not* have to know every single word in a text in order to understand it. In real life we often enjoy texts which contain words that are unfamiliar, particularly when reading in a different language. Most teachers now think that language students should learn to cope with unknown vocabulary in context. So you need not feel constrained by closely prescribed procedures in deciding how much of a passage to tackle in one lesson. Do what you feel is right for your learners, what is best for you as a teacher.

## Interest level

Is the passage boring? If so, dismiss it quickly and do something more motivating. If the passage is involved but full of interest, you might choose to base several lessons on it, with discussion and written assignments. Textbooks written for a local market often have quite long indigenous stories, known and loved by all the students but now presented in the target language. These stories were never meant to be analysed for linguistic content. They were meant to be enjoyed. It is ridiculous to leave a good story unfinished simply because you want to practice half a dozen new words and a grammar point.

## Aims

The text should match your aims. If you want to help the learners to acquire real reading skills, then a long text with a fair loading of new words will be essential. If you want to practise a grammar nicety or a useful structure, then a short text will leave time for such practice. If you want to give listening practice, then you will need a fairly short text (or part of a longer text) with lots of episodic content. If heated discussion is your aim, it will be sparked by an interesting and provocative text.

## ■ SELECTING LANGUAGE FOR FORMAL PRESENTATION

Having decided the length, you now have to choose the lexical items to present before the text is seen or heard. The easiest way to decide which words and structures should be presented is to consider two factors.

## The value of the language

Is this new word or expression useful to the students? Will they need it in future in order to enter into classroom debate, to take the examinations or to interact with a foreigner? If not, then it can be ignored until it is met in the passage. At that time, it can be glossed in the mother tongue, saving valuable time. If the word or structure is valuable, then you should make a formal presentation.

## The linguistic context

Is the new word or structure understandable in the context of the passage? If so, do not present it. Let us take an example, using the words *hen* and *to lay*, both uncommon words. In the sentence *Hens lay eggs*, you cannot really be sure that either word will be understood. People buy eggs, factories pack them and naughty boys smash them. If the context is no better than this, then you will either present the words (though they are not really very useful) or gloss them in the mother tongue when you meet them in the passage. Let us look at a different linguistic context though.

> My mother keeps chickens. Every morning I take a basket and check if the hens have laid any eggs.

There is no need now to present either word. They are perfectly understandable in context. Some teachers may worry that the infinitive form of the new verb is not in the text. Does it really matter? The verb *to lay* is not especially useful, so why inflict it on the students? For today's lesson, a level of recognition and comprehension is all that is needed. There is no need to ask ridiculous questions in order to make the class produce all the forms of the verb. In practising reading or listening, you can treat unusual verb forms (bent, caught, etc) as lexical items rather than grammatical forms.

## ■ READING AND LISTENING IN THE FOREIGN LANGUAGE

There are sound pedagogical reasons for working with texts. By reading, the students **acquire** language in a natural way. They learn to write accurate English by reading it. In the same way as we learn to speak by listening, we probably learn to write by reading. The more everyone reads, the better! However, you should make sure that the students do it properly. Some teachers assume that each passage is to be read aloud by the students. Some think it is dangerous to allow learners to see the printed words before they have heard a spoken model. Others ask the students to follow the text as it is read aloud. But few teachers set out to develop *real* reading skills in a systematic way.

In real life we treat passages in different ways, reading with purpose. We read an item of gossip in the newspaper quickly, to get the general sense. If we are reading about income tax changes, we run our eye down the page until we come to the part that is relevant to our own wage packet. Then we scrutinise it. We

79

read a report from our child's school slowly and carefully, trying to understand every implication. As language teachers, we must endeavour to give these different reading strategies to our students. They should not leave us with the impression that they have to read English slowly, decoding every word and phrase.

## Reading aloud

Do not ask students to read texts aloud. Reading passages, unlike dialogues, were never intended to serve as models for speech. The great majority of language educators condemn the practice, for the following reasons.

1 It is not a real life skill; people rarely read their mother tongue aloud. If they do, few do it well. Our students will never need to read English aloud.
2 When one student is reading, the others are inactive. Some are day-dreaming, others reading ahead.
3 Student readers offer a poor model.
4 Reading is stopped for mistakes of pronunciation.
5 The reader's attention is on pronunciation, not meaning.
6 It is wasteful of valuable learning time.
7 The practice is harmful. People who learn to read by reading aloud often continue to say the words mentally as they read, thoughout their lives. Sometimes they work their mouths as they read, slowly and silently.
8 It is unnecessary. Through proper questioning techniques teachers can elicit the words of the text in more natural ways.

Despite this, some teachers are *required* to get students reading aloud. In such cases there is only one safe place for that activity – *after* the text has been fully exploited. By then, the students will have heard and used most of the words in the text several times, so they should be able to read aloud fairly easily and with total understanding.

## Listening with a purpose

Most of what has been said about reading applies to listening. We listen for a purpose. Sometimes we need to catch every word that is said. At other times we half listen until something of real interest arises, at which point we pay close attention. Sometimes we need only to get the **gist** (essence) of what is said.

The language of genuine speech is quite unlike that of written texts. There are repetitions, hesitations and ungrammatical slips. The speaker will check for comprehension, inviting a short response of some sort. Intonation patterns and stress markings also convey meanings. The learners should be prepared to cope with language spoken in a realistic way. Unfortunately, the average teacher has no access to samples of authentic speech. Later, though, we shall see how a reading passage can **be spoken** by a teacher for purposes of listening comprehension.

We look now at ways of dealing with the text. What follows applies equally to reading lessons and listening ones. Where different treatment is needed, this is made clear. An example will be worked through later, step by step. First, let us take an overview of the options.

## ■ DEALING WITH A TEXT

There are usually three major stages, each with several possible phases, though this is not inviolable. There will always be some sort of presentation stage, followed by the reading or listening activity, which in turn is sometimes followed by an exploitation stage. Let us look at the stages separately.

### Introduction and task setting

The first phase in this stage is the presentation. Techniques for presenting vocabulary, grammar points and structures were covered in earlier chapters. Criteria for selecting vocabulary to present were given at the start of this chapter, with a strong recommendation that some lexical items be left unpresented. However, it is important to remember that listening is more difficult than reading. A reader can always cast an eye back over a misunderstood phrase, but the listener gets no second chance. Consequently more words will be presented if the text is to be heard than if it is to be read.

The next phase in this introductory stage is the arousal of interest. You can announce the title of the passage and give a brief idea of the content. It is important not to give too much information at this time, one sentence will usually suffice. It will sound like this:

> This passage is called ' . . . . .'. In this little story we meet Sung Hee and find out about her experiences when she goes to the city to find a new job.

Thirdly, you supply a reason for listening or reading by assigning a task of some sort. To do this you usually ask some **guiding questions** (or *pre-questions*). Guiding questions should be straightforward and factual. They should focus on major details, not trivial or secondary ones. Two questions will be enough for most texts. The aim is to make the class read or listen for the main events without worrying too much about the details. Often these simple questions can be given orally. To write them on the board is time consuming, though you might just write the WH-words as a memory aid.

### Reading and listening

You can now move into the second stage. Up to this point in the lesson books have been closed. With the introductory stage finished, the text can be heard or read silently. If it is to be heard, then books remain closed. There is little point in your reading aloud if the learners can see the text. This only has the effect of slowing down their reading to a talking speed.

If you do read aloud, offer a good *speech* model. Guidelines are given at the end of this chapter. Do not restrict yourself to the words in the text. **Tell the**

**story**, using the text as a guide. Read a line or two, adding any needed additional colour or detail. Break off to explain a strange word, using only the foreign language. Make any necessary sketch on the blackboard midway through a story. Rephrase a difficult sentence more simply. By treating a text in this way, you can create something like authentic, spontaneous speech. You can also add to the interest.

If students read the passage themselves, set strict time limits and gradually cut these down until the students automatically read at something like the speed at which they read their first language. For a short passage, seconds only will suffice. For a longer text, perhaps a full page long, a minute or so may be needed. To time it, read the text yourself silently beforehand. Allow a little more time, depending on the reading skill of the class. When the allotted time has passed, get them to close their books.[1]

Check the answers to the guiding questions at once. Because they are concerned with main incidents or characters, the answers will normally be correct. Language errors are unlikely if the response patterns are natural and short. The entire procedure for this short stage, from the moment the class began reading to the end of the check, will take only a few minutes for the average short text.

If the passage is not very interesting or valuable, further exploitation may not be worth doing. In listening or reading for key events, the learners have already accomplished something worthwhile. After all, the main aim of any listening or reading lesson is to get the students to listen or read. By now, that aim has been accomplished. Why not move into a new activity? They could even begin work on the following text. Let us assume, though, that the passage is worthy of more intensive scrutiny and some form of follow-up. Here are some suggestions for further activities, but do not think that you should do all of them each time you work with a good text. Just select one or two, so that there is variety from lesson to lesson.

## Exploiting the text further

You move now into a third, exploitation stage. Often the students can work from memory with books closed, but having had only fleeting contact with the text, they will not be able to quote at length. If you wish, you can let them all read the passage once more, very quickly. This stage will include a mixture of any of the following activities.

### 1 Limited response phase
Use true-false statements, yes-no and choice-questions to feed the details and lexis of the passage to the class once again, but in a new form. As well as giving listening practice, this increases the learners' familiarity with the passage and their understanding.

### 2 Reproduction phase
WH-questions are best for this purpose. These questions could, of course, be composed and asked by students. Their questions, as well as the answers, will enable you to judge the depth of understanding. If they have problems compos-

ing or answering WH-questions, revert to true-false and choice-questions or go through the text again. The answers will normally be in a short, natural form. Later, you can elicit longer chunks of language by using prompts (*Tell me about . . ., Describe . . .*).

### 3 Query time

It is always a good idea to invite questions about anything in the text that puzzles or worries the students. They can rote learn phrases for this function (*Please sir, what does X mean?*, *Miss. I don't understand the phrase . . .*). Make clear the fact, though, that they need not know every word in the passage in order to enjoy it.

### 4 Grammar awareness

Draw attention to any grammatical nicety but do not feel obliged to *teach* it. Simply pointing out a regularity or form is often enough to enhance awareness of the formal features of a text. Ask the class why an apostrophe s is suffixed to a word or why there is a plural verb form with a singular collective noun. Draw attention to discourse features, asking what words such as *here* or *there* refer to. Point out an irregular adverb, and so on.

### 5 Scanning

Ask the class to find a name, a detail or a date. Simple though this is, it provides practice in scanning. Get the students to find all the words of a specified group. With a topic based passage they can write or call out the names of all the vehicles, crops, foodstuffs, etc.

### 6 Dictation

Two or three sentences from the text are quite enough. Corrections can be made by the students themselves. You or a good student can write on the board, beginning each phrase a short while after the others. Then let everybody compare their version with the one on the blackboard. If you really want students to read aloud, then giving dictation is one authentic way of having them do this. They can take turns, in pairs, to dictate a sentence and mark each other's work. The activity should not last more than two or three minutes, or boredom will set in. An alternative is to do the short dictation a day or two later, as a warm up and review exercise.

### 7 Spot the mistake

This is a sort of memory test, but it is done like a game. Books are closed and the following instruction is given.

*Help me if I make a mistake or if I stop.*

You then read the text aloud but stop at times and wait for the next word to be called. At other times you can make a deliberate error of detail (but never of language) for the class to correct.

### 8 Extension and discussion

Conversation, argument and debate allow students to go beyond the language of the text. This is easy where a passage is topic based and interesting. To move into this production phase, ask hypothetical questions, make provocative statements and use prompts.

### 9 Review

Reactivation is always helpful to learning. The passage can be reviewed a few days after it was first dealt with. Challenge the class to think back to the text and remember any new key words or phrases, as well as details.

## ■ DEMONSTRATION EXPLOITATION

Here is a worked example of a passage used for listening practice. Most of the activities described above are used, but in a genuine lesson you would rarely use so many. The approach would be very similar if the text were used for reading. The main difference would be that instead of hearing the passage spoken at a steady speed, the students would have only a few moments to read it before being asked to close their books and reply to the guiding questions. If you time your own reading of this short text, you will find that it requires no more than twenty seconds to read it once, rapidly but carefully. In view of the aim of reading lessons – to cultivate real readings skills – it would be inadvisable to allow the class more than half a minute for the task of silently reading a passage of this length.

> TEXT: MILITARY LIFE
> John Smith had completed his first month as a soldier. He was doing his compulsory military service. He didn't like the discipline, the drills, the combat training and the long marches. He was an artistic young man and dreamed only of the day when he would finish his service and become a civilian again. One evening the sergeant walked into the barrack room. *Are there any musicians here?*, he asked. *Yes, Sergeant*, called John. *I play the guitar.* Two other soldiers were also musical. *Right*, said the Sergeant. *You three go to the canteen right now. There's a piano there. Move it to the officers' mess!*

### Stage one: presentation and guiding questions

In the blackboard example, below, you will see that the teacher decided to present two words that are not even in the text. This is because they may be useful in discussion. You must not allow yourself to be constrained by the deficiencies of a text. The presentation sounds like this.

TEACHER: The passage you will hear is about a young soldier. But first there are some new words you'll need to know (blackboard presentation).

---

VOCABULARY

Civilian ≠ military
Compulsory = obligatory, forced
Barrack room = dormitory for soldiers
The mess = dining room (military)
Recruit = new soldier
Conscription = forcing people into the army

Ex. School is compulsory to age eleven.

---

TEACHER: I want you to listen carefully, then tell me two things about this young soldier, John Smith. First; *why* was he in the army? (*repeat*). Second; *what* did the sergeant make him *do*? (*repeat*). Right, listen carefully to the passage.

## Stage two: listening

The teacher reads aloud (or plays a tape recording). The passage is spoken at a careful but steady speed, and with occasional comments and asides to make it more speechlike. It is heard only once. This is followed by a random check on the two pre-questions. Nominated students answer them while the others say if the answers are correct, making any needed corrections.

## Stage three: exploitation

This stage comprises several of the activities described earlier.

*Phase one: increasing comprehension*
The teacher fires short-answer questions at the class. The answers are given by

nominated individuals or called out by everyone, giving a sense of urgency and competition.

> Was the soldier's name George?
> Was his last name Smith?
> Had he completed one month's service or two?
> Did he like the discipline?
> Did he like the training?
> Was he practical or artistic?
> Did he paint or play an instrument?
> Was it a guitar or a trumpet?
> Was John a sergeant?
> Who came into the barrack room?
> What did this sergeant ask for?
> How many did he find?
> Did John volunteer?
> Where was John sent?
> What did they have to move?
> Where to?

*Phase two: Reproduction*

Next the teacher uses WH-questions to elicit details from the passage. The language of the replies is mainly, but not necessarily, that of the text. Most of the replies will be in a short-answer form.

> What was John Smith doing?.
> What sort of person was he?
> What sort of character did he have?
> What happened one evening?
> Who can remember the sergeant's exact words?
> And what did John reply?
> What happened after this?

*Phase three: Communication*

Now the teacher encourages the class to be adventurous with language. Any type of extension question can be put in order to elicit original and communicative language from the students. Not all of the questions would be needed, but teachers must always be ready to ask another question to keep discussion going. There is no need to keep the different question types separate, as they are here.

**a) Personal**

> Have you got a brother/father who has been in the army?
> What did he think of it?
> What did he do during his service?
> Do any of you play an instrument?
> How did you learn to play?

**b) General**

> Do we have military service in this country?

Is this a good or a bad thing? Why?
Which countries in the world do have compulsory service?
Is it fair to excuse women from service?
How do people become officers?
What are sergeants like? Why?
Whereabouts in the world are there American/Russian military establish-ments?
Why are they there?

### c) Hypothetical

Why do you think the sergeant asked if anyone could play an instrument?
What did John think the sergeant might propose?
What do you think happened to John Smith in the rest of his service?
If there were a war, would you fight? Why (not?)
Why do the countries spend so much on arms?
Could the world exist without armies?
Is it possible for all men to live in peace?

*Phase four: limited writing*

There could be some written follow-up. The class could write their responses to some short-answer questions, put orally, or take a line or two of dictation. Such activities need no further description. Here, though, is an example of something different.

**Guided writing** from a blackboard cue.

John _ _ _ One month.
    Artistic.
Sergeant _ _ barrack room.
    Musicians?

The learners will not all write in exactly the same words, especially if they have only heard but not yet seen the text. In the main, though, they know the story. There has been some oral follow-up and the vocabulary is simple. They would probably write something like this:

John had completed/finished one month as a soldier/ in the army. He was artistic/ an artistic young man. One day a/the sergeant came/ walked into the barrack room. He asked for musicians/ he asked if anyone played an instrument/ he said 'Are there any musicians here?'

*Optional phase: review*
A few days later you could use a similar cue on the blackboard to elicit the entire story. Alternatively, a poster picture like this would remind the students of the main points.

## Summary of the three stage lesson

Begin by presenting any needed lexical items and setting the scene in some way. You also give the students some sort of task to perform as they listen or read. This makes the reading or listening active, instead of passive.

Next the class reads or listens to the text, seeking answers to your guiding questions. Keep reading time short. Make a random check on the answers to the pre-questions so that individuals are not tempted to opt out of the reading or listening.

If the text is worthy of more class time, you can go into a third stage, exploiting the passage further by means of a selection of the activities described above. You can relieve the intensivity by including a few moments of writing. You can even focus briefly on a grammar point. In these ways, you will conduct a fast moving and enjoyable lesson, with plenty of variety.

Let us go on now to consider ways in which teachers can offer a good listening model when they read aloud.

# ■ TEACHER'S READING ALOUD

In order to provide listening practice, teachers usually have to read aloud. Of course, textbook passages were not intended to represent speech. So it becomes necessary to render them more authentic. By following these guidelines, you can make your own model resemble a more natural form of speech.

## Guidelines to observe

In the examples which follow the sounds of speech are represented by approximations to regular spellings, rather than phonetic symbols. Here are the principles that you should respect if you want your speech to sound authentic.

### Stress
Use natural stress patterns. Emphasise the *key words* in each phrase. Key words are those that carry important elements of information. It may be helpful if you go through the text beforehand and mark the words to be stressed with a fluorescent marker pen. Stress marking is probably the most important feature of spoken English, much more important than the pronunciation of individual phonemes. In this example, the stressed syllables are capitalised.

The SEMinar HAD to be CANcelled beCAUSE of POOR atTENdance

### Reduced vowels
Reduce the vowel sounds of unstressed syllables. This is a distinctive feature of English speech. If we look again at the example sentence above, all the unstressed vowels are pronounced as a short i sound (as in *big*) or as a **schwa** sound. *Schwa* is the name of the short vowel sound in the words *the* and *a*. As a result of this vowel weakening, the utterance *He is a photographer* will sound something like *HEE za fa TOG ra fa*. In speech, almost all auxiliary verbs take on that *schwa* sound (*am, are, was, were, does, can, should, must*, etc).[2]

### Rhythm
Do not give all syllables the same time value. There should be approximately the same amount of time between all stressed syllables. Where there are several

unstressed syllables between two stressed ones, the unstressed syllables are squeezed into the short time space available, giving a hurried effect.

### Intonation

Use intonation to express emotions and attitudes. Listen to any anglophone disc jockey to hear an exaggerated form of this. If you want to sound lively then this musicality is essential.

### Contractions

Make all natural contractions. This helps to convey the written language into spoken forms. *I am* becomes *I'm*, *He was not* should be spoken as *he wasn't*, and so on.

### Word boundaries

Do not mark word boundaries. Words beginning or ending with a vowel sound should link up with neighbouring words, even if you are reading slowly. The syllables of speech cross boundaries that are evident only in print. *I am against it* will be spoken in four syllables and sound something like *I ma gen stit.*

### Theatrics

Read in a dramatic and exciting way. Use a different voice or voices for direct speech. Move around the room as you read. Use facial expressions and body language if they can help comprehension. Become an actor. In this way you will hold the students' attention and they will understand more readily.

### Modifications

Adapt the text. Break off to add an explanation, to comment, or to expand the story. Use the passage as the core of a more spontaneous speech model. Texts must not become a restriction. The more you embellish and improvise, the more natural the text will sound, hesitancies and all! *Tell* the story, rather than reading it.

## ■ CONCLUSION

The aim of a reading lesson is to help students develop good reading strategies. We have taken the view that reading is a silent and fast activity. In some cases the students will read for full understanding, at other times for key details. Reading is purposeful and the teacher has to arouse interest and provide that purpose. Presentation of too many words is harmful, as the guessing of meaning from context is a major reading skill.

Similar arguments apply to listening. The aim is to develop listening fluency. The teacher has to contrive reasons for listening. When a passage is used for listening practice, the teacher should try to make it representative of natural speech. The text is not inviolable. The story can be *told* if it is adapted and rephrased as it is read. This will make the reading more representative of authentic speech.

The length of the text chosen depends on the aim of the lesson, the complexity of the language and of the content, and the passage's interest and value. In some cases a long text will be dismissed in minutes, at other times a short text or part of a longer one will be the basis of an entire lesson.

Teachers should not try to crowd all the exploitation activities described in this chapter into a single lesson. There is no need to make an exhaustive and exhausting study of every passage in the textbook. Follow-up to the reading or listening is optional, depending on all of the factors above. Once the reading or listening activity has been completed, you have achieved your main aim. When there is follow-up, it should be varied, to offer unpredictability, interest and enjoyment.

## Notes

[1] When you first set strict time limits on reading, there may be muttered complaints. If you take the trouble to explain and justify this insistence on increasing reading speed, the students will come to understand. Gradually, they will learn to run their eye down the page quickly and with understanding. So, when sufficient time has elapsed for one fast reading, books should be *closed*. They can be opened again later, if there is a need to refer to the text or if there is to be any written work.

[2] Auxiliary verbs keep their full vowel sound when they are in a stressed position (e.g. *Are* you . . ? *Does* she . . ?)

# 8 Exploiting dialogues

## ■ THE NATURE OF DIALOGUES

Unlike reading passages, dialogues are intended to be spoken aloud. The writers have tried to use and to represent natural speech forms. A dialogue can be viewed as a short theatrical play. Ideally, it will be acted out in class, rather than simply read aloud. To reach that stage involves an investment of time and effort, though, and some dialogues are not worthy of such treatment. In this chapter we shall consider how to evaluate, adapt and exploit dialogues. Vocabulary and structure receive the major focus, but with special attention to the **functional** value of the structures. Teachers have to be able to conduct efficient and meaningful drills and to model structures clearly on the blackboard, as well as to establish and manage simultaneous pair work, if dialogues are to be exploited efficiently.

## ■ DETERMINING AN APPROACH

Your approach, when handling a dialogue, will depend on several variables. You have to take into account the age and experience of the students, the length of the text, its relevance to the learner's needs, its value, complexity, interest level and authenticity in terms of speech.[1] Having evaluated these aspects, you choose an approach. The approaches described here are not mutually exclusive, though. You can treat one part of a dialogue in one way and the rest in another, if you wish.

### Possible approaches

*1 The comprehension approach*
Use the text for comprehension purposes; just set out to get an understanding of the dialogue. Treat it as though it were a reading text. Do this when the text lacks interest or is too long.

*2 The rote learning approach* / Memorizing
You can have the students learn a dialogue by heart. Do this only when the text is short, interesting and full of useful vocabulary and structures.

*3 The creative approach*
A somewhat higher level aim is to get the learners to adapt a dialogue, to

individualise it in order to make it more personal and relevant to their own lives. This is frequently necessary if schools are using textbooks written outside the country.

### 4 The expanding approach

There will be times when you need to widen the scope of a dialogue. This is the case where it fails to exploit a potentially useful situation. Sometimes it is merely a question of adding new vocabulary items, but frequently you will be introducing new useful structures. This approach has role play as a final step.

### 5 The mixed approach

You will often combine two of the three approaches above. Part of the long dialogue will be used as though it were a reading text, leaving you a short, valuable sample to treat in one of the other two ways. You will do this when the dialogue is long but contains things that are worth the effort of learning by heart or when one short extract lends itself to adaptation or expansion.

## ■ DEMONSTRATION LESSONS

We shall look now at the step-by-step procedures to follow for those different approaches, in the order listed above. The fifth approach (the mixed one) need not be shown, as it is a straight combination of the first approach and one of the other two.

## The comprehension approach

There is plenty of justification for using a dialogue for comprehension alone. The students engage in speech, even though they do not speak the exact words of the text. The dialogue is treated as though it were a reading or a listening passage. The second option is the better of the two, because the language listened to can be made to sound reasonably authentic. If possible, have the entire dialogue recorded on an audio cassette. Most dialogues have only two or three speakers. If you and one or two colleagues get together, you can record all the dialogues in the textbook in a matter of hours.

As far as presentation and exploitation are concerned, the guidelines given in the previous chapter are wholly valid and can be referred to. However, because dialogues are direct speech, there are some minor differences of procedure at the exploitation phase:

### Step one: presentation
Present any vocabulary that is of special value or will be difficult to understand.

There is no need to teach grammar points or even to practise a structure since the aim here is comprehension.

*Step two: task setting*
The students are given a reason for listening (or reading). Ask a few guiding questions.

*Step three: listening*
Play the tape or speak the parts. It is a good thing to let the listeners *see* the speakers as they listen. This can be done in various ways:

a) Draw the faces of the speakers on the blackboard or bring in more carefully drawn pictures of the characters. You can often find magazine pictures of people to represent the speakers. With the pictures drawn or pinned on the blackboard, you have only to point at them in turn as you speak or play a recording of the dialogue.
b) Bring students to the front to represent the people on the tape. Just point at them in turn as the dialogue is spoken. The students themselves say nothing. If you are speaking the parts yourself, simply move behind the student who represents each speaker.
c) Use puppets. Younger children love to see simple glove puppets. Many of the child-to-child dialogues in beginner classes are not easily spoken by an adult. You can be divorced from unsuitable roles by using glove puppets to represent the boy or girl speakers. By slightly moving one hand at a time, you show which character is speaking.

*Step four: comprehension check*
Verify that the learners are able to answer the two or three guiding questions. Do this by random checks to ensure full involvement. If the dialogue is not of any real value you might well stop at this point.

*Step five: exploitation*
If the dialogue is worth exploiting further, any of the optional activities given in Chapter 7 can be used. Be careful how you do this, however. Any *What did they say?* questions, which are so easily answered when the class is working with a reading passage, become difficult. This is because the dialogue is in direct speech and the students have to make a transformation into indirect speech. There may be times when you wish to practise such manipulation of syntax. If so, a dialogue is the ideal source. If that is not your aim, avoid such questions.

## The rote learning approach

If a dialogue is too long, you will have to select one short part. This part should be of special value, with a number of useful expressions.

*Step one: presentation*
Ignore the grammar points. The aim now is to get the students to learn a short

sample of natural speech. Irregular verb forms can be treated as lexical items. Even a new tense will normally be understood in the context. However, you will need to practise one or two of the most important and useful structures, but stressing the functional value of the utterances. The board will look something like this, offering support for the practice, as the students internalise the basic structure by making up new enquiries.

```
MAKING  ENQUIRIES.


Could you tell me if + present simple
                      Miss Ford lives ... ?
                      We have homework?
```

*Step two: listening*
The dialogue is modelled exactly as in step three in our first example. The students listen as the extract is played or spoken.

*Step three: repetition*
A rapid drill follows. Let the class see the text as you work, but their eyes should be on you for the drills. Backward build-up will be needed for longer phrases. This use of repetition drills is another reason for keeping the extract short. It would be boring to have to repeat more than a few lines. A danger of repetition is that the speed of delivery tends to be slowed and intonation patterns forgotten. With speechlike production as the aim, it is essential that the phrases be spoken and echoed at natural speed and with proper intonation.[2]

*Step four: public pairs*
It is advisable to accept volunteers for this activity if the students are to work from memory alone. The speakers can either stand up at their desks or come out to the front and speak the parts, making appropriate gestures. An alternative is for the teacher to take one of the roles and let the class or selected individuals speak the other parts.

*Step five: private pairs*
Instruct the class to work in simultaneous pairs. They should go through the dialogue once, and then change roles for a second practice. You may decide to allow them to have their books open for the first run through, but the danger is that they then begin to read aloud instead of speaking naturally. If the drills

have been effectively conducted, the class ought to be able to work without the text.

### Step six: public check
Randomly chosen pairs should go to the front and work through the dialogue as a check. The other students will be able to make any needed corrections or offer prompts.

## The creative approach

You will often have to change factual details in a dialogue, to make it meaningful and suited to the local context. It is ridiculous to expect rural learners to tell each other that they live in such and such a city, that their father is an engineer or that they themselves hope to become a doctor, if such statements are untrue and inappropriate.

### Steps one, two and three: presentation and practice
An inappropriate dialogue can be treated as in the example immediately above, up to the end of the drill phase (step three).

### Step four: substitution
Nominate a few students, inviting them to make the offending sentences truthful, saying where they really live, what their father really does for a living and what they themselves really hope to become in the future, and so on.

### Step five: private pair work
This is done with the students personalising the dialogue as they speak it at their desks. Every pair will be producing a unique dialogue, but on the framework of the original one.

### Step six: public check
Nominated pairs should be asked to go to the front and to play out their adapted dialogue. This public check is what keeps students working during closed pair work activities.

## Expanding dialogues

This time you will be presenting (or revising) additional new vocabulary and structures that are related to the situation in the dialogue. It is no longer a question of simply adapting the dialogue by letting the learners substitute items from their active vocabulary store. The dialogue will become the basis of an acting out activity. Imagine a dialogue where a shopper refuses a garment because it is too expensive. You will want to revise or introduce *too large, small, loose, long, short,* and so on. With this extra vocabulary fresh in the students' minds, paired practice will be richer. At other times the teacher may wish to add structures, to extend the range of functions in the situation. Let us take this extract from a dialogue as an example.

ROBERT:  Hey, Charles. What shall we do this weekend?
CHARLES: How about going fishing?
ROBERT:  That's a great idea! What time shall we meet?
CHARLES: How about seven thirty?
ROBERT:  Fine. Will you . . .

There are two useful functions here: *making a suggestion* and *accepting a suggestion*. You would want to isolate and practise both expressions, with the class offering and accepting alternative activities on the model *How about -ing?*

However, in real life we often turn down a suggestion. So, your students need the function of *declining a suggestion*. What is more, they may want to know how to *make a counter proposition*. The teacher who wants to give the class the ability to cope with a genuine situation of this sort has to bring in language from beyond the text. The new structures must be presented and practised with a clear emphasis on their functional value. This will be followed by prompted substitution, supported with a blackboard cue that looks something like this.

SUGGESTING AND DECLINING

How about -ing ?                    No thanks,
                        I don't feel like -ing.

New Suggestion:
I'd rather + verb.

e.g. How about watching T.V. this evening?
No thanks, I don't feel like staying in.
I'd rather go to the cinema.

Pair work follows. Nominated public pairs make suggestions and counter suggestions, putting forward new and original suggestions. The students can even change the context if they wish, as long as they are using the day's language items. This leads into a short spell of intensive private pair work followed by a public check on randomly chosen pairs. However, because so much improvisation is taking place, the public check will be much more exciting than usual, as you will see below.

### Acting out: The grand finale

Teachers who never allow the students to act out adapted dialogues are neglecting a very motivating activity. The original lines and situation provide the support and suggest a basic plot. Less confident students can stick closely to the words and structures in the printed dialogue; extroverts will take some degree of risk. But there is little scope for serious errors. The students are in a communicative situation, using language for real purposes. They will happily become a waitress, a doctor's patient or a taxi driver, inventing some badge of their role. The waitress will drape a cloth over her left arm, the driver will sit at a chair and turn an imaginary wheel and the doctor's patient will limp along with the aid of a branch or imaginary crutches. There will be no shortage of would-be actors. The problem will be to share out the opportunities. The actors get the attention and admiration of the class while the observers get interest, enjoyment and more exposure.

## ■ CREATING YOUR OWN DIALOGUES

Do not allow yourself to become a slave of the prescribed texts. There are times when language needs practising in a simulated way, but the needed dialogue has not been provided. At such moments you can improvise your own. Improvised dialogues require very little preparation. You plan the activity carefully, but there is no presentation or practice beforehand. No writing of any sort is involved, the whole thing is oral. A drama activity like this can be dropped into any spare 5 minute slot at the beginning or end of a lesson.

## Procedure for directing an improvised dialogue

Decide in advance a communicative situation with which the students ought to be able to cope, using only language they have learned to date. From this rough outline you can decide the prompts that you will need to make. This will become clear as you read the demonstration, step by step.

### Step one: describe the setting

This may be a restaurant, shop, doctor's surgery, a hotel bar (as below), even a schoolroom in a different country.

### Step two: invite volunteers

This is one case where it might be wise not to nominate. Confident and extrovert volunteers will put on a better show, and offer a better model, than will reluctant conscripts.

### Step three: assign roles

You may want one person to be a secretary and the other to be a job seeker trying to get an interview with a manager. A doctor can interview a patient, and so on. The new identities add to the interest. In the short example that will follow one student is asked to become a Canadian engineer, in town for a seminar. The other is to be a lady doctor, on holiday at the same hotel. Their new names and any essential details are given to the volunteer students only when they come forward to play out the scene.

### Step four: prompt the exchanges

As they play, you feed them their lines. This feeding can be done in English or in the mother tongue. The latter way has several benefits. Most important, everyone in the class can then follow the dialogue. Additionally, you are not providing the actors with the words they need to play their parts, they have to find their own words. Your prompts act as a script, keeping the students within the bounds of their power of expression, as in this example.

> TEACHER: Okeh Joe. You're Robin from now on. I'd like you to introduce yourself to this attractive young lady. Try to get to know her.
>
> JOE: (assuming a new identity) Oh, good morning miss. My name's Blackwood, Robin Blackwood. Are you here for the engineering seminar too?
>
> TEACHER: Anna, explain that you're a doctor and that you're here on holiday from another country.
>
> ANNA: Hello. No, I'm not an engineer, ...

And later:

> TEACHER: Right. You know a little about each other. Find out about each other's family, hobbies, and so on.

## ■ THE AUDIENCE

It should not be thought that the watchers are not involved when any play acting is going on at the front of the class. They are very active mentally, getting exposure to the teacher's language as well as that of the role players. They are seeing English used for communicative purposes and they are all enjoying their learning experience.

## ■ CONCLUSION

Dialogues are to be used selectively. The nature of the passage will influence your aims and approach. Where the dialogue is too long or without special merit, it can be treated as a reading comprehension passage. A dialogue that is to be learned by heart should be short, interesting and useful. One part of a longer dialogue can be isolated for repetition and learning. Learning is by repetition, substitution and simultaneous pair work. It is only through pair work that the learners will have an opportunity to say their parts often enough to internalise them.

Where possible, dialogues should be substituted, adapted or added to in some way. This results in their being more truthful, more communicative, more useful and more interesting. You will often need to add potentially useful vocabulary or expressions, in order to widen the communicative value of the dialogues that are printed in textbooks.

Where a textbook does not provide dialogues, or has dialogues that do not cover the communicative situations that you want to set up, you can create your own dialogues. This is done by prompting, with students taking on new identities and improvising their parts at the front of the class.

The grand finale of any dialogue which has been adapted in different ways will be the **acting out**. Even in an overcrowded classroom, there is enough space at the front for the two or three players to come out and give a short performance. To act out a dialogue takes moments, two or three pairs or groups can be given a showcase setting in the space of less than five minutes. This offers variety to the lesson, arouses interest and enhances motivation.

## Notes

[1] Criteria for evaluating a text are explained in greater detail in the preceding chapter.

[2] Whether books are open or closed during a repetition drill is an individual decision, Orthodoxy says they should be closed, but many teachers disagree, and regard the written form as offering valuable support at this time. If you have made the effort of learning a new language recently, it is probable that you share their opinion. If so, do let the students see the text but do not permit them to read lines aloud. They can glance at the text occasionally but their eyes must be on you as they speak.

# 9 Using the blackboard

## ■ THE IMPORTANCE OF BLACKBOARD WORK

The most valuable teaching aid, world wide, is a blackboard or other good writing and drawing surface.[1] Sketches, diagrams and tables enable teachers to avoid excessive use of the mother tongue, while prompting meaningful oral contributions from the students. In many ways, a blackboard is more essential than a textbook. When students look at a page, their eyes and thoughts could be anywhere. When they look at the blackboard it is apparent that their attention is on what the teacher has written or drawn.

In earlier chapters, guidelines were given for using the blackboard to present vocabulary, structure and grammar points. It is assumed that readers are familiar with the content of those three chapters. Here, we shall be considering clarity, layout, the use of tables, techniques of drawing, and other aspects of blackboard use.

## ■ USING THE BLACKBOARD PROPERLY

Blackboards are sometimes neglected, so much so that the chalk is scarcely visible to the class. Washing them with a sponge helps, but if the surface is worn there is only one thing to do. You must buy a tin of paint and renew it. *Blackboard paint* is cheap and easy to apply and dries in an hour. There is a choice between black and a restful green colour.

### Some golden rules

There are seven useful tips to observe if you are to use the blackboard efficiently.

#### Carry a tool kit
A small toiletry bag will easily contain what you need. The various items should be carried in separate plastic bags, so that the interior of the cosmetic bag remains clean. You will need a few sticks of white chalk, some brightly coloured chalks, a blackboard eraser and a damp sponge or cloth. The sponge should be rinsed out once or twice during the day. Carry an old radio antenna for a

blackboard pointer. Retracted, it fits easily into the cosmetic bag. This entire package will fit into your briefcase or handbag.

### Start clean

At the start of each lesson ask someone to clean the board and write the date in one corner. This provides an opportunity for real language use, with a range of *please* and *thank you* formulae. While the cleaning is being done, conduct a warm-up activity, a game or a song.

### Write legibly

Blackboard writing should look more like print than cursive script. Avoid stylish loops and spirals that can be misread. Beginners, especially, are confused by elaborate lettering. Write large so that those seated at the back can read easily. Do not cram too much writing onto the board.

### Write straight

It is easier to write straight if your lines are kept fairly short. Avoid writing all the way across a wide board. Later you will see that it is advisable to use the blackboard in three main sections, which automatically gets your lines short.

### Stand sideways

Do not stand with your back to the class as you write. Stand at 45 degrees and write with the arm extended. This makes it easy to glance back over your shoulder from time to time as you work. It also helps you to write straight.

### The talk'n chalk principle

Never work in silence. It is vital to keep the class involved. Comment on your drawing as you draw. Invite students to read out what you are writing, to answer a related question, to tell you what word to write next, how to spell the next word, and so on. This is not easy at first, but persevere. It will soon become second nature.

### Economise on blackboard time

Avoid long periods of inactivity on the part of the class. Anything that requires careful drawing or planning should be done at home beforehand, in picture or poster form.[2]

### The layout of the blackboard

Divide the board in three sections. These need not be exactly the same width. New vocabulary is written in the left hand section and any grammar point or structure goes to the right. These language items will stay on the board until the end of the lesson. The centre is used for ongoing work, such as pictures, working examples and notes.

The blackboard will look something like the one shown below, halfway through the lesson. In a real classroom the blackboard is much wider, so it will appear far less crowded than is the case here. New vocabulary is to the left of the board. The key structure is on the right. The middle of the board has served as a scribbling area. Eventually, the pictures will be cleaned off, leaving only the vocabulary and structure. This language is the core of the lesson content, offering a reasonable learning load for students to review at home.

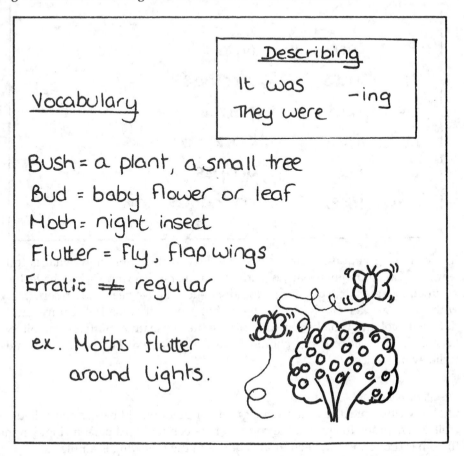

Notice that the teacher has been economical with words, giving short definitions and avoiding long illustrative sentences. Notice, too, the use of the mathematical sign for *equals* to mean *the same meaning as*. The equals sign is crossed through to denote *opposite*.[3]

## Laying out grammar structures

Working models on the board should be stark, devoid of unnecessary words that distract from the focus. Chapters Two and Three contain plenty of examples, so a few samples of both good and bad models will be sufficient here. These grammar points and structures belong on the right hand side of the board if they are being introduced and copied. They go in the centre, to be erased later, if they are being used for revision.

### A bad model
Look critically at the models that follow. Can you see why this first one is not efficient?

PRESENT   SIMPLE

| I | like | apples |
| He | likes | oranges |
| She | likes | pears |
| We | like | bananas |
| You | like | grapes |
| They | like | mangoes |

It is confusing because of an excess of words. It does not show what is to be learned. The pronouns that go with the unmarked forms should have been grouped together. The pronouns *he* and *she* should have been shown separately, with the *-s* marker emphasised. Highlighting of a grammatical feature can be done with coloured chalk or by underlining the key feature. Suffixes can follow a *plus* sign. The *you* pronoun should have been omitted; *You like* ... is a most unlikely utterance.

### The improved model

Oral or written practice of the same grammar point would be less controlled, as well as less prone to error, if the contrast between the third person singular and the other pronouns had been more stark as in the following example.

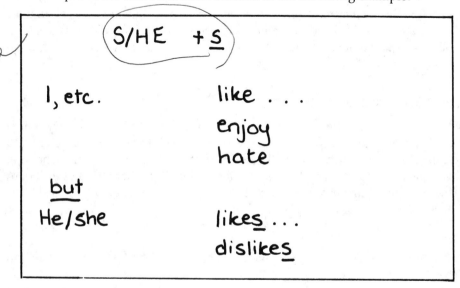

S/HE   +<u>S</u>

| I, etc. | like . . . |
| | enjoy |
| | hate |
| | |
| <u>but</u> | |
| He/she | like<u>s</u> . . . |
| | dislike<u>s</u> |

*A good model*

Here is an example of a well presented grammar point with a meaningful title. The only criticism we might level is that the learning load is too great if the possessive pronouns are being presented for the first time. For revision, though, such visual support would be ideal.

---

OWNERSHIP

| This belongs to | me. | | mine. |
|---|---|---|---|
| | you. | | yours. |
| | him. | It's | his. |
| | her. | | hers. |
| | us. | | ours. |

---

## Evaluating blackboard models

Each time you plan the representation of a grammar point, be critical of your own first draft, in the same way as we have been of the models above. Here are some models for you to judge. Do not look at the comments that follow each model until you have come to your own conclusions. What do you think of this first example?

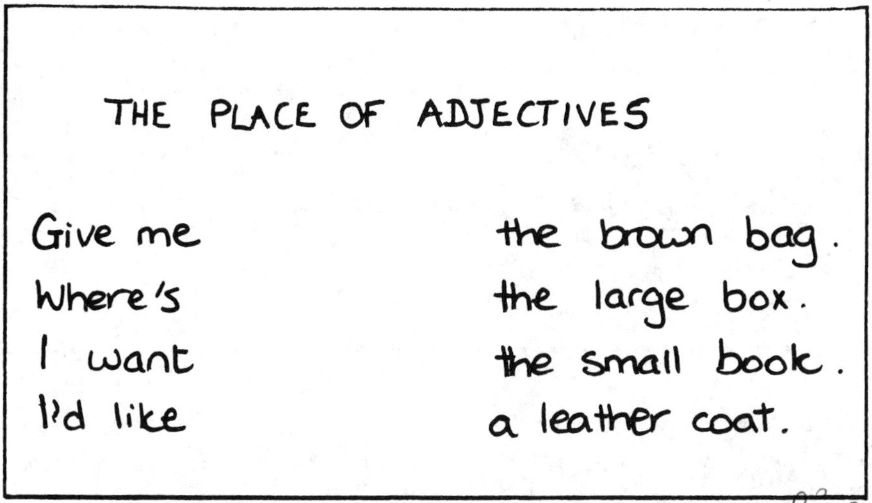

---

THE PLACE OF ADJECTIVES

| Give me | the brown bag. |
|---|---|
| Where's | the large box. |
| I want | the small book. |
| I'd like | a leather coat. |

*Confusing*
*Starts*
*mixed*
*w/*
*quest.*

*no highlighting of point*

You probably agree that this is another poor model. The teacher has simply written a few phrases to show the word order. The rule (adjective before the noun) does not stand out clearly enough to facilitate revision at home. The students would find it simpler to practice and to revise from a more basic model, like this:

```
ADJECTIVE + NOUN


                    nice        School
It's a/an           American    car
                    big         house
                    etc.
```

What do you think of this next one?

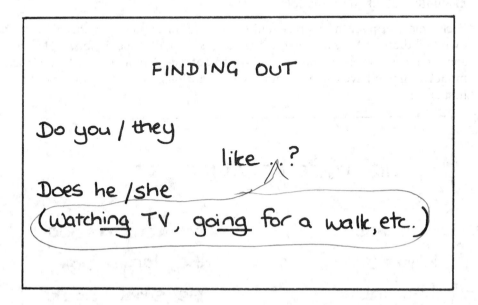

```
FINDING OUT


Do you / they
                    like ⋏ ?
Does he /she
(watching TV, going for a walk, etc.)
```

This is a good model. The layout is clear and economical. The teacher has not included unlikely forms (eg *Do I like . . . listening to music?*). With blackboard support of that sort, practice will flow easily.

## Language practice tables

Other types of table are used to cue speech. They are not usually copied and so they belong in the centre of the blackboard. They are built up gradually, with contributions elicited from the students. As far as possible, they are person-alised. With a little thought, tables can be contrived for most practice situations. Let us look at some examples.

*Talking about meals*

Supposing that you are presenting the names of the principle meals. The new words would be written on the blackboard. You would probably wish to add *generally* or *usually* so that you could ask students the times at which they usually take lunch, supper, and so on. The next step would be to build up a practice table, using the names of a few students. Completed, it would look like this:

| MEAL: | LAURIE | EMMA | SANDY |
|-------|--------|------|-------|
| Breakfast | 6 o'c. | 6:30 | — |
| Lunch | 12:45 | 10'c. | 10'c. |
| dinner | 6 p.m. | 7 p.m. | 7:30 |
| Supper | — | 9:30 | 10 p.m. |

e.g. What time do you/does Laurie have ...?

Sandy / I  usually  has/have  lunch at ... o'clock

Practice would be teacher directed at first, leading into pair work, with the learners asking and telling each other the times that they really take those meals in their own families.

*Talking about people*
The next table gives practice in talking or writing about people. In the example, the teacher has used the names of members of the class, but characters from a reading passage or personalities known to the students could be chosen. Students love talking about favourite soccer or pop music stars. The categories have to be adapted to fit the local context or to practise different vocabulary. In many countries families do not keep pets and mothers do not have jobs. In such cases *height, colour of hair, ambition, favourite food,* and so on might be used instead.

```
                DESCRIPTIONS

 Name       Age   Pets    Hobby    Mother's Job.
 Adrian     11    -       music·   secretary
 Margaret   12    cat     cinema   housewife
 Guy        12    parrot  books    dentist
 Claire     11    dog     aerobics dead


 e.g.  Guy is twelve.  He has/keeps a parrot.
       He likes to read / reading   books.
       His mother is a dentist.
```

*Talking about the past*
You can use a table like this next one to present or to revise the past progressive tense (though you would call the activity *talking about the past* if the focus is on use). If this were a new tense, then the table and examples would be on the right of the board, to be copied at the end of the lesson. If, though, the table is to support revision, it would go in the middle to be erased at the end of the practice. You would begin by eliciting what a student did yesterday and the times at which he or she began and finished those activities. This information is added to the table so that the tense can be used meaningfully.

| Art | Yesterday |
|-----|-----------|
| School | 8 - 12:30 |
| Lunch | 1 - 1:15 |
| Rest | 1:15 - 2 o'c. |
| Soccer | 2:30 - 4 o'c. |
| Classes | 4 - 6 o'c. |
| Piano | 8 - 10 o'c. |

e.g: What __was__ Art __doing__ at exactly 9 p.m?
He __was__ practising the piano.

Tense changes are easily made with tables of this sort. By using *Next Monday* you could elicit the use of the future progressive (*He'll be having a rest from one fifteen to two o'clock*).

## ■ SIMPLE BLACKBOARD SKETCHES

No artistic ability is needed. Blackboard sketches are quickly done and so they carry the minimum of detail. More complicated pictures are done at home and on paper and brought to class. If you are not used to sketching quickly, practice on scraps of paper. This will make you familiar with the basic shapes used. Drawing on paper, though, is not the same as drawing larger scale faces and figures with chalk. So spend an hour or two at a board in an empty classroom, too. You will soon gain the skill and the confidence to make rapid, effective drawings. While practising, talk aloud as though you were in front of a class to get used to involving the class as you sketch.

## Faces

A face is circular or egg shaped. The mouth and eyes are the most expressive, but nose and ears can be added if you wish. Faces show emotions, but speech bubbles can be added to introduce words or expressions.

## Age and sex

Hair often denotes sex as well as age. In some societies a lack of ear rings or a necklace will immediately mark a face as male, regardless of hair length.

## Stick figures

Stick figures are also called *pin men* or *matchstick figures*. Facial details are omitted, as are clothes, except for a skirt or cloth for women. They are drawn in a second or two, but attention must be paid to the ways in which the legs and arms are bent. Inexperienced sketchers will sometimes put figures into positions which even acrobats would be unable to adopt. The main factor to consider is the length of the limbs compared with that of the body. You can indicate the direction they are facing by the feet.

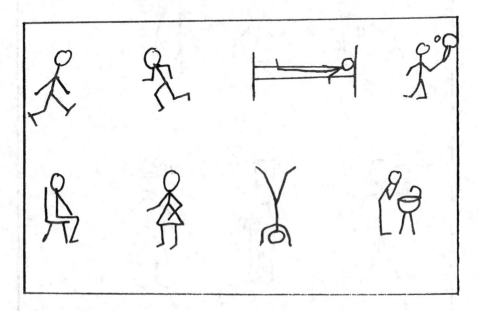

## Actions

Stick figures can wash, take a shower, sweep the floor, cook, wait on table, and so on. Remember that the students will interpret a picture via their own culture. For example, in many parts of the world the verb *to carry* would be portrayed by objects on the head or by a mother with a baby slung on her back. Objects in the hands are being *held*, not carried. *Digging* in many countries is done in a bent over position, using a V-shaped implement, and so on. Teachers have to be familiar with the environment and concepts of their students if they are not to signal incorrect meanings.

## Buildings

Most buildings are box-like. A name can be added to indicate its function, if necessary. A local name that students recognise is often better than one in the target language.

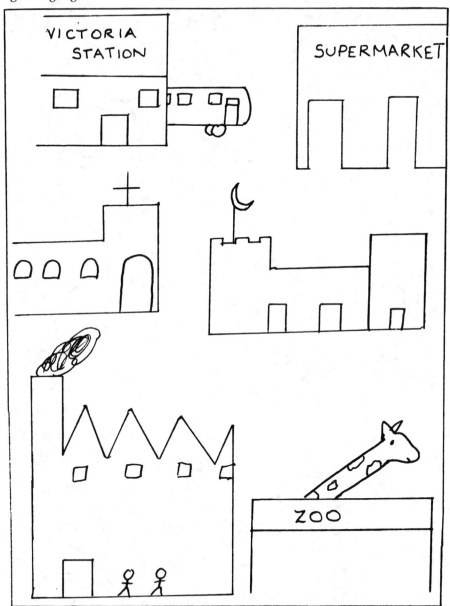

## Objects

Practice copying some of these common objects. Your copies need not be exact, but should be easily recognised. Look around the local environment and go through the textbook for other objects you might want to sketch on the board. Practise drawing them until you can do so rapidly.

# ◼ BUILDING UP PICTURES

You can tell stories by building up a drawing as you talk. Fruit, vegetables and people can be added to a market stall; vehicles of various kinds can be added to a street scene. At other times, though, you will need a succession of different pictures, with separate episodes, as in the two examples that follow. However, remember that you cannot simply draw in silence for several minutes. Each element is sketched in moments, as you talk and elicit, stopping between each new addition.

## Movement

An impression of movement can be given by repeatedly erasing a figure and drawing it again in different locations relative to a fixed object such as a building. Or, a movement can be portrayed by numbering successive positions relative to a fixed object, in the way shown below. The first thing drawn in this little story is the outline of the restaurant. Although the restaurant becomes number 4 in the final composition, it was the first thing sketched on the blackboard because it immediately gives a setting and some expectations. The name of a well-known local restaurant can be written over the door. The teacher tries to involve the class as the drawing is built up, and the teacher talk is shown after the picture. The talk will also give you an idea of the steps of the build-up.

## The teacher's talk'n chalk

This is the sort of teacher talk that would have accompanied the drawing.

TEACHER: Look, here's a building (*writes an identifying name*). What sort of building is it? That's right, a restaurant. Look, who's this man (*drawing the waiter and table, but not the seated figure*)? Right! He's a waiter.

OK (*adding figure 1 on the left of the board*). Who's this? Can you give him a name? Boris? Right, if you say so. Is Boris walking or running?

Right. Walking. Where do you think he's going? To the restaurant? Yes, I think you're right. To the restaurant (*adding the clock*). What's the time? Twelve o'clock? You're right, it's noon. So, what meal is Boris about to have? That's it. Lunch. It's lunch time. Let's carry on with our story.

Now (*drawing figure 2*). He's stopped. What's he doing? Correct, he's talking to a lady. What do you think he's saying? Um. Maybe. What do you think, Nadia? Who is it? His wife? I don't think so. Who do you think she is, Yusef? Just a friend? Right, a friend. What do you think they are saying to each other?

Now (*drawing figure 3*). Is Boris still walking? Why not (*drawing clock to show that 50 minutes have elapsed*). That's it, he's late for lunch.

And so on.

## Using composite pictures for review

Composite pictures, like the one on page 117, portray successive scenes, so they are ideal for prompting the reconstruction of a reading passage for review purposes. They are normally done on the blackboard, with the teacher eliciting the details or portraying the story as it is told by the class. If you are not able to sketch quickly, though, the composite picture can be drawn at home beforehand on a poster size sheet of paper. The sort of text being revised here will be self-evident.

*Time changes*

Tense changes are easily made. Just write any past or future date next to the composite picture and you will offer plenty of guided practice in talking about past or planned events.

# ■ CONCLUSION

Where there is little or no money for school maintenance, caring teachers should make a small investment of time and of paint to improve the blackboards that they regularly use. Teachers should not be reduced to cleaning the board with a dirty piece of rag or a paper tissue. Nor should they need to hunt around the room for a piece of chalk. They will arrive equipped and their first action will be to have the blackboard wiped clean with a blackboard eraser and a damp sponge. This preparedness alone gives you an air of professional competence.

Experienced observers can tell a great deal about a teacher's professional competence, and the way a lesson is being conducted, just by glancing at the blackboard midway through a lesson and again at the end. Written work on the board will be neat and large enough to be easily read from the back. Key vocabulary will be listed on the left of the blackboard, with new structures or grammar points on the right hand side. The written examples will be limited to useful and learnable language. Important or regular features of any structure or grammar point will be highlighted with coloured chalk or by underlining. This writing will remain on the blackboard throughout the lesson, to be copied at the end.

Simple blackboard tables are an effective means of prompting oral work and of personalising the language of the textbook. Pictures and diagrams help to convey meaning and serve to prompt oral work. Tables and drawings are not normally copied by the class so they will usually be in the centre of the board, which is also used for scribbling or sketching.

The efficient teacher will work rapidly at the blackboard, involving the class the whole time. Drawings or tables will be carefully planned beforehand. In this way no time is lost and the visual is done with no hesitation or reworking. Teachers who can make rapid but recognisable drawings are able to motivate students and enhance their comprehension and retention. As the old adage says, *One picture is worth a thousand words.*

## Notes

[1] Although the term *blackboard* is used, what is said applies equally to the whiteboard, the overhead projector or the flip chart.

[2] The production and use of pictures and posters is taken up in the following chapter.

[3] To write long sentences on the blackboard invites non-involvement and mischief. If necessary, extend a sentence or add any necessary illustrative sentences when the class is already copying.

# 10 Making and using simple teaching aids

## ■ ENLIVENING LEARNING

Language learning can be dull, especially if the learners feel little real need to be learning the foreign language anyway. The difficulty is to catch and rivet their attention. The personality and enthusiasm of the teacher is probably the most important single factor in enlivening a lesson, but the learning process itself should be exciting and enjoyable. You can make it so, by frequent changes of activity and a diversity of materials.

The range of aids described will be sufficient to ring the changes, lesson by lesson, over the course of a week. To use only flashcards, for example, and to use them every single lesson, would be almost as bad as never using them at all. Variety is what is needed. To create most of the visuals described here, you need only a few sheets of used paper, two or three felt tip pens, scissors and paste. Within the space of an hour or two, and at virtually no cost, you can prepare a wide range of re-usable items. We shall not be looking at the use of video players, overhead projectors and such like equipment. Instead we shall concentrate on visuals that are portable, inexpensive, and easy to make and to use. We begin with the most simple before describing some which are rather more sophisticated.[1]

As well as instructions for making each visual aid, we explain the techniques that can be used with them. First, though, there is one useful supplementary aid that you should put into each classroom that you use, leaving it in place. This is just two nails! Put them on the top rail of the blackboard, about two metres apart. The distance must be exactly the same in each room. Hammer them well into the rail of the blackboard to ensure that they cannot be removed by mischievous students. In your bag you carry a length of string, looped at each end to fit over the nails. At the beginning of a lesson you put the string in place to make a line on which to hang visuals. It is quite unobtrusive. Afterwards, you take the string down and carry it to the next classroom. You also need two or three clothes pegs with which to attach visual aids to the line, as will be seen later.

## ■ AIDS REQUIRING LITTLE PREPARATION

### Flashcards

Except for the blackboard, the flashcard is probably the most widely used visual aid in language teaching. It is just a simple picture on a piece of card or paper.

Storage is easy if you always use the same size of paper. The A-4 size (29 × 21 centimetres) is easy to get and can be seen from the back of the room. Make up large envelopes to keep the flashcards in, labelling each set for easy retrieval. You will need duplicate pictures of important lexical items. This enables you to keep an entire lesson set intact while you also build up separate sets by topic or situation (furniture, packaging, the restaurant, travel, transport, medicine, etc). The topic sets are added to, lesson by lesson, as new vocabulary is introduced.

### Making flashcards

Use old pieces of paper, as long as one side is clean. Stick two sheets together (printed sides inwards) to give durability and strength. Use a thick felt tip pen, making simple line drawings. Black is best for outlines but colour can be used, too. Begin by making a rough sketch in pencil, then go over it with the pens. It takes only moments. The paper can be used horizontally or vertically, depending on the shape of the subject.

The advantages of flashcards over a blackboard drawing are several. Class time is saved. They are motivating and eye catching. Because they are done at home, carefully, the quality of the drawing is higher than that of a blackboard sketch. They can be colourful. And, they can be used again and again.

### Using flashcards

Flashcards are used mainly for presenting new lexical items, though they may also be used for review. You hold them visible as the words are presented. If you want to stick them on the blackboard, use a short length of sticky tape, rolled into a ball with the sticky side outwards for an instant fix. There is also a professional re-usable substance called *blu-tak*. A small ball of this plasticine-like substance will even hold objects such as a passport or a wallet to the board. Afterwards it is rolled off, to be used elsewhere.

### Examples of flashcards

On the following page are examples of a few flashcards that have been used for presentation and have now been stuck to the board next to the illustrative sentences. The students copy the sentences at the end of the lesson, leaving space for the pictures. Do not let them waste class time doing art work in class. They can make rough copies and draw them more carefully for homework.

Charles *stammers.*

The *bill* came to 4.30.

Large apples are 50 pence a pound. Small *ones* are 35 pence.

Jo has *more* pens *than* Ann.

Charles *thinks* Mary is beautiful.

121

## A clock face

With a clock face you can teach students how to ask or give the time while you yourself are facing the class. If you cannot get hold of a large old clock face with hands that still move, you can quickly make one.

### Making a clock face

To make a clock face, stick some white paper on a piece of cardboard and cut a circle from it. A square of card, about 20 centimetres in size, provides a circle which is large enough to be seen from the back of the room and which fits in to a brief case.

Write the hour digits around the circle. Start with 12, 6, 3 and 9. In this way the other numbers can be fitted in without difficulty.

Cut two hands for the clock, one short and fat, the other long enough to reach the rim. Blacken them and attach them to the centre of the face, using a split pin. A small square of cardboard stuck behind the centre gives added strength.

### Using the clock face

To teach the time, do not make the mistake of working round the face in a clockwise direction. The following sequence is easier for the learners.

a) Practice the hours out of order, not 1 to 12 o'clock. Get the class to learn the questions too, *What's the time, please?*, *Could you tell me the time?*
b) Contrast *past* and *to* for the minutes (5 past, 5 to; 10 past, 10 to, etc).
c) Contrast *a quarter past* and *a quarter to*.
d) Teach *half past*.

If you are not a native speaker of English, remember that if you specify a number of minutes other than five, ten, twenty and twenty-five you must add the word *minutes*, eg:

Five past ten     Ten to twelve

but

Eight *minutes* past/to nine, and so on

## The digital clock

As a result of the microchip revolution, the terms used above are fast disappearing. Most students who own a watch will have a digital one, so you have a duty to teach the modern way of telling the time, even if it is not included in the text book. As well as being more current, it offers good number practice.

### Telling digital times

The time is simply read out from the figures, so we hear *one forty-five* rather than *a quarter to two*. What is more, we have an exactitude of time that was not possible before. Today, we are told that it is *six twenty-nine*, when we would have been told *about half past*, a few years ago. The twenty-four hours are also used, so that *a quarter to six in the evening* (*five forty-five pm*) may well be said today as *seventeen forty-five*.

### Practising digital times

The obvious way to practise times in a digital way is to simply write times on the blackboard. However, it is good to change the focus from the board at times and so it is worth bringing in a few sheets of paper of the sort seen here. They can be created in moments and thrown away afterwards. Or they can be kept, along with any flashcards, in the lesson envelope for use next year.

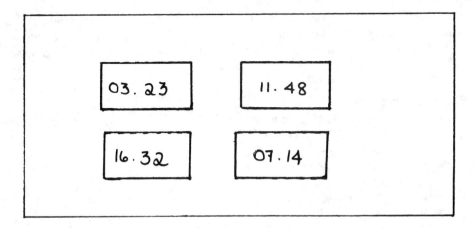

## Wordcards

Keywords or short phrases can be written on the back of any flashcard. This allows presentation of the written form at the same time as the meaning and sound are presented. Some teachers believe that this helps learners to internalise the new word.

Commonly, though, wordcards have no pictures. They are used at the early stages of reading for word recognition, especially where the native script is different from that of the target language. The advantage of wordcard activities like those below is that the learners are *really reading* for information.

## Wordcard read'n choose

This is a good way to combine intensive listening and early reading skills. You use a set of related words (already known) and the learners have to select the words that you indicate. The procedure could not be easier. Here is an example, in which the topic words are all connected with *transport* (ferry boat, car, taxi, yacht, lorry, motor-bike, aeroplane).

## Step one: reading and remembering

First you show six or so wordcards, one at a time. Hold each one up in silence for one or two or three seconds. Tell the learners that they should try to remember them. When all the wordcards have been seen by the class, put the cards face down on your table.

## Step two: the challenge

Now you ask questions about the wordcards, with the students answering from memory. It will sound like this:

TEACHER: Which have four wheels?
STUDENTS: Lorry, car, taxi.
TEACHER: Which travel in the air?
STUDENTS: Aeroplanes.
TEACHER: Which have four seats?/Which carry merchandise?
Which have two wheels?/Which go on the water?
Which carry passengers? Which . . ?

## Wordcard misfits

The game is similar, but this time the class has to identify the one that does not belong in the set. For example, with these six wordcards, *television* is the odd man out, as the others are buildings

| | | |
|---|---|---|
| hotel | house | post office |
| television | restaurant | supermarket |

The method is the same as that above, but after the wordcards have been seen you ask the students to identify the one card which does not belong in the set. If you wish, you can create arguments and encourage the learners to attempt to justify a choice by contriving sets in which there is more than one candidate for the odd card out status. (eg boy, girl, man, baby, woman, doctor).

## WH-question wordcards

Make and carry a set of these, they will often come in useful. After rapid silent reading of any text you can use these WH-question wordcards to prompt questions from the class, avoiding the need for any kind of talk on your part. You hold up the question prompt in silence and then nominate the student who has to phrase a question, which another student then answers. The cards look like this:

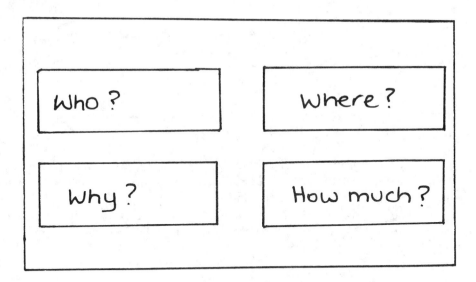

*Wordcard sentences*

Wordcards can be used in combination, to make sentences. They can be attached to the board, like flashcards. However, you can also make wordcards from sheets of A-4 paper folded in half, lengthways, so that they can stand. They can then be placed along the edge of your table, so that substitutions can be made during a drill. Your table will look like this during practice. You will have other wordcards (my friends, I, We, Children, dislike, sweets, sugar, etc) ready to be switched in and out of the sentence. The grammatical point being practised will be on a separate card, if possible. Here it is the *-s* of the third person singular verb.

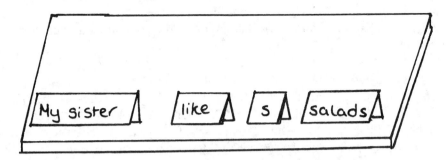

Alternatively, the folded wordcards can be hung along a string suspended between two nails, as described in the opening to this chapter. The cards are easily dropped on or lifted off. This is a particularly good way to practise a structure, as the slot to be substituted can be removed from the **string of words**. In the following example the teacher has removed a card which carries the words *by car*. The students will call out *on foot, by bike, by plane*, etc.

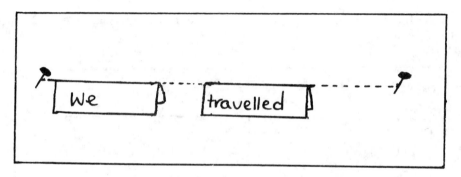

## Letter cards

Single letters are put on smaller cards and are used to introduce the alphabet to students to whom it is unfamiliar. You can also show sound-spelling correspondences (at ate, pet pete, kit kite, etc) and the build-up of words. Two or three copies of vowels and certain letters will be needed. The cards are propped along the ledge of the blackboard, or made with a flap so that they can be placed on the string.

## Number cards

Number cards are used to present numbers, but can also be used in number games. With a pack of number cards in your briefcase you will always have a warm-up activity or time-filler game available.

### Making number cards

To make these, you need only a few squares of white card, somewhat larger than playing cards. Write a single digit, 0 to 9, on each. Numbers 6 and 9 are reversible, so these two digits should be underlined. It is a good idea to write the same number on both sides so that you can see the number yourself and there is no danger of its being displayed upside down. Make two sets. With a single pack of ten cards you cannot show multiple numbers such as 22, 55, and so on. With a second pack you can combine them to show almost any number, right up to millions.

### Using number cards to introduce numbers

When you use these cards to introduce numbers for the first time, do not make the mistake of presenting the numbers in sequence. If you do, the students will rote learn them like a chanted phrase and will always run through the sequence mentally before answering. Introduce and practise them out of sequence, beginning with numbers to five (3, 2, 5, 4, 1, 0, 2, 4, and so on). Do the same with 6 to 10 and, later, with numbers to fifteen then to twenty. Always teach and test out of order. Do not give the class a chance to chant numbers in sequence until they have been well learned. And even then it is better to go backwards before going forwards. If you do this, the learners will always be able to produce the correct number on sight.

Having taught up to twenty, you will need to make some extra cards with noughts. Now you can relate the new numbers to old to assist learning (in most languages of the world there is a relationship of the sort seen here).

13, 30, 300, 3,000, 3 million, (then 31, 35, and so on),
14, 40, 400, 4,000, 4 million (43, 47, 49, out of order)
15, 50, etc.

### Challenging combinations

Two cards at a time can be held in the hands to make numbers up to 99 (37, 54, etc.). To show longer numbers, it is best to stack the cards along the ledge of the blackboard, adding one at a time (e.g. 3, 37, 374, 3,749, 37,491 and so on). If there is no ledge on the board, make up the number cards with flaps, so they can be dropped over the string. The build up sounds like this exchange.

TEACHER: What's this (*placing a 9*)
STUDENTS: Nine!
TEACHER: And now? (*adding an 8*)?
STUDENTS: Ninety-eight!
TEACHER: Great! (*adds 1*) And now?
STUDENTS: Nine hundred and eighty-one!

and so on.

Another challenging way to use the cards is to use them for mental arithmetic. Hold up any two cards and tell the class to add, to subtract or to multiply the figures.

## Magazine pictures

Ask your friends to pass on old magazines so that you can keep any useful pictures. Single objects can sometimes be cut out to be used with the felt board or magnet board (explained later). Often, a full picture will portray a scene or concept that can be used to trigger discussion or introduce a text in an interesting way. Keep the full page pictures in folders, labelled by theme (picnic, beach, food, traffic, fashions, sport, etc.). This will be a useful resource to have at home when planning lessons or revision.

## Moving pictures

To show movement in a hand held picture is easier than it sounds. You need only a flashcard and a little imagination, but the result is riveting and you immediately gain the full attention of the class.

### Making and using a moving picture

Supposing you want to present *The sun is going in/coming out*. You start with a flashcard picture of a clouded sky. In this, you cut a small slit, to allow the sun to disappear behind a cloud and to reappear. The sun is portrayed on the end of a separate strip of paper. The strip itself is the same colour as the sky, to make it less visible. The end of the strip is inserted into the slit, so that when the card is held up, the sun is seen near the clouds. Then it is slowly drawn in, through the slit, to give an impression of the sun *going in*. Afterwards, the process is reversed, and magic! The sun *comes out* again. The same technique can be used to crash a car into a lorry, to make a person walk towards and go into a bank, to make a person jump into and out of the water, and so on.

Look at the example, below. The picture is being used to present the verb *to fetch*. The picture of a house in the rain is shown. Then the strip is pushed through the slit in the door to show the lady coming out of the house into the rain. She is made to stop and then disappear back into the house. The strip is reversed (or a second strip is used) and pushed into view again, to show her coming back out with an umbrella. The lady went back to *fetch* an umbrella.

The strip insert looks like this:

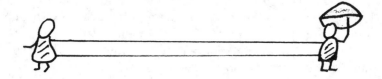

## Finger puppets

Proper **glove puppets** are cheap to make or buy, and they are a valuable teaching aid. Perhaps a friend or relation can make you some? If not, you can make finger puppets from paper, in the way shown below. Finger puppets are just small head and shoulder pictures of people, fitted over two or three fingers by means of a looped strip. As always, two sheets of paper are stuck together for strength. Point A is glued to point B to create the loop that goes over the fingers. The head and shoulders figure can be drawn or a magazine picture can be cut out and stuck onto the finger loop.

(glue point A to point B)

*Using finger puppets*

Two finger puppets are marvellous for dialogue work. You can model male and female roles, as well as child roles. You just waggle the hand with the picture of the person that is doing the talking. Children can make puppets of their own in order to practise dialogues in the same way at their desks. After this intensive practice, designated students can come to the front of the class, one at a time, to demonstrate the whole dialogue with their own puppets.

## Realia

Never waste time drawing real objects that can be carried into class. Why draw *weeds* when even a city dweller can pluck a handful on the way to school? If possible, make a collection of realia (pronounced ree-*ah*-lee-ah) from the country whose language you teach. Waste bins are an excellent source. You can find bus tickets, food labels, stamps, and so on. Empty packets and tins (or simply the labels) are much better than pictures for teaching shops and shopping, especially if the foreign price stickers are still attached. Young learners will be fascinated by a railway ticket or coin from the target language society.[2]

## ■ AIDS REQUIRING SOME PREPARATION

Do not be put off by the title of this section. These items are easily made and cost very little. They will last for years, and their use adds spice to any lesson.

## The magnet board

This is just an oblong sheet of thin zinc. It can be painted white if you wish and fitted with a carrying handle. Any developing country has its tinsmiths, making buckets, bowls and so on. For a very small price they will cut your oblong

(80 centimetres by 60) and turn the edges so that they are not sharp. An alternative is to use the white side panel of an old fridge or gas stove, but this will be much heavier.

All that you need now are a few small magnets or pieces of a broken up larger one. Garages often have an old magnet, from the engine of a car. Radio and TV mechanics always have a stock of small magnets. Again, they are cheap; they may even be given free of charge. The board is leaned on the ledge of the blackboard or suspended from a nail. Cut outs from magazines or hand drawn pictures can be attached, using the pieces of magnet to hold them in place.

### Using the magnet board
In Chapter Nine, we looked at composite pictures, built up on the blackboard. With the magnet board the picture elements are predrawn and cut out (cutting roughly around the shape of the object). You put them on the board one by one to build up the picture. Sometimes you will want to put on a back cloth first, to give a background. The back cloth is a single sheet of paper (it can be made of several sheets of A-4 stuck together) the same size as the board. On it you draw the background to the picture you will build up. For example, you could show two of the four walls of a room before adding furniture or creating a restaurant scene. A background of a street could be used when introducing traffic, children playing, a lamp post, and so on.

## The felt board

This is used in the same way as a magnet board, but is made of card or thin plywood and so it is even lighter. On the front you stick a sheet of felt. Any pictures that you prepare for it must be backed with felt or pieces of sandpaper. It is sufficient to glue just one or two small pieces to each picture. When you press the backed pictures onto the felt covered board they automatically stay in place.

### Using the felt board
As with the magnet board, pictures are built up as you talk. People and objects can be made to move on command, in this way:

TEACHER: Where's the dog? Under the tree, did you say? Right! But he's not there now, is he? Why not? That's right, he's chasing a cat? Where's the cat now? Yes, on the wall!

### Pictures for felt and magnet boards
The magnet board has some advantages over a felt board. Pictures can be superimposed and held in place with a single piece of magnet. An open wardrobe can receive a suit, a child can be dressed, and so on. With a felt board, multiple overlays are not possible. Also, pictures for the magnet board do not have to be backed with felt or lint.

The pictures you use with either board are rarely square in shape. Normally you cut out silhouettes so that they fit nicely into place in the composite picture.

Because each picture is part of a larger picture, some care has to be exercised. Cups and plates must be small enough to look right on a table but the table must be smaller than the bed, and so on.

Perspective is another consideration. Pictures in any composite picture look better if they are viewed from one side and slightly above, as in this picture of a bedroom.

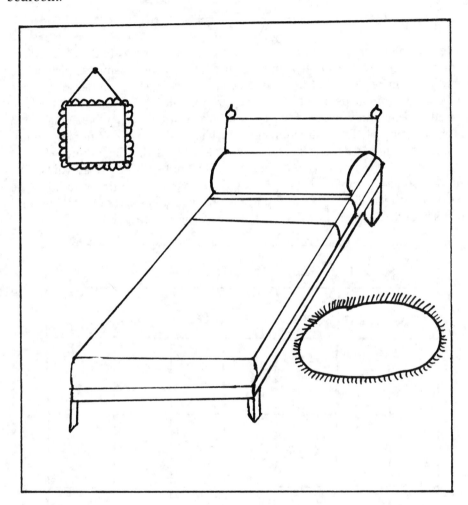

## Wall posters

These visuals are real time savers. If you have no large sheets of paper, stick several smaller sheets together to make a large poster. Storage is simple. They are rolled up, with an elastic band around the middle and a small label on an outside corner for identification. Once one is unrolled, practice begins with no delays.

### Displaying wall posters
There are several options for displaying a poster. One or two students can be

asked to hold it up. It can, of course, be stuck to the blackboard with blu-tak or by means of a roll of sticky tape at each corner. The centre of focus can be changed if you wish: posters can be put on the wall to one side of the board or the classroom. An even easier way to display them is to use clothes pegs to hang them on the length of string, described above. Use a pointer to draw attention to the point in question.

### The content

**Posters** usually carry a text, or a picture which is too complex to draw quickly at the blackboard. They can also carry a set of four or more smaller pictures to resume an entire story that may have been spread over several lessons in the textbook.[3] Grammar points, too, can be written beforehand onto wall posters, instead of being built up at the blackboard. Wall **charts** have a table, a map, or a graph of some sort. The distinction between charts and posters is not important, most teachers just use the term *posters* to cover all wall visuals of that sort.

Here are three examples of wall posters. With a little thought you will be able to create some to match your own textbook and aims. The first one might be used to introduce *ground floor* and practise ordinal numbers (Room 201? Second floor; The offices? Fifth floor; The restaurant? Ground floor, etc).

| HOTEL MAJESTIC | | | | | | |
|---|---|---|---|---|---|---|
| MANAGER | ACCOUNTS | MARKETING | | | | |
| | | | | | 406 | |
| | | 303 | | | | |
| 201 | | | | | | |
| 101 | 102 | 103 | 104 | 105 | 106 | 107 |
| RECEPTION | | | BAR | RESTAURANT | | |

Simplified maps are useful to practice asking for and giving directions. Name places (cinema, pharmacy, city hall, and so on) can be used instead of numbers or the letters of the alphabet, as in this example:

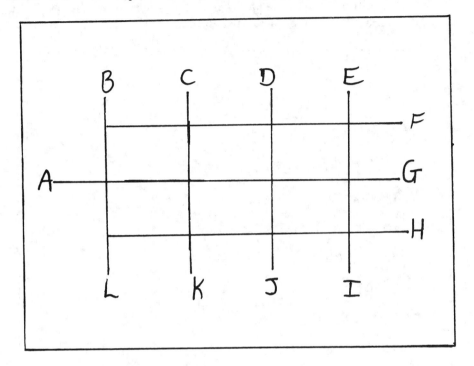

In a well resourced school this next visual, a menu, might be handed out in a photocopied form to each pair of students. However, it is just as effective in a large format. Everyone can refer to it as they practise ordering a meal in a restaurant. One student takes the part of a waiter, after which they reverse the roles and order a different meal and pay a different bill.

MENU

STARTERS:

Avocado

Smoked Trout

Ham + Melon

Grapefruit

MAIN COURSES:

Roast Lamb

Lancashire Hotpot

Steak 'n Kidney Pie

Shepherd's Pie

Pork Chops

DESSERTS:

Trifle

Rice Pudding

Fruit Pudding

Choice of vegetables with main course.

## The portable blackboard

A roll-up blackboard can be made in minutes. It offer a reusable alternative to the posters, described above and is used in the same way, with the same type of visuals. The finished item is light and easily carried.

### Making a portable blackboard

To make this useful aid you only need two lengths of round stick and a square yard of black vinyl or oil cloth for the writing surface. This should be non-glossy. A broomstick will do nicely for the lengths of wood. Cut in half, a broomstick provides two rollers, each 60 centimetres in length. You can make several different sizes of board; they are extremely useful and very cheap.

To assemble it, cut the black vinyl to fit the width of the rollers. Roll the top and bottom of the material onto the rollers, glueing it or tacking it in place with small nails. This shortens the working length to about 2 feet 6 inches. Attach a loop of string at the top, so that you can hang the unrolled visual from a nail. You can fix nails in the walls on the two sides of the room, to offer a change of focus, if you wish.

### Using the portable blackboard

With this visual aid you do the writing or drawing before the lesson and just unroll it when it is needed, like a poster. You can use a range of brightly coloured chalks, and so produce careful drawings, rather than just simple sketches. The portable board is also ideal for laying out grammar points that are too lengthy for the regular board. The portable blackboard can be used time and time again. And, you do not have to find poster sheets. To carry it, you just roll the bottom to the top and snap an elastic band around the cylindrical package.

## The whiteboard

This is another secondary writing or drawing surface. Dark colours stand out especially well on the white surface. Because of this, a whiteboard is excellent for written texts, and even fairly small writing is legible from the back or other side of the room.

### Making a whiteboard

Buy some of the white peel-off and stick-on plastic that is sold in most stationary shops. It is intended for use with what are known as *dry-wipe* pens, and you will need one or two of these as well. The plastic is stuck onto board, and it takes only seconds to stick a piece onto an oblong piece of hardboard, plywood or cardboard. It is very light, but of course it cannot be folded. However, you can make a roll-up version if you prefer, in the same way as the portable blackboard is made, above. In this case, you will need a backing sheet of thick plastic, preferably of a light colour, onto which you stick the white plastic sheet. No glue is needed, the white plastic has an adhesive backing.

### Using the whiteboard

You must use only the special *dry-wipe* pens on this surface, any other pen will ruin the surface. After use you just use a dry tissue or cloth to erase what you wrote or drew with the dry-wipe pen. The special ink cleans off instantly. You can also work with a short original text, then erase words one by one to make any practice more challenging.

## Worksheets

Worksheets are used whenever there is too much text for you to use the blackboard or a portable whiteboard (above). Spirit copiers are available in most schools. The advantage is that the worksheets can be used time and time again, if students learn never to write on them. Photocopies are expensive, and many readers will be unable to afford them, even if the machines are available. You can reduce costs, though, by covering all the available space with small print. Sometimes you can put two or more texts on the same page and separate them after copying.

## ■ CONCLUSION

Unlike most other subjects, where students can work alone with books, language lessons are often teacher centred. Consequently, language teachers have to be able to capture and hold the learners' interest, offering stimuli for conversation and discussion, as well as for practice. This is done by varying the material used, from lesson to lesson and by frequent changes of approach and activity. Teaching, as well as learning, then becomes enjoyable. Fortunately, visuals are easy to contrive. Often they can be made from scrap materials. Even the more sophisticated teaching aids described above can be made cheaply in most countries of the world.

Movement helps you gain and hold attention. You can leave the blackboard area when using hand held visuals, such as flashcards, wordcards, letter cards, number cards, a clock face or finger puppets. Folded wordcards, charts and posters can be displayed at the sides of the classroom or pegged to a string line across the board. A magnet board or felt board is usually balanced on the ledge of the board but can be hung from a hook or nail in any wall. A portable blackboard or whiteboard can act as a reusable poster or chart. Any change of focus is attention holding.

The students will appreciate the efforts you put in to make learning enjoyable. They will know, from the range of materials devised, that their lessons are well prepared and that you are a true, caring professional.

## Notes

[1] If you have access to an overhead projector (OHP), you should certainly use it. Transparencies are easy to store and carry, and images can be projected onto any light coloured wall. Everything that was included for the blackboard in the previous chapter is applicable to the OHP, as is what has been said here about posters. The same wall can be used for slide projections and the British and American Embassies (cultural sections) may well lend you slides of their country if you have a slide projector. Embassies also carry stocks of videocassettes which can be borrowed by schools. Modern electronic equipment is simple to operate, but if you intend to make regular use of sophisticated aids you should invest in a specialist book which explains how such equipment is best exploited for teaching purposes.

[2] If you cannot get hold of realia from the foreign country, use tickets, labels, calendar pages, timetables or any other material from your own. A real driver's licence or passport is far better than a picture of one.

[3] Composite pictures, of the sort seen in Chapter Nine, are typical of what is put on a poster.

# 11 Planning lessons

## ■ THE BENEFITS OF PLANNING

Proper lesson plans are essential. You will be more relaxed and confident if you follow a clear plan. As you finish one phase, a glance reminds you of the next. The plan will enable you to improve your *timing*, too. By comparing the estimated time with the actual time taken for different types of activity, you soon learn to judge lesson stages and phases with great accuracy – both in planning the lesson and in executing it.

In addition, the plans are an aid to continuing improvement. After the lesson you can add an evaluation to the plan, identifying those parts which went well and those which were less successful. This plan, with your comments and corrections, provides a useful, timesaving reference when you next plan the same lesson.

In this chapter we formalise a basic 3–stage framework which can be used for a range of different types of lesson. We begin by planning a reading lesson and a listening lesson. Then we do the same for a lesson which exploits a dialogue. These lessons were all described in earlier chapters. We add what is often known as a *standard oral lesson*. This is the lesson type which is most used, and abused, world-wide. Here it has been humanised and given a communicative emphasis.[1]

A 3–stage framework is far more flexible than it may at first appear. Even lessons of the same type become quite different if the learning activities and teaching techniques are varied within each stage from lesson to lesson.

## ■ PLANNING THE LESSON

There are three basic steps in making a lesson plan. First, you decide the aim of the lesson. Second, you choose what language you will highlight (if any). Third, you decide your strategies. Let us look at the three planning steps separately:

### Decide the aim of the lesson

If there is a teacher manual with the textbook, an aim may be stated there. Commonly, the aim will be to practise one particular language point or to introduce a few new words. You are under no obligation to adopt the same aims. The writer was not writing specifically for your class or for your context, and you may wish to modify both the aim and the approach. You might choose to use the passage for reading, perhaps running two or more passages together to get the needed length. You may choose to use the passage as a starting base for free oral expression. You could even decide to use a dialogue for reading comprehension and a reading passage as a stepping stone to guided role play. The aim of each lesson will depend on the nature of the text and your philosophy of language teaching.

## Select the key language

Do not feel restricted by traditional guidelines. Introduce as much or as little as you need, in order to treat the passage in the way *you* want to treat it. If you are conducting a reading or listening lesson, there is no need for formal presentation of a grammar point or structure. It will be understood in its textual context. You can leave out the presentation of vocabulary in a reading lesson, to allow students to develop their guesswork strategies. Even in a listening lesson, there is no need to start with the presentation of new vocabulary every time. Why not just explain the meaning of the new words as you reach them in the text you are reading aloud? Where there is to be acting out in a lesson, you will probably want to introduce two or three useful structures, emphasising the communicative value of each one.

## Choose your approach

Your pedagogy should be in harmony with your aim. Consequently, there is no single method (a *method* is a fixed sequence of activities, rather like a recipe) that will suit each lesson. If the aim is to offer fluency practice, clearly the teaching strategies will be quite unlike those of a lesson which has a grammar practice focus. The approach to a lesson culminating in a role play activity will be radically different again.

## ■ A 3–STAGE LESSON

As stated earlier, the majority of lessons can be planned as a 3–stage process. Each stage has several steps or **phases**. If you look back, three stages will be evident in the model lessons already seen in this book. The reading and listening lessons demonstrated in Chapter Seven had a **pre-reading** or pre-listening stage, in which vocabulary was presented and interest was aroused. Then came **task reading** (or listening) and limited exploitation of the text. Finally, there was a **follow-up** stage, during which the students could use English spontaneously.

For the dialogue-based lesson, in Chapter Eight, there was the **presentation** of new structures, paired **practice** and then a final **performance** stage, with acting out.

## The three p's

The three stages are usually called the *Three P's*, standing for **presentation**, **practice** and **performance** (this last is sometimes called the **production** stage).

### The presentation stage

You introduce needed new vocabulary and grammar structures. Scene setting and task assignments are carried out for reading and listening lessons.

### The practice stage

You move from controlled practice to guided practice and exploitation of the text.

### The performance stage

You encourage linguistic innovation, shifting attention to what is being said, rather than concerning yourself with total accuracy.

## The lesson as a unit

Like everything in teaching, this 3–stage lesson structure is not absolutely fixed. Nevertheless, it is a helpful framework when you first begin planning lessons and ensures that you do not overlook anything. And of course, the *lesson* is not an inviolable 45 minutes whole, either. Rather, you should think in terms of lesson *units*. There will be days when you want to cover two short lesson units in a single teaching period, or when the three stages of one lesson unit have to be spread over two periods.

You fill each stage with a selection of activities that are suited to the lesson aim. These comprise your stage phases. **Supplementary activities** (like setting and checking homework, conducting revision, giving a test, playing a game or singing a song) can be viewed as a fourth stage, even though such elements are scattered across the other three stages.[2]

## ■ THE SHAPE OF A LESSON PLAN

Your master plan should be written on **one** sheet of paper and carry an absolute minimum of detail. This does not mean that you have only that one page on your desk. There are supplementary pages, numbered on the sequence that they will be needed. These pages, too, should be self-contained, for ease of handling. The first may carry the illustrative sentences for the lexical items being introduced, a miniature sketch of a needed blackboard drawing or the pre-questions for a listening session. The second page of notes may have the layout of a grammar point to go on the blackboard, together with a few prompts or substitutions to use when practising. A third page may have short-answer questions, another the longer-answer questions. Yet another may have discussion points or prompts for a role play, and so on.

It may seem wasteful that an entire page is used for the layout of a structure when it could easily be fitted at the bottom of, say, a page which carries only four or five illustrative sentences. However, it really is much simpler to work with self contained notes and you are less likely to lose your place. Also, you can write more clearly, using bigger and more easily read print. This makes it easy to snatch a glance as the lesson proceeds. The added bonus is that the plan, notes and any visuals are used again, when this lesson is next taught. So, it is important that they be user friendly.

The number of supplementary pages and their nature will depend on the sort of lesson being conducted. In your main (one page) plan, you just mark the page number of the supplementary notes you will need at that point of the lesson (eg *Note 2*). Just one key word in the plan or in a page of supplementary notes will remind you when to produce a wall chart, a clock, number cards, a map, or any other needed visual aid. This procedure will become clear in the example plans which follow.

## ■ SOME SAMPLE LESSON PLANS

We look now at some sample plans, beginning with a blank outline plan. We then examine some completed lesson plans. Each model plan is followed by a description of the contents of the supplementary pages that accompany it.

The first completed plan is for a listening lesson, but it is also applicable to a task based reading lesson. In looking at this plan and the notes, readers should refer back to the demonstration lesson in Chapter Seven, where a soldier is told to move a piano.

The second plan is for a dialogue-based lesson, and relates to the model lesson (expanding a dialogue) in Chapter Eight. Readers should refer back to this.

The third completed plan is for a traditional oral lesson, bringing in many of the basic techniques introduced in the early chapters of the book.[3]

### The skeleton plan

On the following page is the skeleton plan which gives an overview of the shape of a 3–stage lesson. This, or something similar, you could photocopy in hundreds, to use for your own planning. A blank master plan to complete as your lesson takes shape will save time and prod your memory. On the second page is a completed lesson plan for a listening lesson.

LESSON No.                    CLASS

AIM(S):

LEXICAL ITEMS:

STRUCTURE/GRAMMAR:

### PROCEDURE

WARM-UP/REVIEW:

STAGE 1, PRESENTATION:

   a)
   b)
   c)
   d)

STAGE 2, PRACTICE, EXPLOITATION OF TEXT:

   a)
   b)
   c)
   d)
   e)

STAGE 3, PERFORMANCE:

   a)
   b)
   c)

OTHER ACTIVITIES (warm-up, homework, game, etc):

RESERVE ACTIVITY

TEACHING AIDS NEEDED:

COMMENTS:

# A completed lesson plan for a listening lesson

AIMS: a) To give practice in listening to a story.
      b) To give opportunities for expression of opinions about military service.

NEW LEXIS: a) from text: mess (officer's), barracks room, compulsory, civilian.
          b) additional vocab.: recruit, conscript.

STRUCTURE/GRAMMAR: No formal focus

## PROCEDURE

WARM-UP (3 minutes):
    Song, Happy birthday dear Yao (14 years)

STAGE 1, PRESENTATION (approx. 7 mins):

  a) New vocabulary: (Note 1).
  b) Introduction: Story of a young conscript, etc.
  c) task setting: Why was John Smith in the army? What did the sergeant make him do?

STAGE 2, EXPLOITATION (approx: 10 mins):

  a) Reading aloud, once.
  b) Check on pre-questions. Random.
  c) Read text second time, dramatically.
  d) Familiarity, short answer Q's (Note 2).
  e) Limited production, longer-answer Q's (Note 3).

STAGE 3, PERFORMANCE (approx. 15 mins):

  a) Hypothetical Q's and Discussion (Note 4).
  b) Written arguments, papers exchanged, discussed.

OTHER ACTIVITIES: Check yesterday's homework (approx. 5 mins).
                  Set homework, page 73, ex. 4.

RESERVE ACTIVITY: Substitution, game-like:

    John Smith dreamed only of the day he would . . .
    *I* often dream of the day I shall (win the lottery, etc).
    What about you?

TEACHING AIDS: Cassette recording of text. Tape player.
            (reminder: check batteries, zero rev. counter).

COMMENTS: (filled in immediately after the lesson).

## The supplementary notes for the lesson above

The one page plan referred the teacher to the supplementary notes needed at certain phases. For a reading lesson, the plan and procedure would have been very similar, but the practice and follow-up might have included some written work, as the students would have seen the text. This is what each page of notes would look like for that lesson.

### Note 1

This would list the new vocabulary, together with any illustrative sentences and drawings to be put on the board. The page would look rather like the blackboard model given in the worked model in Chapter Seven (Step One). In this lesson there is no grammar focus. If there had been a grammar structure to introduce, the skeleton layout would have been on a new numbered page, together with any questions or prompts to be used in the practice.

### Note 2

This page would carry the range of short-answer questions, with the aim of providing more listening practice and increasing comprehension. The question types could be separate or jumbled together for variety, as in phase one (stage three) of the model in Chapter Seven.

### Note 3

This page of notes would have cues to elicit longer answers, exactly as in phase two of the model lesson.

### Note 4

This set of notes would enable the teacher to keep the discussion moving. The questions could be just as shown in phase three of the model lesson. Alternatively, the grouping into three sets could be dropped and the questions mixed together. The teacher would allow arguments to develop, following any new and unexpected angle. There would be no attempt to use every one of these questions or discussion prompts. The short written task would also be on this page (eg *in pairs: write one good argument for or against compulsory service*).

### Other notes

You may well want yet another page of notes, for example with answers for the homework check or cues for any reserve activity. A reserve activity is worthwhile, in case you mis-time a lesson. It can be a simple word game, a song, or a review of a previous lesson. It can be shifted to tomorrow's plan if it is not needed today.

*Lesson comments:* The space at the foot of the plan is important. As soon after the lesson as possible you should note any improvements to be made when you next plan and execute this same lesson. Perhaps another word or two should have been presented. Maybe the timing was wrong. Possibly a good new discussion point emerged and could be added to Note 4. Another visual aid may be needed. The next time you teach this lesson, and on subsequent occasions, you can produce improved versions of the plan and notes.

## The supplementary notes for the lesson on p. 146

In the printed dialogue, the suggestions were accepted immediately. This is not always the case in real life. So, the teacher has extended the acting out possibilities by adding phrases for declining politely and making another proposal[3].

First, there is a short warm-up, invented as a lead-in to the lesson. Some of the items suggested (quite unpredictable) during that play-like activity may prove useful in the stages to follow. Plenty of changes of activity are evident in the plan and there is a written activity to begin in class and complete for homework, so there will be no timing problem.

### Note 1

The teacher chose to teach *How're things?* as a lexical item, rather than as a structure. This is the best way to handle a formula (*What's new? What a nice/awful day!* etc). This first note would just show the skeleton layouts of the three structures to be presented at the blackboard.

### Flashcards

The teacher has prepared a set of flashcards, to prompt different refusals and counter suggestions at several points of the lesson. The set should be suited to the local context. In Mexico or Spain there might be a card to represent *going to the bullfight*. In Africa or India there may be one to represent *the village*. General flashcards might represent *go to the football match, discotheque, playcards, a walk, shopping, the cinema, watch TV*, and so on.

A note about blackboard drawings has been included at the point where the dialogue is introduced (Stage 1, Phase C). This page would contain model sketches of three heads. Once on the blackboard, these allow the teacher to model all three parts (or play the recorded text), indicating who is speaking.

### Note 2

This page would remind the teacher where to make cuts for the backward build-up of the longer phrases. It would also have prompts for substitution practice, cued orally. The substitution reminder would look like this:

Substitutions (for *this weekend*): During the holidays, On Monday (etc) after-noon; Next/This Tuesday evening, etc.

## The supplementary notes for the lesson on p. 147

There are plenty of changes of activity, with visuals to capture interest. The teacher revises some related topic vocabulary before presenting new words from the text and adding additional words that might be useful in practice or discussion. Notice that at the end of practice the teacher gives an opportunity for the class to look through the text and ask about any words or phrases that still

# A completed plan for a dialogue-based lesson

AIMS:  a)  To have the class learn key structures by heart.
 b)  To have them practise the dialogue with substitutions.
 c)  To introduce some role play.

NEW VOCABULARY:  How're things? (formula) = How are you?
 a bike ride = an excursion on bicycles.
 a picnic    = a meal in the open air.

NEW STRUCTURE: How about -ing . .? Function: Making a suggestion.

ADDITIONAL LANGUAGE:  Declining: I don't feel like -ing.
 Countering: I'd rather + basic verb.

## PROCEDURE

WARM-UP: Game (3 minutes), Going on a Picnic:

 You bring a/the/some ...!
 I'll bring ... (nominated students).

STAGE 1, PRESENTATION (approx. 10 mins):
 a)  New vocabulary (three lexical items above).
 b)  New structure (Note 1 and flashcards).
 c)  First model, spoken (BB drawings of speakers).

STAGE 2, PRACTICE (15 mins):

 a)  Repetition drill (Note 2, backward build-ups).
 b)  Cued Substitution, chorus work (Note 2).
 c)  Public pairs: cued acceptance/refusal and counter suggestions (flashcards).
 d)  Private pairs, substituting dialogue. Books open.
 e)  Ditto. Books closed.
 f )  Public check.

STAGE 3, PRODUCTION (to end of lesson, 17 mins):

 a)  Public pairs, new suggestions.
 b)  Private pair role play; new suggestions, counter suggestions, agreeing weekend activities.
 c)  Acting out. Volunteer pairs.
 d)  Write out created dialogues.

HOMEWORK: Complete writing of dialogues.

RESERVE ACTIVITY: none

VISUAL AIDS: Set of flashcards with suggestions.

COMMENTS:

## A completed plan for an oral lesson

AIMS: a) To present nine new related lexical items.
  b) To practise the grammar point, orally and in writing.
  c) To exploit the text thoroughly.
  d) To give opportunities for creative use of English.

NEW VOCABULARY: ironmonger's, goods, tools, corrugated iron, wire, concrete.
  Additional vocab.: screw, screwdriver, wrench.

GRAMMAR POINT: People + their (possessive adjective).

### PROCEDURE

WARM-UP: Revision (1 minute):
  hammer, nails, wood, cement (flashcards).

STAGE 1, Presentation (approx. 10 mins):

  a) New vocabulary (Note 1, new flashcards, visuals).
  b) Introduce new grammar point.

  *People* buy *their* tools at the ironmonger's.

STAGE 2, PRACTICE (approx. 20 mins):

  a) Cued reproduction of grammar point (Note 2).
  b) Write 2–3 new sentences on the model, in pairs. Check.
  c) Pre-questions on text:
    i) Name of the ironmonger? ii) Why was customer angry?
  d) Silent reading.
  e) Exploitation, increased comprehension (Note 3).
  f) Scrutiny of text to identify problems.
  g) Copy vocabulary and grammar point.

STAGE 3, PRODUCTION (14 mins):

  a) WH longer-answer questions (Note 4).
  b) Discussion questions (Note 4).
  c) Guided paragraph writing, from BB cue (Note 5).

RESERVE ACTIVITY: True-false on pictures, page 47 textbook, students to ask questions in public pairs.

VISUAL AIDS: Short length of wire. Small piece of concrete. 4 flashcards for review, 3 for new vocabulary.

COMMENTS:

puzzle them. And there is a chance at the third stage for students to be creative in using English. The teacher has ensured full involvement by giving a short written task in the final stage, but one which leaves little scope for error.

## Flashcards

Altogether, there are seven flashcards. Four of them had been used in an earlier lesson and are now brought back for revision of related vocabulary. The new ones introduce the words *tools, corrugated iron* and *concrete*. This last flashcard might simply look like a sack of cement (labelled) plus a pile of stones. The three new flashcards can be stuck on the blackboard next to their related phrases (These are tools, Concrete is reinforced cement, This roof is made of corrugated iron).

**Note 1**

This page would remind the teacher of any definitions or illustrative sentences that will be put on the board for the six new words:

> An ironmonger sells tools, cement, paint, etc.
> Goods = merchandise. Shopkeepers sell goods.
> Wire   = conducts electricity.

**Note 2**

This would remind the teacher of the substitutions to be given or elicited during the grammar practice:

> People buy their rice/meat/medicines, etc at . . .
> People who live in countries where there's a lot of heavy rain, build their walls/roofs/homes/huts of . . .
> People who live in cold/hot/countries build their . . .

**Note 3**

This page would have questions for the exploitation of the text after it has been read, silently. It would begin with yes-no questions, then move to choice questions (or true-false, for a change) and WH short-answer questions.

**Note 4**

The fourth page of notes would carry WH-questions to provoke longer answers, prompts, personal questions, general questions of an educational sort and hypothetical questions. There would also be a few provocative statements to throw into any discussion.

**Note 5**

The last page would have the outline for the guided paragraph, to be copied onto the blackboard:

> In my village/town, people build their houses with . . .

They cover their roofs with ...
They buy their ... at ...
Our house is ...

## ■ CONCLUSION

All the skills, strategies, techniques and activities that we have at our disposal are considered at the planning stage. We exercise choice in deciding the lesson type and in choosing the learning activities to include within each stage. In this way we can be **eclectic**, varying the approach from day to day. This is so much more motivating for the class than a predictable sequence of teaching steps.

It takes only a few minutes to plan a lesson, and the rewards far exceed the effort. With a clear plan you will be confident and the lesson will go well. Read through the day's text, noting any new vocabulary and useful structures. Jot down your aims, then decide the strategies you will adopt. From the jottings, draw up a plan, using the headings seen in the blank lesson plan given earlier, but making any needed modifications to the basic framework, which is not rigidly fixed.

The next step will be to produce the supplementary pages of *notes*. The first will usually show the illustrative sentences for the new lexical items and any blackboard sketches to be used in presenting the words or formulae. The second will probably show the layout of the day's grammar point or structure. With a listening lesson, there may be no grammar focus, but with a reading lesson you may wish to pick out a grammar point to highlight. With a dialogue you would probably insist on the functional values of two or more useful structures. There will be separate notes to support you in the production stage and to remind you of any additional activities.

Visuals will be prepared at the same time. On the master plan, you indicate the points at which they will be used. At the end of the plan, the visuals are listed together to act as a reminder to take them to school on the following day and on any future occasion you teach the same lesson.

The space for comments at the foot of the page, or overleaf, is most important. This is completed after the lesson. The sooner the better, while you still have an impression of what was successful and what might have been better. Each time you teach this same lesson, you can refer to those notes to create a fresh master plan, incorporating any needed changes. It may be necessary to add a new page of supplementary notes or to revise a page in some way. The whole lesson package is kept for future use. Your teaching will improve continuously because of this process of self evaluation, you will grow professionally over the years. An investment of time this year, planning all of your lessons in detail, will result in improvements and real economies of materials and time in the future.

## Notes

[1] The Standard Oral Lesson (SOL) is widespread, not least because it was the method taught to Peace Corps volunteers, who planted it everywhere they went, including

teacher training colleges. Their students became English instructors (they were not really **teachers** in the ideal sense of the word), and some of them went on to become trainers and inspectors. And so the method lives on.

The SOL procedure is a hybrid of the Direct Method and the Audiolingual Method. Any use of the mother tongue is forbidden. There are always half a dozen new words and one grammar point or structure to practise in each lesson. The dialogues and reading passages in the textbook sound artificial because they were written to provide such a linguistic diet. Every new word is the subject of a formal presentation. Illustrative sentences are repeated in chorus. Structures and grammar points are rote-learned, by means of substitution and transformation drills. The passage in the textbook is read aloud and reproduced in full sentence answers to questions. Finally, there is a short guided production stage, but it is teacher directed and the teachers continue to correct. At the end of the lesson the students copy the illustrative sentences and grammar points.

Even when given by experienced instructors, a diet of unchanging SOL lessons is dull. In the hands of a majority of poorly trained teachers, the lesson can be a disaster. The good thing about it is that it offers a recipe that is easy to follow. However, a 3-stage oral lesson does not have to be predictable and uncommunicative, as is evident in the lesson plan in this chapter. Teachers can be adventurous and innovative, ringing the changes in their approach to each oral lesson.

[2] Plan all the odds and ends of activities as a **stage four**, but spread them throughout the other stages to vary the learning pattern from lesson to lesson. A **warm-up** activity has to be at the start of the lesson. You might go straight into a **homework check** afterwards, before beginning the presentation stage. It is usually best not to split any presentation from the treatment you give the text, but a relaxing **game** or a **song** might come after any formal work on the text. At the very end of the lesson you could **set homework** or even conduct a short **test**. By viewing optional extras like those as the components of a stage you are less likely to overlook them when you are planning text-based 3-stage lessons.

[3] In the model lesson of Chapter Eight, (expanding a dialogue) we saw the teacher introduce additional structures to expand the value of the role play follow-up to a dialogue. The dialogue that follows is the one that the teacher was faced with, and on which the lesson plan is based. It is evident that without the extra functions of *declining* and *making counter suggestions*, any follow-up role play activities would be very limited and predictable.

### Text of dialogue

| | |
|---|---|
| JOHN: | Hi Bill. How're things today? |
| BILL: | Fine. What shall we do this weekend? |
| JOHN: | No plans. I may go to the pictures. |
| BILL: | It's a lovely day, how about going fishing? |
| JOHN: | That's a great idea, but how about taking a picnic with us? We could go to the beach. |
| BILL: | OK. You bring the drinks. I'll bring some chicken sandwiches. |
| JOHN: | Fine. Why don't we see if Charlie wants to go? |
| BILL: | All right. I'll make the sandwiches, you phone Charlie. Ask him if he can bring some fruit. |
| JOHN: | (*on telephone*). Hello. Is that you Charlie? Hey, how about going fishing? |
| CHARLIE: | Sure. That's ... |

# Part Three

# INTRODUCING VARIETY INTO TEACHING AND LEARNING

# 12 Language learning games

## ■ THE VALUE OF PLAY

Through games, learners practise and internalise vocabulary, grammar and structures. Motivation is enhanced, too, by the play and the competition. An added benefit is that the learners' attention is on the message, not on the language. They acquire language unconsciously, with their whole attention engaged by the activity, in much the same way as they acquired their mother tongue.

Information gap activities are dealt with in another chapter.[1] Here, we are concerned with simple games that require little preparation but can be used for the revision and practice of various language points. Useful though these games are as time fillers, they are also effective teaching–learning instruments. They merit a proper place in your lesson plans, two or three times weekly.

We begin by looking at letter and number games. Then we move on to word games before looking at games that involve speech, rather than single words.

## ■ NUMBER AND LETTER GAMES

Most syllabuses include digits and the alphabet fairly early on, and classes often learn the sequences by heart. In real life, letters and numbers rarely occur in that fixed order; they are found in dates, phone numbers, names, prices, and so on. Realistic practice should, then, involve unpredictability. This is best achieved through games like the following.

### Bingo

Each player has a *card*. These can be photocopied from a master sheet and cut out with scissors (one master page can hold 6 to 8 cards) or the students can be asked to draw their own. There can be as many boxes as you wish, but five across and four down will usually be enough, giving twenty spaces. Next, the students are instructed to fill their card with random numbers. It is best if this is done in a prescribed way, working from low numbers at the top to the higher numbers lower down. This enables players to find the numbers you call more quickly. It helps if you instruct them to write any number between 1 and 10 in the first row, 11 and 20 in the second, and so on, as in the examples seen below.

Naturally, the game can be played with numbers between 50 and 100 if you want to practise higher numbers. Alternatively, the game can be made to last much longer by allowing a wider choice on each line. If the first line has numbers from 1 to 20, the second 21 to 40, and so on, it is apparent that on a five line card you could use all numbers from 1 to 100.

A completed card will look like this, but every student's card will be unique thanks to the chance distribution of the numbers they themselves have chosen.

*A bingo card*  **B   I   N   G   O**

| 3 | 5 | 7 | 8 | 9 |
|----|----|----|----|----|
| 11 | 12 | 15 | 16 | 18 |
| 22 | 24 | 26 | 27 | 29 |
| 32 | 35 | 38 | 39 | 40 |

You yourself will need a rough master sheet, with all the numbers on it. Tick the numbers as you call them, to ensure that they are not given more than once. As they are called, in quite random order, the students cross off the numbers on their own cards.

There are two winners for each game. The first student to cross out all the numbers in any one line across the card calls *Bingo!* He or she then calls back the numbers crossed out as a check. This winner gets a small prize, such as a sweet. The second winner is the first person to have *all* his numbers called. This student signals the fact by shouting out *Full House!* The full house winner gets a somewhat better prize, perhaps a pencil.

## Secret messages

This game practises both numbers and the alphabet. Each letter is given an agreed number, but it is not necessary to work from $a = 1$ to $z = 26$ each time. You can stipulate any combination (eg $a = 10$, $b = 20$, $c = 30$, and so on). Once you have put the message into the agreed code, you then call out the numbers. A space between two words is marked by the word *zero*.

Here is an example based on the code 1 to 26. It translates as *Bring me a pencil*, and the first student to obey and take one to the teacher would get the prize. Sometimes a clever learner will decode before you finish sending.

| 2 | 18 | 9 | 14 | 7 | zero | 13 | 5 | zero | 1 | zero | 16 | 5 | 14 | 3 | 9 | 12 |
|---|----|---|----|---|------|----|---|------|---|------|----|---|----|---|---|----|
| B | R | I | N | G | | M | E | | A | | P | E | N | C | I | L |

## Prices

This is a good way to practise the recognition of prices, an essential skill for any market place. It is played with a box rather like that for bingo. You can use the local currency or any other. In the example, the currency is the American dollar. The figures across the top row represent the number of cents. The figures down the side show the dollars. We rarely get a sum like $2.36; small coins are usually rounded to multiples of five. Each time the game is played, the dollar and cent values are changed, to practise a new range of numbers.

The students copy the table from a model on the board. You work with your own private copy and call out the prices at random. The students tick them off on their cards. The idea is to call out all the prices, in random order, *except for two or three. The winners* are those who can correctly identify the prices that have *not been called*.

This is one of those rare games where the aim is to have as many winners as possible – a lot of winners is indicative of good listening competence. In the game below there are 40 boxes, so the class would have to identify 37 prices before the winners are identified. In the example the teacher has called the first three prices. These are $1.20, $3.25 and $5.95.

*The prices Grid*

## PRICES

| CENTS: | 10 | 20 | 25 | 30 | 50 | 75 | 90 | 95 |
|--------|----|----|----|----|----|----|----|----|
| 1 | | X | | | | | | |
| 2 | | | | | | | | |
| DOLLARS: 3 | | | X | | | | | |
| 4 | | | | | | | | |
| 5 | | | | | | | | X |

## Count again

This is a useful two-minute filler that can be used for warm-up or even introduced halfway through the lesson for variety. You give the class one digit. The class counts aloud from that number, in unison. After a few numbers you clap your hands and the class stops. You call a new number and the class immediately begins counting from that point. The game becomes more difficult if they are required to count by twos, as here:

TEACHER: Twenty.
STUDENTS: 20, 22, 24, 26, 28, 30, 32, (clap)
TEACHER: Eleven.
STUDENTS: 11, 13, 15, 17, . . .

## ■ WORD GAMES

Vocabulary revision can be fun. All of the games that follow can be adapted to fit any syllabus. Some even give you the opportunity to add lexical items that are not on the syllabus, but which are useful to the students.

### Word sets

A box layout, similar to that of Bingo, is put on the blackboard. The name of one student is written across the top to provide initial letters (avoid long names or those which have letters repeated). At the side the chosen topic areas are indicated. The players have to find words in each topic area which begin with the prescribed letters. This can be done at the board, with students calling out words, or on paper, in pairs. Sometimes it is impossible to find a word for every single box, so the pair which completes the most squares will be the winners. Here is an example of a nearly completed game, using the name *Robin*.

*A word set box*

| Name: | R | O | B | I | N |
|---|---|---|---|---|---|
| JOB | | operator | builder | inspector | nun |
| ANIMALS | rhino | ostrich | badger | insect | |
| COUNTRY | Romania | | Belgium | Italy | Norway |
| FOOD | rice | olives | butter | | nuts |

The check is oral. There are usually several options for each slot. It is a good idea to ask desks to change papers for the marking. To play a second time, you just erase ROBIN and write in a new name, adding or deleting a row of boxes if necessary. Alternatively you can leave the name and change the topic areas.

### Word building

This is a good way to practise spelling. A long word is written on the blackboard and the class is given a fixed time, say two minutes, in which to write as many other words as possible, using only the letters of the original word. This can be an individual task or a pair work one. Working from the word *aeroplane*, the class might find:

real, pen, ran, no, an, plan, panel, learn, ...

Papers are exchanged for the marking, which is done orally. The scoring is *not* one point for one word. A point is won only for a word which no other students have found. In the space of ten minutes, it is possible to play and check two or three games.

## Card scrabble

Readers probably know the professionally produced word building game. The one described here has been adapted and simplified for the classroom. The teacher has to make a pack of letter cards, but once made they can be used for years. The cards should be about the same size as playing cards. They are easily carried as an ever ready warm-up or time filler. Through playing, the class engages in vocabulary revision and spelling practice.

### *The composition of the set of cards*
One card for each letter of the alphabet is not appropriate. Some letters occur less frequently than others. If you look at the letters in this paragraph, there are lots of vowels (but not many letters *u*), while some consonants are infrequent or missing altogether (*x, z, w,* etc). This distribution of letters is different in all languages, so if you are a modern languages teacher you have to find out the letter frequency of your language. The easy way to do this is to check the local version of *Scrabble*. A more irksome way is to spend an hour counting letters on a randomly chosen page of print.

In English, the letter frequency is as below, given slight adjustment to keep the pack manageable. You should make up the numbers shown for each letter, giving a pack of 72 cards for the 26 letters.

| No. of Cards | Letters | | | | | |
|---|---|---|---|---|---|---|
| 5 | A | E | N | T | | |
| 4 | I | O | R | S | | |
| 3 | C | D | F | H | P | L |
| 2 | B | G | M | U | W | Y |
| 1 | J | K | Q | V | X | Z |

### *How to play card scrabble*
To play, one student shuffles the pack and draws seven cards. The seven letters are written on the board. The learners work in pairs to build as many words as possible from the letters. After a check (in which the winners are those who discover words that nobody else thought of), the teacher has only to draw one

more card. With just one new letter added to the seven, a new range of possibilities is opened up for word creation. The game continues in this way after each check, with a new letter being added each time. This gives you total control over timing.

## My shopping basket

The first speaker gives one item of shopping, the second repeats it and adds another, the third builds yet another item into the list, and so on. The game can be played in alphabetical order or not, as you wish. It is easier to provide new words if no such restriction is imposed. On the other hand, it is easier to remember items in alphabetical order. The items themselves are important, but the quantity or packaging need not be remembered exactly. The game will sound like this.

STUDENT 1: In my basket I've got an apple.
STUDENT 2: In my basket I've got an apple and a ball.
STUDENT 3: In my basket I've got an apple, a ball and a packet of crisps

(and so on – a duck, some eggs, a pack of flour, etc)

The game can be made competitive, to involve more students where the class is large. Each row of desks becomes a team. The message is passed to the back of the class from the front. One of each pair, having added an item, has to turn round and pass it to a student seated in the desk behind, and so on. When all the rows have finished, the last student (right at the back, of course) has to stand and repeat the whole list as it arrived. There should be as many items in the basket as there are students in the row.

## Anything to declare?

This is the question posed by customs officers at ports of entry. The traveller has to declare what is in the baggage. The students are supposed to avoid mundane objects, and declare items that might conceivably interest the officer. The game can be played in alphabetic order, as shown here, or without such a control.

TEACHER: Have you anything to declare madam?
STUDENT 1: I've got this alligator.
TEACHER: And you? Anything to declare?
STUDENT 2: Only an alligator and a boomerang.

(cat, dog, explosives, fish, gun, etc)

## Sound chains

This is a good activity for ear training. The students have to identify the last *sound*, but not the last letter, of the word spoken before. The player nominated then gives a word beginning with that same sound. It is suitable for advanced learners as it is very difficult to identify some final sounds. What is more, certain sounds do not occur in an initial position, in which case the player must say so. The game sounds like this;

STUDENTS: desk, kite, tin, nice, splash, shape, pulling, there is no word begin-
ning with the sound *nq*.
TEACHER: Good. Start with a new word.
STUDENTS: love, van, nice, sit, top, pie, ice, etc

## Letter chains

This is played in the same way as sound chains, but with the emphasis on the spelling. It is best played in teams (say the two halves of a class), so that they can attempt to trap each other. There should be a time limit of 5 seconds for a response to be made. The chain will be like this:

through, here, egg, gap, photograph, hair, etc

## Word associations

We associate certain words with others in our memory. For example, the word *father* probably triggers an association with *mother* in your own mind. In turn, this word is usually associated with *child*, or *baby*. This game exploits these associations.

To play the game is easy. You just say the first word and quickly designate someone for an immediate association. Having received that response, you at once designate another student for the next word association, and so on. It is important that the game move swiftly. In this way everyone keeps thinking fast and genuine first associations are more likely. You yourself say nothing once the game is moving, you just point to indicate who is to provide the next word. However, the game has to be interrupted if a questionable association is offered, as in this example:

TEACHER: Snow
STUDENTS : Cold, arctic, dog
TEACHER: Why do you say *dog*, Billy?
BILLY: Because dogs pull the ah . . .
TEACHER: Oh yes, the *sledges*. Good. Carry on, Joe. Dog

and so on.

## The grammar focus game

This game can be played in alphabetical order, but an alternative way is sug-
gested below. While playing, the learners will be practising any structure chosen by the teacher or focusing on a specified grammatical category of word. Because

it can become difficult to think of a good substitution, it is best played with voluntary contributions rather than nominated ones. In this way it will move quite fast. When there is a breakdown, the teacher can either move to the following letter of the alphabet or offer a new structure. The structure is written on the board, as in these examples of different varieties of the game.

*Noun focus*

PROFESSIONS

When I grow up I want to be an <u>a</u>rtist.

STUDENT 1: When I grow up I want to be a *baker*.
STUDENT 2: When I grow up I want to be a *cook*.

(and so on, with doctor, engineer, fireman, goalkeeper, etc)

*Verb focus*

VERBS

Why did she <u>a</u>rrive late ?

(buy a dog, catch a cold, drop the bag, eat the food, etc.)

*Adjective focus*

ADJECTIVES

My mother is very <u>a</u>rtistic.

(beautiful, cruel, dreamy, elegant, etc)

*Adverb focus*

> ### ADVERBS
>
> and _artistically_.
>
> They did it,
>
> but _angrily_.

(badly, cheerfully, dangerously, endlessly, etc)

*Function focus*

> ### MAKING A REQUEST
>
> May I answer that question?

(borrow a pen, call you this evening, drive the car, etc)

The alternative way to play these games is to assign any letter of the alphabet, at random. The students call out all the possibilities that they can think of, with that letter. Then you give another letter, and so on. The example immediately above would sound like this, if that procedure were adopted.

TEACHER: Letter T.
STUDENTS: May I telephone, take a seat, try this cake?
TEACHER: Letter P.
STUDENTS: May I play the piano, put the TV on? ...

## ■ SPEAKING GAMES

The next two games practise asking questions, but involve careful listening for content. They make excellent competitive team games, with the class divided into two. In each game the class is limited to twenty questions, so the question strategies are important. The teams have to ask global questions in order to narrow down the possibilities. Wild or redundant questions will quickly be discouraged by protesting team-mates.

## What's My Line?

The aim is to ascertain the profession of a person by using only yes-no questions and choice questions. The student at the front chooses a profession or job of some sort. Encourage them to be imaginative. As well as being bank employees, they can be bank robbers, snow clearers, astronauts, watch repairers, dog trainers, and so on. The sort of *global questions* the students need to ask in order to narrow down the range of choices might include:

- Do you work inside or outside?
- Is the work mental or physical?
- Do you need a special qualification?
- Are you a state employee?

## Animal, vegetable or mineral?

This time the students have to guess the object, person or thing that the person at the front is thinking of. Any type of short answer question may be used. The chosen student begins by giving a clue, to hint at the nature of the object. The five permitted clues are ritualistic:

### 1 My object is animal
This clue designates any living being or article composed of an animal product; such as a leather suitcase, an ivory brooch, a woollen suit, a pair of shoes, a pop star.

### 2 My object is mineral
This clue is for objects made of stone, glass, metal, plastic, water, and any other mineral. In this category we get a bottle, a cork, a watch, a diamond ring, a lorry, a pen.

### 3 My object is vegetable
Products made of wood or any plant product come into this category, such as a piece of string, a shirt, a desk, a canoe, a door.

### 4 My object is abstract
These are intangibles and concepts, for example music, a dream, a song, an idea, a ghost.

### 5 My object is (animal) and (mineral)
Finally, there are mixed categories. A house is both vegetable (the wood) and mineral (bricks and glass). A tin of sardines is both mineral and animal. A pencil is vegetable (wood) and mineral (graphite).

The person replying is expected to be somewhat helpful. For example, if the object was a *puddle*, the replies might be:

Q1: Do we find this indoors or outdoors?
A: Normally outdoors, unless you leave a window open.

Q2: Do we find them in the day or in the night?
A: In the day or the night. It's more a question of seasons.

## Chain story

This final game is open, in that what is said is entirely unpredictable. You write a finishing sentence on the blackboard. The students are nominated at random to suggest sentences, building up a simple, short story that must *end* with that closing sentence. The game can also be played in small groups. If so, restrict the story length to three or four new sentences, otherwise the students will want to write everything down. After only two or three minutes, the activity is stopped and the groups tell their stories, voting for the best one. The stimulus sentences should be designed to prod the imagination. Typical ones might be:

- And then I woke up!
- Of course, I had to eat it, pretending I enjoyed it.
- Afterwards, I found out that the gun was loaded.
- That's when I decided not to become a doctor.

An example of the story leading up to the last example might be:

I went into a hospital the other day.
I saw a doctor giving an injection.
This hurt the patient, so he hit the doctor.
That's when I ...

## ■ CONCLUSION

Language learning should be enjoyable. Games help make it so. It should not be thought that playing with words is a loss of learning time. Concentrating and listening intensively, the students acquire a great deal of language, but quite unconsciously. Much of our mother tongue competence was gained through using language in play.

Though most games are easy to prepare and to administer, they should not be viewed as mere warm-up activities or time fillers. They merit a planned place in the lesson. Unlike most learning activities, games can be as short or as long as you wish, so they are easily fitted into any lesson plan. This gives you lots of flexibility. For examples, when planning a listening or reading lesson, you may find that you need only half of the full lesson time. You can now choose areas of vocabulary for enjoyable review or even present and playfully practise an entirely new but potentially useful structure. In this way, lessons become less predictable. Variety enhances the interest of the learning process.

## Note

[1] An information gap occurs where one speaker possesses information that is denied to the others. The principle of information gap was discussed in Chapter Six, when we considered the topic of *real* questions. Information gap activities are described more fully in Chapter 15.

# 13 Songs and rhymes

## ■ THE BENEFITS OF MUSIC AND RHYME

Although the songs and rhymes are mainly the sort that teachers of English would use with young learners, the *techniques* and *approaches* apply to the teaching of any other language and to many kinds of literary text. When students sing or recite, they automatically assume command of the prosodic features of the language. The prosodies are stress, rhythm, intonation and syllable length – features which affect whole sequences of sounds. These patterns are among the most difficult aspects of language for students to master.

Poems and songs exaggerate the rhythmic nature of the language. This is especially important for English, which is a **syllable timed** language with stressed syllables being spoken at roughly equal time intervals, even in everyday speech.[1] When the students recite or sing they are obliged to use the prosodies correctly in order to reproduce the *swing* of the piece. Once the song or rhyme has been learned, it is in their minds for the rest of their lives, with all the rhythms, grammatical niceties and vocabulary.[2]

Songs and rhymes also give insights into the target culture. They are authentic texts, and as such they are motivating. You can publicise and popularise your subject simply by including songs and rhymes in the lessons. Young learners show off their songs and rhymes to their family, even teaching them to younger brothers and sisters. In schools which begin the day with a general assembly of some kind, language teachers can enhance the students' sense of achievement and give prominence to language teaching by getting a class to sing a song or two. Not least, rhymes and songs offer a welcome change of diet in the classroom.

The songs and rhymes you meet here are traditional ones that have proved their worth for generations. Any native speaker could make a cassette recording for you. If you know someone who plays a guitar or piano, the tunes are simple, with only two or three chord changes.

### Pop songs and poems

Poems can be handled in any of the ways seen in this chapter, as can short extracts from a work of literature. More advanced classes will enjoy working with pop, rock'n roll and jazz songs. The music creates a happy and relaxed environment, but even so a great deal of worthwhile work is accomplished. The lyrics of jazz and pop records have enormous linguistic value, as contemporary examples of authentic folk poetry and speech. In addition to useful colloquialisms, they sometimes contain interesting representations of dialectal speech. The record or cassette sleeve often carries the words of the songs, and you can easily copy them onto a poster or worksheet.

## ■ WAYS OF TEACHING SONGS AND RHYMES

There is nothing difficult or unusual in the techniques you will use. The aim is to bring students to the stage where they can reproduce the piece, understanding most or all of it. Most of the techniques will be demonstrated later; those that are not are easily imagined.

### The ostensive way

You illustrate the story line with pictures and mime. This is the best approach for young learners who do not worry about understanding every word in a text. Most songs and rhymes can be treated like this.

### Translation

Translate the text into the students' mother tongue. This is most appropriate for pieces which are linguistically complex, but it can also be done to save time. With certain texts it may be worth giving a **literal** translation, one which respects the word order, as well as the meaning.[3]

### Cloze texts

Write the text on the board, poster or hand-out, but with key words or phrases deleted. The student pairs have to identify the missing words as they listen. With difficult texts, provide a text which has just a few easy words deleted. With easy texts the deletion rate can be quite high. This is a good way to present a longer poem or song.

### Focus questions

Put some focus questions on the blackboard or worksheet to guide the class listening. With beginner classes, especially, you can use **inverted WH-questions**. In this way the questions contain the words of the text in exactly the order they will be heard.

### True-false statements

With more difficult texts, true-false statements or choice-questions enable you to reproduce virtually the whole text before it is heard. If there are more than two or three statements or questions, they should be written on a poster or a roll-up blackboard beforehand.

## Private study

This is another good way to approach a longer piece. After a fairly rapid and silent reading, the students ask for any needed explanations. This may be done in English or the mother tongue, depending on the level of the class. Afterwards, the piece is heard and learned without any form of presentation and with no problems of comprehension.

## Jigsaw listening

You provide a jigsaw version of the text before it is heard. This is yet another useful technique to use with more difficult texts. Either the words within lines are jumbled, giving a structural emphasis to the task of unscrambling, or the order of the lines is changed. This latter method is better for longer songs or poems. The listening acts as a self check.

## Disappearing texts

You put the whole text on the blackboard. The students read it as they listen. Afterwards they sing or recite it. Then, one or two words are erased and it is sung again. More words are erased, and so on until it can be sung with no support. This is an enjoyable and challenging way to get shorter texts learned by heart.

## Dictation

You dictate the text and correct it publicly before the class hears it. This is only suitable for short texts in which most of the words are already familiar to the learners.

## Mixed modes of presentation

A mixture of two or more techniques can also be used. For example, a song can be presented visually and an odd word or phrase quickly translated as it occurs. A text can have its lines alternately gapped and scrambled. A word for word translation can be followed by listening with visuals to remind learners of the meaning, and so on. The main thing is to vary the approach each time you introduce a new song or rhyme and to make the activity an enjoyable one.

## Demonstration procedures

The step by step demonstrations will clarify those approaches, but first a word about the prosodies. In all of the rhymes, the **rhythmic patterns** receive close attention as this is probably the most important linguistic feature of any form of poetry. The stressed syllables are all highlighted. With songs, though, the stress will automatically be correct if the tune is respected. For that reason there is no highlighting of the stressed syllables in the catalogue of songs later in the chapter.

## Selected songs and rhymes

*TEN LITTLE INDIAN BOYS (counting song)*
The technique demonstrated here is the **ostensive** one.

*a) Presentation*
Tell the class they will hear a song about Indians. Show a picture of a Red Indian and mention cowboy films. Explanation of the one structure (*there were*) is optional. In the song this particular phrase is hurried, being entirely unstressed, as it would be in everyday speech.

*b) Visual cue*
Write the numbers 1 to 10 on the blackboard, with the picture of the Indian in the middle;

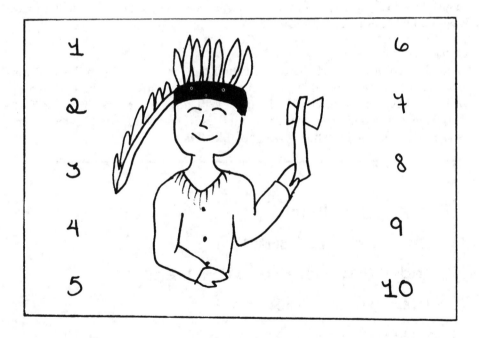

*c) Look and listen*
Play or sing the song two or three times, pointing to the numbers as they occur in the song.

*d) Repetition*
Have the class repeat line by line, paying great attention to the rhythmic pattern

167

which represents the sound of Indian drums, with one stressed syllable followed by two unstressed ones: *Dum* ditty *dum* ditty, *dum* ditty *dum*.

### e) Singing
Get the class singing, ensuring that only the correct syllables are stressed;

> *One* little, *two* little, *three* little *Indians*,
> *Four* little, *five* little, *six* little *Indians*,
> *Seven* little *eight* little, *nine* little *Indians*,
> *Ten* little *Indian boys*.
> (There were:)
> Ten little, nine little, eight little Indians,
> Seven little, six little, five little Indians,
> Four little, three little, two little Indians,
> One little Indian boy!

### MARY HAD A LITTLE LAMB (nursery rhyme)
These are the steps to follow if you use the **cloze text** technique.

### a) Presentation of new vocabulary
Present the words *lamb* and *fleece*. A small ball of wool and a picture would be easy to take to class. To present the word *everywhere* could be wasteful of time, so it would be better just to translate it.

### b) The cloze passage
Write the text on the blackboard, indicating deleted words with a dash. Generally, when teachers use this procedure, they omit stressed (*message*) words, which are easy for the class to distinguish. With advances classes it is possible to delete the unstressed *grammar* words, but these are very difficult to catch (*a, was, as, that, the, to*). The blackboard will look like this:

```
- had a little -
Its - as - as snow
And everywhere that - went
The - was - to -
```

### c) Read and listen
Say the rhyme once or twice. Afterwards, the listeners call out the missing words, which are written in the gaps.

### d) Repetition
Have the class repeat the whole piece. Pay special attention to the rhythm, one

stressed syllable followed by three unstressed ones. This gives a *dum* de diti rhythm (as in the word *VENtilator*).[4]

> Ma**ry** had a *li*ttle lamb,
> Its *fleece* was white as *snow*,
> And *ev'*rywhere that *Ma*ry went
> The *lamb* was sure to *go*.
> It *fo*llowed her to *school* one day,
> Which *was* against the *rule*
> *How* the children *laughed* to see
> A *li*ttle lamb at *school*.

## *JACK AND JILL (nursery rhyme)*

This time we use the technique of **focus questions**.

### a) Presentation

Present the unusual vocabulary visually, (eg *pail* = picture of a bucket, *crown* = point the top of your head, to *tumble* = use gestures to show a rolling fall).

### b) Focus questions

You can give questions like these orally when the text is simple. Notice the inclusion of two inverted WH-questions.

> I want you to tell me where Jack and Jill went.
> And why they went there.
> And last, what happened to Jack?

### c) Task listening

Play the tape or say the rhyme. Check the answers to the questions, ensuring total comprehension. Draw a picture of a hill, with two pin figures going up and tumbling down if necessary.

### d) Repetition

Write the text on the board. Let the class repeat the rhyme, line by line, stressing every second syllable. Notice that both syllables of the word *water* have to be stressed, unlike in normal speech. The same thing happens with the very last word, *after*. We lengthen both syllables of these words to maintain the cadence of the rhythm across the missing unstressed syllables. The missing syllables, all of which must be **ghosted**, are indicated by asterisks in the text.[5]

*Jack* and *Jill* went *up* the *hill*
to *fetch* a *pail* of *wa* * *ter* *
*Jack* fell *down* and *broke* his *crown* and
*Jill* came *tumbling af* * *ter.*

### e) Reciting

Finally, the class can recite the whole piece, in rhythmic unison. Then randomly nominated learners can be asked to recite it without the support of the text.

### ONE, TWO, THREE FOUR FIVE (song or rhyme)

The words of this piece are somewhat more complex than those of Jack and Jill, so you should offer true-false statements or choice questions (but not both). These serve to introduce some of the words and concepts that will be heard. Although the song has irregular verb forms it is perfectly acceptable for beginners, who will easily understand the words if they are met in this game-like way.

### a) Task setting

The statements or questions can usually be given orally. If they are to be read, the questions should be written beforehand on a poster or roll-up board if this is possible. The questions and statements themselves need no formal presentation, provided the meaning is conveyed as the cues are spoken:

> TEACHER: Are these statements true or false?
>    The child caught a *frog* (flash card and mime).
>    He *ate* it (*mime*).
>    His *hand* was bitten (*mime*).
>       *or:*
>    Did he catch a *fish* or a *rabbit* (sketch and mime)?
>    Did he take it *home* or *release* it (*mime*)?
>    Was he *bitten* or *scratched* (*mime*)?

### b) Repetition

Use chorus repetition, line by line, until the class seems confident. If you feel it helps, write the lines on the blackboard as you practise them. The rhythm is alternate stressed and unstressed syllables. However, sometimes there is no unstressed syllable at all. So, we ghost those intervals, to keep the rhythm constant.

*One* *, *two* *, *three* four *five,*
*Once* I *caught* a *fish* a*live* *,
*Six* * *se* ven, *eight* nine *ten* *,
*Then* I *let* it *go* a *gain* *.
*Why* * *did* you *let* it *go?*
Be *cause* it *bit* my *finger so* *.
*Which* (*) *finger did* it *bite* *?
*This* li'l *finger on* my *right.*

## c) Reciting

When they have repeated each line a few times, let the students recite the whole piece.

## IF YOU'RE HAPPY AND YOU KNOW IT (song)

This songs needs a **mixed mode** technique, as it contains a mixture of simple and complex language.

### a) Presentation of the structure

> If you're happy and you know it
> and you really want to show it . . .

This long repeated line is too abstract for a simple presentation. So it needs **translation**.

### b) Demonstration

You demonstrate the actions as you sing the song, or play it on a tape, so the comprehension of the other lines presents no problems. You can even invent and introduce new commands **ostensively** if you wish (eg *touch your nose, bang the desk, draw a cat, write your name, fold your arms, stamp your feet, slap your leg, turn around*). Note, though, that all the commands must have three syllables (two unstressed followed by one stressed) if they are to fit the rhythm. This rules out a lot of practice type language (pick up your bag, point to the door, etc). The underlying rhythm is *dum de diti dum de diti*. It is important to note that each sentence begins with two unstressed syllables (three words in two syllables). You pick up the **pulse** (the beat) on the first syllable of the word *happy*.

> If you're *happy* 'n you *know* it clap your *hands* (clap, *clap*).
> (repeat the line)
> If you're *happy* 'n you *know* it 'n you *really* want to *show* it,
> If you're *happy* 'n you *know* it clap your *hands* (clap *clap*).

### c) Singing

With the cue visible on the blackboard, the class can sing in chorus. Later, individuals can sing, while the other students mime the commands.

# ■ THE WORDS OF OTHER POPULAR SONGS

By now you should have a fairly clear idea of ways of exploiting songs and rhymes. For most of the pieces that follow there is some background information, which you may want to pass on to your learners as an introduction. Any obscure vocabulary is explained. Sometimes a possible teaching approach is recommended.

### TEN GREEN BOTTLES

This is highly repetitive and practises numbers. The basic phrases are probably best translated without comment.

> Ten green bottles, standing on the wall (*twice*).
> And if one green bottle should accidentally fall,
> There'd be nine green bottles standing on the wall.

> Nine green bottles, standing on the wall (*twice*),
> And if one green bottle should accidentally fall,
> There'd be eight green bottles, standing on the wall.

And so on, down to a last line of:

> There'd be no green bottles, standing on the wall.

### BAA BAA BLACK SHEEP

This needs visuals to represent a sheep, wool, a sack, the master, the dame (archaic for *lady*) and a country lane.

> Baa baa black sheep, have you any wool?
> Yes sir, yes sir, three bags full;
> One for my master, one for my dame,
> And one for the little boy who lives down the lane.

### OLD MACDONALD HAD A FARM

This is repetitive, with animals being added successively, turning the later choruses into a memory challenge. In addition to animal noises it has the nonsense phrase *ee aye ee aye oh*.

> Old Macdonald had a farm, ee aye ee aye oh.
> And on that farm he had a cow, ee aye ee aye oh,

> *Chorus*:
> With a moo moo here, a moo moo there,
> Here a moo, there a moo, everywhere a moo moo,
> Old Macdonald had a farm, ee aye ee aye oh.

> Old Macdonald had a farm ee aye ee aye oh,
> And on that farm he had a chicken, ee aye ee aye oh,
> With a cluck cluck here, a cluck cluck there,
> Here a cluck, there a cluck, everywhere a cluck cluck,

A moo moo here, a moo moo there,
Here a moo, there a moo, everywhere a moo moo,
Old Macdonald had a farm, ee aye ee aye oh.

And so on with duck (*quack quack*), sheep (*baa baa*), dog (*woof woof*), cat (*miaow miaow*), turkey (*gobble gobble*), pig (*oink oink*) and anything else the singers can add. This makes the final chorus very long indeed.

## ON TOP OF OLD SMOKY

This waltz has the name of a mountain, perhaps a volcano or one that is shrouded by cloud and dark trees on the summit. To *court* someone, is to make loving advances. In this song, the young man or woman lost a lover as a result of natural shyness.

On top of old Smoky, all covered with snow,
I lost my true lover, for courting too slow.
Now courting's a pleasure, but parting is grief,
'n a false-hearted lover is worse than a thief.

For a thief will just rob you, and take what you've saved,
But a false-hearted lover drives you to the grave.
On top of old Smoky, all covered in snow,
I lost my true lover, for courting too slow.

## HERE WE GO ROUND THE MULBERRY BUSH

When children sing this they walk around in a circle with linked hands. Since the song is so short, they often go straight into *This is the way* (below) which shares the same tune. The origins of the song are sad. In eighteenth century London there was a women's prison. In the small exercise yard stood a single mulberry tree, not a *bush*, as it says in the song. The mulberry tree is the plant on which silkworms live. The women convicts would shuffle round and round that tree once a day for a few minutes' exercise.

Here we go round the the mulberry bush,
The mulberry bush, the mulberry bush.
Here we go round the mulberry bush,
On a cold and frosty morning.

## THIS IS THE WAY WE CLEAN OUR TEETH

This song is based on everyday actions and is sung with accompanying gestures. As such it is an ideal beginners' song. The two phrases of the song should be translated when the song is introduced. The tune is the same as that of *Here we go round the mulberry bush*.

This is the way we clean our teeth,
Clean our teeth, clean our teeth,
This is the way we clean our teeth,
On a cold and frosty morning.

This is the way we wash our hands,
Wash our hands, wash our hands,
This is the way we wash our hands,
On a cold and frosty morning.

And so on, with other actions (*sweep the floor, wash the dishes, stir our tea, drink our milk, brush our shoes, comb our hair, eat our food,* etc).

## THE ALPHABET SONG

For the students, this is an enjoyable way to learn the letters of the alphabet by heart. However, the letters do not all receive equal timing – some letters are repeated and others are rushed, as though they were unstressed syllables. All this is indicated in the text below by the spacing between the letters.

```
A     B     C     D     E     F     G
H     I     J     K     L M N O P
L M N O P         Q     R     S     T
U     V     W           X     Y     Z
```

## ONE MAN WENT TO MOW

This is a backward counting song in which the singers add a man for each new verse. Usually it is sung up to ten. One simple picture will explain the meaning if it shows a man with a scythe about to mow a meadow (cut the grass of a field).

One man went to mow, went to mow a meadow,
One man and his dog, went to mow a meadow.

Two men went to mow, went to mow a meadow,
Two men, one man and his dog, went to mow a meadow.

Three men went to mow, went to mow a meadow,
Three men, two men, one man and his dog,
Went to mow a meadow.

## THE BEAR WENT OVER THE MOUNTAIN

This song and the next share the same tune. It is easily presented by means of a blackboard sketch.

The bear went over the mountain,
The bear went over the mountain,
The bear went over the mountain, to see what he could see.

But all that he could see,
But all that he could see,
Was the other side of the mountain,
The other side of the mountain,
The other side of the mountain, was all that he could see.

## FOR HE'S A JOLLY GOOD FELLOW

This is sung to honour someone of note. The words are simple. *Jolly good* is a colloquialism, meaning *excellent*. *She* can replace *he*, with no problem, despite the masculine ring of the word *fellow*.

> For he's a jolly good fellow, for he's a jolly good fellow,
> For he's a jolly good fellow! And so say all of us.
> And so say all of us. And so say all of us.
> For he's a jolly good fellow, he's a jolly good fellow.
> He's a jolly good fellow! And so say all of us.

### LONDON'S BURNING

In 1666 the old City of London burned down. The fire burned for six days and destroyed four fifths of the buildings. The *engines* are the carts with hand pumps, buckets and ladders that were the forerunners of today's red fire engine. The song can be sung straight through, but it sounds very attractive as a **round**, with four sets of singers coming in, one after the other.

> London's burning, London's burning,
> Fetch the engine, fetch the engine,
> Fire, fire; fire, fire,
> Pour on water, pour on water.

### LONDON BRIDGE IS FALLING DOWN

The old bridge across the Thames was made of wood, with shops of all kinds lining the two pavements. Inevitably, it caught fire and collapsed, to be replaced with a stone one. The song is easily presented by using pictures, a piece of brick and a piece of stone. A playing card house could be used to demonstrate the meaning of *fall down*.

> London Bridge is falling down,
> Falling down, falling down,
> London Bridge is falling down, my fair lady.
>
> Build it up with bricks and stone,
> Bricks and stone, bricks and stone,
> Build it up with bricks and stone, my fair lady.

### POLLY PUT THE KETTLE ON

When visitors call to see someone in Britain, the kettle is *put on* to boil water for tea. At the time this song was composed the kettle would have been put on the fire. Polly and Sukie might have been daughters or serving girls.

> Polly put the kettle one, Polly put the kettle on,
> Polly put the kettle on, we'll all have tea.
>
> Sukie take it off again, Sukie take it off again,
> Sukie take it off again, they've all gone away.

### SHE'LL BE COMING ROUND THE MOUNTAIN

This was written when the railway was built across the USA in the last part of the nineteenth century. The *she* in the original version was steam locomotive. In those days the time of arrival was unpredictable, so in answer to an enquiry from a traveller, the station master would just say *When she comes*. Today, the fact that the song was originally about a locomotive is not apparent and the word *she* has come to signify a woman. It is a simple matter to compose new, six-syllable substitutions for the song, and some are suggested below.

> She'll be coming round the mountain when she comes,
> She'll be coming round the mountain when she comes,
> She'll be coming round the mountain,
> Coming round the mountain,
> Coming round the mountain when she comes.
>
> *Chorus*:
> Singing aye aye yippee yippee aye.
> Singing aye aye yippee yippee aye,
> Singing aye aye yippee, aye aye yippee,
> Aye aye yippee, yippee aye.
>
> She'll be drinking coca cola when she comes, ...

And so on, with *eating bread and butter, riding six white horses, wearing silk pyjamas, drinking ice-cold water*, and anything else that you or the class can think to add.

## OH SUSANNAH

This was sung as the pioneers migrated across the USA in their wagon trains. The banjo is played seated, with the instrument resting on the lap (the knees). We do not know who Susannah was, nor why she might have cried at the banjoist's departure. Probably, she was just a passing girlfriend to a travelling man. The second verse is funny.

> Oh I come from Alabama, with a banjo on my knee,
> 'n I'm going' to Louisiana, my true love for to see.
>
> *Chorus*:
> Oh Susannah, don't you cry for me,
> F'r I come from Alabama with my banjo on my knee.
>
> It rained all night the day I left, the weather it was dry,
> The sun so hot, I froze to death, Susannah don't you cry.

## ROW, ROW, ROW YOUR BOAT

This is short but sounds very sweet as it is sung as a four part round. A quarter of the class begins, then the other sections come in one by one. It was originally sung by slaves rowing on the Mississippi. The word *but* means *only* in this sense.

> Row, row, row your boat, gently down the stream,
> Merrily, merrily, merrily, merrily, life is but a dream.

## THE WHEELS ON THE BUS

This is another nursery school vocabulary builder. It is about the sights seen and the sounds heard on a big London bus. Translation may be needed for some lines, but most are self evident from the noise. Small children make gestures for each line. *Fares please* is the conductor's call as he goes through the bus selling tickets.

The wheels on the bus go round and round,
Round and round, round and round,
The wheels on the bus go round and round, all day long.

The hooter on the bus goes peep peep peep,
peep peep peep; peep peep peep.
The hooter on the bus goes peep peep peep, all day long.

The conductor on the bus says 'fares please,
Fares please, fares please.'
The conductor on the bus says 'fares please', all day long.

The wipers on the bus go swish swosh swish,
Swish swosh swish; swish swosh swish,
The wipers on the bus go swish swosh swish, all day long.

## The words of other popular rhymes

As with the songs, any interesting anecdotes or explanations are given. Because rhythms are not evident, as they are in songs, where music sets the patterns, stressed syllables continue to be marked. Missing, unstressed syllables which are to be ghosted are indicated by an asterisk.

### HUMPTY DUMPTY

*Humpty Dumpty* is a nonsense name. suggestive of awkwardness and fatness to the British ear as a result of this rhyme. It was the nickname given to the Duke of Gloucester, a very fat gentleman. During the seventeenth century civil war, the town of Gloucester (pronounced *gloster*) was attacked by the Roundheads, enemies of the king. An enormous cannon, used in the defence, was given the same nickname as the Duke by the attackers. One day, it recoiled off the city wall, and the king's horses (the cavalry) and men (infantry) were unable to mend it. The city was lost to the king as a result.

*Humpty Dumpty sat* on the *wall* *,
*Humpty Dumpty had* a great *fall* *,
*All* the King's *horses* and *all* the King's *men* *,
*Couldn't* put *Humpty* together a *gain*.

### DOCTOR FOSTER

Still in Gloucester, we meet a gentleman who fell into a deep puddle. The rhyming of *puddle* and *middle* is not very good, but the vocabulary is useful and the language simple.

*Doctor Foster, went* to *Gloucester, in* a *shower* of *rain.**
He *stepped* in a *puddle*. right *up* to his *middle*,
And *never* went *there again*.

## *WHAT ARE LITTLE GIRLS MADE OF?*

*Snips* is an out-of-date word for pieces of rag. Snails and docked (cut-off) dog's tails are equally unlovely. The second verse follows exactly the same rhythm as the first.

> *What* are *li*ttle girls *made * of?* (repeat the line)
> *Sugar* and *spice* and *all* things *nice\**
> *That's* what *li*ttle girls are *made * of.*

> What are little boys made of? (repeat)
> Snips and snails and puppy dogs' tails,
> That's what little boys are made of.

## *THIRTY DAYS*

This rhyme helps us remember how many days there are in any month. It is spoken with alternating stressed and unstressed syllables.

> *Thirty days * have* September, April, *June * and* November.
> *All* the *rest* have *thirty one*, but
> *Feb'ry twen*ty *eight* alone.

Lack of space prevents us from continuing this catalogue of songs and rhymes, but children's books will provide plenty more for the enthusiast. Native speakers of any age are ideal informants, too.

## ■ CONCLUSION

On linguistic grounds alone, songs and rhymes deserve a regular place in the classroom. In addition to providing useful words and structures, they impose the correct use of the prosodic features on the learners. All of the pieces given here are part of the linguistic heritage of generations of Britons and Americans, they are genuine, **authentic texts**. Songs and rhymes are also highly motivating. The learners look forward to the lessons which are enlivened by their use.

## Notes

[1] Stress timing is dealt within Chapter Seventeen.

[2] What is said here about learning the prosodies of English holds true in reverse, of course. English students tend to impose syllable stress patterns on to new languages, speaking with a recognisable English accent in the process. When they are taught to sing or recite in the foreign language, this accent virtually disappears.

[3] Some methodologists recommend word for word translations where there is a contrast between the mother tongue and the new language. For example, an anglophone learner of French is told that *If fait beau* is literally *It/he makes/does beautiful*, but that it expresses the meaning of *It's a nice day*. As well as helping learners to sort out their own **mental grammar**, it prevents them making harmful inferences (that *fait* means *is*).

[4] It is important that you understand the rules of prosody – for everyday speech, as well as for singing and reciting. The rhythm of speech has to be respected. Each new spoken segment in any rhyme begins with a **pulse**, the beat of a stressed syllable. The technical word for a segment (a number of syllables beginning with a pulse and ending just before the next pulse) is a *foot*. Consequently, the spoken lines of poetry do not always reflect the printed layout. The stressed syllables have to come at exact intervals. And, of course, one or more unstressed syllables could be missing. In such cases a slight pause is made or the preceding stressed syllable is lengthened, to occupy the time. I refer to this feature as **ghosting**. The example that follows will make all of this clear.

In this rhyme, *Mary had a little lamb*, the first word of the printed second line (*its*) belongs to the foot which begins in the preceding line with the word *little*. The last foot of the second line begins with *snow*, is followed with a double pause, and finishes with the word *and*. If we lay out the rhyme to show the rhythmic feet, you will see the prosodic structure more clearly. The sign * indicates a ghosting pause for the space of one unstressed syllable:

The sound structure of Mary had a little lamb

| / | . | . | . | / | . | . | . |
|------|------|-------|------|-------|------|------|------|
| Ma | ry | had | a | li | ttle | lamb | its |
| feet | as | white | as | snow | * | * | and |
| ev | ry | where | that | Ma | ry | went | the |
| lamb | was | sure | to | go | * | * | it |
| fo | I'd | her | to | school | ... | | |

[5] See Note 5, above for an explanation of the ghosting feature.

# 14 Revision and homework

## ■ REACTIVATION PROCESSES

The term *review* is used here in the same way as *revision*, to describe the process of **reactivation** that helps assimilation and learning. Unless your textbook has a clear language recycling policy, there is a real risk that the students will forget what they covered in earlier lessons. In the first part of this chapter there are suggestions on what to revise and how to conduct the activities.

Homework is another form of reactivation. During out-of-school time, students rework material or engage in practice activities. The chief factor that militates against successful language learning in the school is probably *time*. During an academic year, schools may have as little as 30 effective teaching weeks. Over the entire secondary school cycle, few language students get more than 500 hours of classroom exposure. By increasing their contact time, we can increase the students' level of competence. Classes that get homework usually reach a higher level of achievement and do better in examinations than those that are denied extra learning time.[1]

## ■ THE PLACE OF REVISION

Many teachers start every lesson by revising a grammar point from the previous lesson or by reviewing the reading passage used in that lesson. This is usually done by means of questions, with full length answers to force the regurgitation of key phrases from the text. Such revision offers continuity but it is somewhat limited, and it is in the wrong place. You should begin lessons with some sort of warm-up activity. When classes are settling in, students need a few moments of relaxation to retune their ears to the sounds of the foreign language. It is better to start with some listening, a chat, a game or a song.

Revision can then follow the warm-up, but there are times when it should be delayed until later. If the review is simply a factual one and the new passage is a continuation of the previous day's reading, then it is best done just before the new passage is seen. In this way, the review becomes a sort of pre-reading activity and assures continuity of the story line. At other times, as we shall see, the review can be self contained and can be put almost anywhere in the lesson plan to offer a short change of activity.

## ■ REVISING GRAMMAR POINTS

Revision of grammar should go easily and be enjoyed. The hard work was done when the points were first presented and practised. Grammar points and structures can sometimes be reactivated with realia or visuals in a game-like way, and ways of doing this will be suggested later.

## Choosing a grammar point for revision

The grammar point can be chosen in an arbitrary way. You may decide to revise the passive voice, a structural transformation, a tense, the use of possessives, or some other aspect. To do this, you need only to look back at past lesson notes and reproduce the language practice phase. List the areas of grammar that you introduce in a notebook and write the date against items each time they are revised. There is no need to feel guilty about this somewhat haphazard approach to revision. Learning is most effective when it is topped up at intervals. Because this sort of review is self contained, you could plan to do it at the end of a lesson as a reserve activity, to be done tomorrow if there is insufficient time today.

You will frequently identify language points which require revision from the monitoring of the production stage, when English is used spontaneously. The mistakes can reveal a need for another look at an old problem area. The students will be glad to know that they can enter into a debate without worrying about intrusive corrections, but knowing that any serious mistakes will be picked up for attention. Mistakes in written work also reveal needs for remedial work. Such remedial review can be a self-contained activity at almost any part of the lesson, though a logical place would be during the day's presentation stage, when everyone is paying attention to the formal properties of English.

You should also revise structures and grammar points that can be incorporated into the day's work. The nature of the text will suggest the language area to be revised and its place in the lesson plan. A controversial topic will indicate a need for students to express agreement or otherwise in the discussion stage. They may want to express likes and preferences in follow-up to a text dealing with food. To discuss the future of the Indian subcontinent, modal verbs will be needed and could be revised just before any debate. The scope of any dialogue can be widened by the review of a related function just before the pairwork phase. This review will suggest ways in which the students can be more adventurous in adapting the dialogue.

## Ways of revising grammar points

Revision should go quickly and easily, as the grammar points will already be familiar to the students. Try to make the process enjoyable.

### Using realia to practise grammar points

You can bring out a few students to revise *in front of, behind, between, next to,* and the other prepositions. You can use the same line-up to revise *taller than, the shortest,* and so on. If the students stand one behind the other, you can review ordinal numbers.

A bag of small objects will enable you to revise structures like *Have you got . . .?* or *Is there a . . .?* Use the students' belongings to revise possessives and the use of the demonstrative pronouns – *Whose is this? It's mine/Brian's/hers, Whose are these* (spectacles, scissors)? *Are they yours, Heidi? No, they're his/Sadu's,* and so on.

### Using substitution to revise grammar structures

Substitutions of the sort seen in Chapter Two offer a good way to revise useful structures and to make students think about the purposes for which language is used. Work with a formulaic utterance of some sort and tell the class to write as many substitutions as they can in one minute. The activity can be made enjoyable and competitive if, at the checking stage, points are awarded only for grammatically correct sentences that nobody else thought of.

It might take five minutes or more to make the oral check. Most students will have provided several fillers for the slot and so there will be many original, often funny, substitutions.[2] Choose sentences that allow the imagination some free rein:

> I was so sorry to hear that (you broke your leg)
> How nice of you to (call).
> I'd be only too pleased to (carry the case for you)

## ■ REVISING VOCABULARY

Criteria for selecting vocabulary for review are the same as for the grammar. The lexis can be chosen in an arbitrary way, because it ties in well with the new text, or because class work indicates a need to reactivate a certain field. Vocabulary can be grouped by **topic** (eg food, furniture, vegetation, feminism, equal rights), by **situation** (the bank, the supermarket, the post office), by **semantic field** (boy, youth, man, gentleman, chap, guy, mister, husband), or by **grammatical category** (adverbs, adjectives, shared affix, etc).

## Ways of revising vocabulary

Profit from the work you did when lexical items were presented for the first time by re-using any visuals. The simplest way to do this is to arrive every Monday morning with all the previous week's visuals for a comprehensive review stage immediately after a warm-up. However, there are other ways to revise vocabulary.

### Illustrative sentences

If new vocabulary is placed in a linguistic context and copied at the end of the lesson (a common procedure), the class can be challenged to recall the exact sentences they copied a few days or weeks earlier. More challenging, and perhaps more valuable linguistically, the class can create new illustrative sentences for the words as you call them out. This is probably best done orally.

In this way lots of words are reactivated in a short space of time and given contexts.

## Vocabulary networks

Choose a topic area (eg *sports, hobbies, school*) and write the key word in a box in the centre of the board. In the example below, the topic is *the bedroom*. Ask the learners to say what furniture is in a bedroom. As items are called they are strung out from the centre box and underlined to act as **head-words**. The board will look something like this at the end of that short first stage.

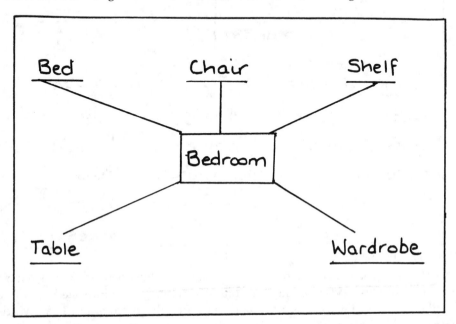

Next, the class suggests what might be found in or on the items of furniture, and lists are built up. Sometimes a second head-word is identified and a subsidiary list built upon this. In the example, the word *uniform* was offered as something to be found in the wardrobe. The teacher used it as a new head-word to start another list. If *underclothes* had been suggested, this could have started yet another subset. The final network will be considerably more complete than the example on the following page.

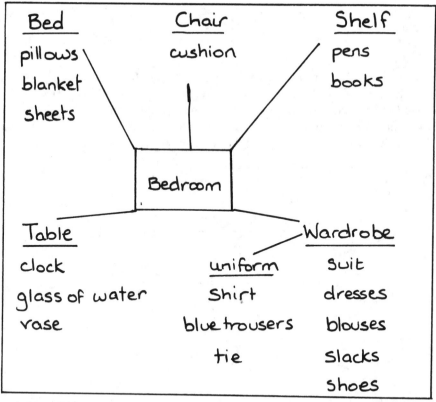

*Vocabulary tables*

This alternative layout to the network one is less exciting visually. Here we have the topic of *Shops*, revised in the same brainstorming fashion but listed in a more traditional style. It is difficult to create space for subsets from new head-words with this layout, though they could possibly be squeezed between the columns. In the example, there are two potential head-words in the chemist's list (*cosmetics* and *baby products*). There might well have been *medicines*, as well. Whichever presentation is adopted, you should prepare your own list of taught key lexis, to be brought forward or prompted if they are not offered spontaneously by the class:

| SHOPS + SHOPPING | | | |
|---|---|---|---|
| <u>Baker's</u> | <u>Chemist's</u> | <u>Grocer's</u> | <u>Butcher's</u> |
| bread | aspirin | conserves | steak |
| cakes | shampoo | cereals | lamb chops |
| croissants | sun oil | cheese | beef |
| | cosmetics | cold meats | chicken |
| | baby products | | |

## Scrambled sets

Yet another approach for revising topic vocabulary is this. You dictate a mixture of topic words and then ask the students to group them, providing their own head-words. With the topic *food*, for example, words like *milk, apples, potatoes, melon, cheese, courgettes, yoghurt,* would be classified under the headings *fruit, vegetables* and *dairy products*.

## Jumbled words

Younger students enjoy being challenged to discover words in playful ways. Single words can be written on word cards, but with the letters jumbled:

## Alphabetical revision

You can also choose a letter of the alphabet and ask the class to write or call out words beginning with that letter (pen, paper, pencil, pet, etc). The game could continue with a few other initial letters. The initial letters would be chosen in order to trigger the recollection of the words that you want to revise. If these are not called, then you can reactivate them by saying *Show me an X, Where is the Y? What colour is this Z?*

## Problem solving review

More advanced classes can be prompted to produce words by means of a sort of oral crossword puzzle. This approach has the added value of making them listen carefully;

TEACHER: Sometimes this is on a door, but it is also found on a fishing line. (*hook*)

## Affixes

The revision of words with affixes is especially valuable because once the learners realise the function of the prefix or suffix they can understand and even create new words. Some suffixes have a grammatical function (*-er, -est, -ing, ed, -ful, -ly*); others carry a meaning. For example, the suffix *-ness* has the meaning *a condition of* . . ., and will convert an adjective to a noun (dirtiness, happiness, emptiness, etc). The prefix *un-* gives many verbs an opposite meaning (unwrap, undo, untie, unbalance) and has a negative meaning when combined with adjectives (unclear, uncertain, unreliable).

## Cognates

You can use cognates for review if your learners have a mother tongue which is related to the language you teach. Between members of the Indo-European family of languages there are thousands of words with an almost identical shape and shared meaning. Within almost any topic area, a few moments' thought will enable you to discover many words whose meaning is immediately **transparent**. Words of this sort are easily taught and just as easily revised, in a brainstorming way. Speakers of most Romance languages will easily recall related vocabulary of this sort:

### TRANSPORT

| | | | |
|---|---|---|---|
| bus | taxi | bicycle | automobile |
| train | porter | baggage | departure |
| ticket | yacht | port | airport |
| docks | ferry | barrier | reservation |
| captain | hostess | passport | restaurant |

## ■ HOMEWORK

Unlike other subject teachers, language teachers cannot get students to learn from the textbook in advance of the lesson. Students are not normally required to learn language that has not already been used in class. Teachers who instruct a class to prepare tomorrow's lesson and learn the vocabulary (from the bilingual list that accompanies some textbooks) are treating language as though it were a knowledge-based subject like history.

## Setting and marking homework

So, what sort of homework should language teachers assign? What are the attributes of good homework? One criterion is that it should not put a heavy workload on the teacher's own shoulders. Whenever possible, assign home-work that can be checked quickly in class. The public check acts as yet another review and has the advantage of allowing learners to identify and correct any mistakes. The students can normally check their own work, but the teacher can have them exchange copy books and correct each other's if this is preferred. Misunderstandings are then cleared up on the spot. There is no need to give a mark out of ten, since the aim is to offer additional exposure to English, not to test the students.

The second criterion is that the tasks should not be too difficult. Mistakes made at home might be mistakes internalised, so the activities should not invite error making. Look critically at exercises in the text book to ensure that they satisfy these two criteria before you use them for homework. And, there should be variety, from one day to the next. Try to give assignments that are useful, interesting and enjoyable.

## Kinds of assignment

Let us look now at a range of homework activities that will not be available in your text book but which are quickly assigned and easily corrected.

### Drawing activities

Your learners often draw in their exercise books to show the meaning of the sentences that they copy (*This is a shirt. It is red*, etc). All this sketching, labelling and colouring should be done at home. By requiring them to do the drawings at home you ensure that they re-read the sentences, remembering the meanings. Children also enjoy drawing and labelling detailed pictures, such as a street scene, a market place or a bus station. Encourage them to design some attractive posters for the classroom walls.

### Babylonian writing

This is a picture spelling assignment for younger pupils. You have only to give one starter word, for example *pencil*. The youngsters go home and spell the work in pictures. To do this, they draw something beginning with the letter *p* (eg *pupil* or *pen*), something beginning with *e* (*egg, elephant*), and so on. The good thing about this is that the students reactivate all their past vocabulary at home in order to find the objects. In class, the public check gives massive coverage, as all the objects are called back. With six initial letters, the word *pencil* might elicit fast recall of about a quarter of the class's active vocabulary.

### Games

Some of the simple games described in Chapter Twelve can become homework assignments, in particular *Word Building*, *Secret Messages* (with the numbers dictated at the end of the lesson), and *Word Sets*. This latter game enables a teacher to conduct a swift review of a great deal of chosen topic vocabulary the next day, especially if a long name is chosen as the head-word.

### Substitution

This activity has already been described, but with single slot substitutions, for revising a structure. It also makes a good homework exercise, and one with lots of writing, if you give a sentence with several slots at which the students must make substitutions:

> 1              2     3
> (We) really enjoyed that (exciting) (film).

## Using worksheets

If the school has any form of copying facility, it is well worth investing time in the production of worksheets for homework. This permits you to break away from the textbook and to offer much more variety. They are not *disposable*, students hand them back so they can be used again and again. Often a single page will hold two or more tasks. Many types of worksheet activity are possible, depending on the level of the class:

### Matching halves

This is a good way to revise topic vocabulary and phrases. The subject phrase is on the left and the predicates are jumbled on the right. It is important that all the phrases on the right should fit those on the left grammatically (though not semantically). The students have to match them up and write out the appropriate sentences. This involves intensive reading and then copying. Often the choice of ending can be ambiguous:

| | |
|---|---|
| When it rains | if often freezes. |
| In sunny weather | people use an umbrella. |
| During sunny showers | it's best to stay inside. |
| On dull days | a picnic is most enjoyable. |
| During European winters | water drips from the icicles. |
| When it thaws | we sometimes see a rainbow |

### Gapped texts

Quite long texts can be given on worksheets, with chosen words deleted. This involves the students in reading and finding an appropriate word for each slot. The gaps can be regular (every seventh word) or you can delete a specific grammatical category of word. If you wish, you can provide a **word bank** beneath the cloze text. This contains all the deleted words, but out of sequence, plus some extra words to serve as distractors.

### Multiple choice and true-false items

These are sometimes included in textbook exercises. If not, it might be a good idea to get the students used to this type of exercise, as it is often used in examinations.[3]

### Parallel writing

On the worksheet you offer one or more paragraphs with plenty of details or facts. The students copy the model, but with a different subject. In this way, the description of New York becomes a guided description of their own capital city, or a film star becomes their head teacher or president. The model provides all the needed structures and key vocabulary.

### Guided writing

Guided writing tasks, of the sort described above, are less liable to error than free essays. Often they can be checked in class, by having students exchange papers. Here is an example of a worksheet task that will produce different though similar responses. It is in the form of a letter, to which the students reply. It can be handwritten, to give a look of authenticity, or it can be typed, like this model:

---

Dear Friend,
Thank you for your letter. I have some questions for you. What is your father's job? My dad is a bank employee. Does your mother work? Mine works at home. We are a big family. Do you have any sort of job yourself? As for me, I work in a supermarket on Saturdays. What are your hobbies? I enjoy reading but I also play hockey. I have two more years of school, after which I hope to get a job in a hotel (I love learning and using languages). What about you?
 Goodbye for now, please write soon,
  Your new friend, Kumi.

---

### Task reading

Extensive reading is possibly the best of all homework assignments. Few schools have class readers and textbooks rarely have longish passages intended only for private reading. More advanced classes can tackle authentic texts, photocopied from media sources. A worksheet form is ideal. The pre-questions are at the top of the page, and the text is printed below. If you wish you can add follow-up tasks as well.[4]

# ■ CONCLUSION

If learning is to be effective, then what is met in class must be revised. Revision should be of more than just the most recent lesson. What was taught weeks or months ago is often pertinent to the new text or grammar point. Revision need not always be done at the start of a lesson. When the text has a clear connection with that of the previous day, the review should be part of the pre-reading phase. A self-contained review can form a reserve activity, to be done at the end of a lesson if there is time.

By giving homework, teachers can increase the time spent by students in contact with the language. Homework assignments should be made as interesting as possible. They should not invite error making. Any correcting is best done by the students themselves, especially where the classes are large. In this way the students get feedback and can ask for clarification.

## Notes

[1] If you compare the time your students are exposed to their mother tongue with the time they spend in contact with their foreign language, the difference is awesome. Aged two and three, they probably hear their first language for ten to twelve hours each day. In just one month, they have the contact time of a five year language course in schools. The miracle is that language teachers achieve as much as they do in so short a time.

[2] The space for which students have to choose or find an appropriate word or phrase is called a **slot**. For each slot (or **gap**) the students provide a **filler**.

[3] Multiple-choice items are described in Chapter Fifteen.

[4] Examples of worksheet pre-reading and post-reading tasks for a long reading passage, also on a worksheet, can be seen at the end of Chapter Twenty.

# 15 Classroom testing

## ■ TESTING AND TEACHING

Evaluation is as much a part of language teaching as are the materials, syllabus and approach. There should be an evident and harmonious relationship between course objectives and all these curriculum elements. You should avoid tests which exemplify poor teaching procedures. Many of the teaching activities that have been, and will be, described in this book are ideal test instruments in themselves. Most of the tests seen now could be used for teaching purposes, too. They are simple to contrive, demand little loss of teaching time and are easily marked. What is more, they can be carried out under quite difficult conditions.

### Testing and learning

A great value of classroom tests is their effect upon attitudes. You can indicate where your own priorities lie by the tests you give. If classes have nothing but written and formal grammar tests, they will perceive this as a lack of interest on your part in their listening, reading and speaking abilities.

Another important aspect is the diagnostic element – the feedback obtained is of value to you and the students. Individuals can identify weaknesses and make efforts to overcome them. You can pin-point deficiencies in the programme and include needed remedial work in the ongoing instruction. Tests can even be used to enhance learning. By giving advance notice of the ground to be covered in a test, you can virtually ensure that the learning is done beforehand.

## ■ TESTING THE FOUR SKILLS

In testing, as in teaching, it is useful to think in terms of the four skills. In this way you can be sure not to overlook a cherished aspect of language use. Even so, many good tests are mixed skill (**integrated**) ones in that they combine reading and writing, listening and reading, reading and speaking, and so on. In this chapter, the tests are grouped by the skills of reading, listening, writing and speaking, as far as possible, but the involvement of any secondary skills is made explicit.

Some teachers feel no need for separate tests of grammar and of vocabulary.

They consider that tests of the other skills require the candidate to demonstrate a degree of sensitivity to the formal aspects of the language. And of course, any test assesses vocabulary to a great extent – the students cannot comprehend or produce language if they do not have an adequate inventory of lexical items. Even so, a few easily administered grammar and vocabulary tests are included here.

We begin with tests of reading and listening. After this, we move to grammar and vocabulary tests before considering a range of writing and speaking tests. Finally, we consider marking schemes and examine ways in which you can sort and use the data collected. Although we are not specifically concerned with examinations, some of the instruments described could easily be combined to form a **test battery**, to serve as a good end of year examination. First though, a word about the nature of some of the tests you will meet.

## Objectively versus subjectively marked tests

Some types of test can be marked with no element of judgement (or **subjectivity**) on the part of the marker; the answers are either right or wrong. Given an answer key, anyone could do the marking. These are known as **objectively marked** tests. On the other hand, essays can only be marked by someone who speaks the language well and who can exercise judgement. The same applies to speaking tests. These sorts of test are subjectively marked.

**Objective marking** is neither a good nor a bad thing. A few years ago, any degree of subjectivity in evaluating language competence was considered undesirable. Today there is a swing towards encouraging and evaluating creativity and fluency, and test designers are more conscious of the ways in which people genuinely use language. Consequently, some types of objectively marked tests are now viewed with a degree of suspicion.

For busy teachers, though, it is often useful to use a test that can be set and marked in a few moments. The use of printed answer sheets with true-false or multiple-choice items formats is a real time saver, even though some expense is incurred. Such tests can be fitted into any spare moment, since the students have only to make ticks or write single letters. Even more valuable is the economy in marking time. To mark 100 test papers takes only a few moments. This is done with a **marking mask**, a sheet of transparent plastic on which you indicate the correct answer pattern. This is just laid over the top of answer paper and the responses can be compared in a matter of seconds.

Unfortunately, the traditional multiple-choice design suffers from the '*good luck syndrome*'. The student selects one of four options. If you gave a reading comprehension test of this sort to a group of illiterate people, the average would be close to twenty-five percent, despite the fact that no-one understood a word. Still, as long as you look at results with a degree of scepticism, there is no reason why you should not use this format. Over several tests, the good luck differences will begin to average out. In any case, there are ways in which you can reduce the guesswork element with a modified multiple-choice format, as you will see in some of the examples that follow.[1]

# Testing reading comprehension

This is perhaps the easiest skill of all to evaluate, and you have plenty of interesting formats to choose between.

## Multiple-choice reading tests

The multiple-choice format is a pure one when it is used for evaluating reading comprehension. This is because there is no mixing of skills: both the text and the choices are in the foreign language, and both must be understood if the student is to get a high score. Here is a sample of a reading passage followed by multiple-choice questions:

---

### MR JONES

Mr Jones delivers the mail in a rural community. A van cannot cope with the country tracks, so he travels from one farm to the next by bike, covering seventy five miles in the course of a five day week. He has been doing the same job for thirty years, since he was twenty. He will be retiring in ten years' time.

By profession, Mr Jones is:
a) a farmer   b) a van driver   c) a postman
d) retired   e) a professional cyclist

His age is:
a) 20     b) 30     c) 40
d) 50     e) 60     f) 75

---

It is quite a good paper. The chance factor has been reduced by offering five or six options. Also, in order to answer correctly, the candidates have to make inferences. However, we can even improve on that percentage level in the multiple-choice format, as we shall see presently.

## Questions and answers

To test reading or listening comprehension by requiring students to write in the foreign language faces you with marking problems. Do you penalise spelling or syntactic errors or are you only looking for evidence of understanding? Looking at the passage about Mr Jones, above, it would be wrong to ask the students to give the profession of Mr Jones if the aim is to evaluate only comprehension. This is because the word *postman* is not in the text. Some teachers avoid this difficulty by offering comprehension questions in the mother tongue.

If the foreign language is used to assess understanding, then you should also avoid any WH-questions which can be answered simply by a process of match-ing words in the question to those of the passage:

– Where does Mr Jones deliver mail?
– When will he retire?
– How long has he been doing the same job?

## Short factual answers

The questions given below are better. Provided the students understand both the question and the text, they can select just the word or two needed for a short answer. Or they can make an inference that places no real demands on their own language resources:

- How old is Mr Jones? (50)
- How old was he when he started this job? (20)
- How old will he be when he retires? (60)
- What distance does he cover daily? (15 miles)

## Split sentences

These are simple to produce, and the chances against guessing correctly are very low indeed if you have twenty or more items. There is no point in making the students write out the sentences; it is wasteful of your time as well as theirs. They simply write the appropriate letter of the completion against the number of the stimulus. The example will make this clear:

---

MARK a, b, c, etc AGAINST THE NUMBERS BELOW
1. She refused cheese     a)  to watch the news
2. He went out            b)  made a speech
3. Their new car          c)  fitted beautifully
4. He switched on         d)  to cut the hedge
5. The Minister           e)  refused to start
6. Her new dress          f )  but took an apple
Answers: 1,     2,     3.     4,     5,     6     .

---

## Scrambled texts

Reading comprehension can also be assessed by asking learners to identify the order of scrambled sentences, taken from one paragraph. Of course, there have to be stylistic or event markers. The paragraph about Mr Jones could not be used, since the last two sentences could have come earlier. To assess extensive reading comprehension, the order of the paragraphs of a long text can be scrambled. To save marking time as well as valuable classroom time, have the students write just the numbers of the sentences or paragraphs, not the whole passage.

## Gapped texts

These are usually referred to as *cloze passages*. The students have to deduce the words that have been deleted from a passage and they cannot do this if they do not understand what they read. Typically, the passage will be about a page in length, with between twenty and forty deletions. The first and last sentences are always given in full, to give the style of the passage. Single words are removed from the printed page at a rate of about every seventh word. The removal can be regular and random (every nth word) or it can be by deliberate choice. This will become clear below.

A major virtue is that the tests are easily contrived. You have only to cross out the specified words in a longish passage (but not counting proper names or figures) and retype it for photocopying. It is even possible just to photocopy the original, having blanked out some words. Gapped text tests are of several varieties, some of which are excellent for testing comprehension.

### Pure cloze

This format is also known as the **regular cloze**. Every sixth or seventh word is deleted, regardless of grammatical category. Consequently, the students have to do far more than simply understand the sense of the passage. To provide a suitable **filler** for the gap (or **slot**) they have to be sensitive to the grammatical category of word needed (noun, auxiliary verb, tense, adjective, article, etc). They also have to *produce* the needed words, so you are assessing their active vocabulary as well as their reading comprehension.

The marking of the pure cloze passage is subjective at times. An offered word may be just about acceptable, but not be the best possible one. And what do you do about a correct word which is misspelt? Despite these minor problems, it is a good test of comprehension and of all-round linguistic competence.

### Multiple-choice cloze

This design offers one way around the problem of judging the appropriateness of offered words. What is more, you are no longer assessing productive skills, only reading comprehension. For each slot, the learner gets a choice of three or four words and has to indicate the one that best fits the gap. Unfortunately, the good luck factor is built into the design.

### Banked cloze

This is even better for reading comprehension purposes. It is marked objectively, you are spared the chore of writing options for the multiple choices, and the chance factor is almost non-existent. The words may be removed on a regular basis, or subjectively. All the words removed are shown, but out of order, at the bottom of the page in a **word bank**. To make guessing more difficult, extra words that will not fit any of the slots (*distractors*) are scattered within the bank. For twenty slots, the bank may offer 30 words.

## Testing listening comprehension

To test listening in a pure mode is less easy, but it can be done. In real life though, listening is often an interactive process, so you should not worry too much about mixing the skills, provided the tests really do evaluate the areas of competence that you want to measure.

### Listen and draw

This is a pure listening test, involving no reading, speaking or writing. Yet you know at once if the students have understood what they heard.

> TEACHER: Write your name in the bottom right-hand corner. Put your age in the middle. Write the figures one to six down the left hand side of the page. Draw a line from figure three to your name. Underline your name.

To earn a mark, the drawing must look like this:

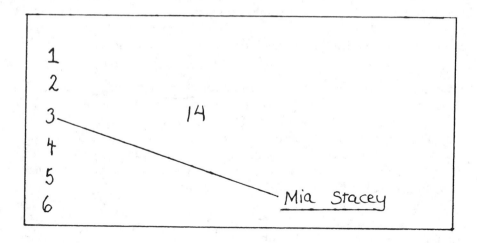

### Focused dictation

The traditional dictation evaluates both listening and writing. A focused dictation is different. Instead of writing everything, the students write only specified words. This could be all the adjectives, all the verbs heard in a past form, and so on. The passage is spoken at a natural speed, twice, and the students write the words as they listen and between the readings. This example shows the answer paper as it ought to look after a focused dictation in which the listeners were told to write only the verbs heard in conjunction with *going to*. The passage would be about a family's holiday plans and might be 100 or more words in length.

```
visit       stay        see        go for walks
play        swim        go fishing
```

### Multiple-choice listening

The multiple choice format is sometimes used for listening comprehension, but it is very much a mixed skill test if the choices (or **stimuli**) are printed in the foreign language. This is because the student has to read and understand the written words on the answer sheet, as well as the spoken words of the test passage. The mixing is even more complicated with questions and answers, as the students have to comprehend the written questions and write the foreign language – in addition to understanding the spoken words!

*Mother tongue multiple-choice*

These problems are avoided if the mother tongue is used for all printed questions or stimuli, as well as for written answers. This mixed language approach is simple and widely used, but some teachers disapprove of the use of the mother tongue. However, there are some multiple-choice formats that avoid the difficulty in other ways and which do not suffer from the good luck syndrome either. We shall see one now.

### Pictorial multiple-choice test

The task is to match a picture with the sentence heard. It is a pure test of listening, as no other skills are involved. The same test could be used as an elementary reading comprehension test if written stimuli were used instead of the teacher's voice. This sort of test, seen above, can be communicative (eg row one, *understanding directions in town*) or grammatical, as in the last row of pictures, where students have to distinguish between singular and plural as well as understand the related prepositions.

The usual procedure is for the learners to look at one line and hear just *one* stimulus for the choice of five pictures (eg *Go straight ahead*). They then indicate the correct picture. There is a one in five chance of choosing the correct picture by luck, even if the students have not understood a word. Then they hear a stimulus for one picture in the next row, and so on.

### Eliminating guesswork in the multiple-choice format

The guesswork factor inherent in the pictorial multiple-choice format can be virtually eliminated by asking the learners to mark the *order* in which all five pictures in each row are described. One mark is awarded only if *all five* pictures are ordered correctly. For example, row three might be:

> John likes swimming. (picture 2)
> Harry goes for walks. (picture 5)
> Bill enjoys playing the violin. (picture 4), etc.

The chances against ordering all five pictures in one row correctly by luck alone are $5 \times 4 \times 3 \times 2 \times 1$, giving odds of 120 to 1. If the picture choices are increased to six, then the odds against guessing the sequence become 720 to 1. Remember that to get just *one* point the student has to get the whole set of five correct.

## Testing grammar and vocabulary

Control of grammar and vocabulary is also evaluated in speaking tests and in certain types of writing test. However, you can easily add separate tests for evaluating both these aspects if you wish. Vocabulary can be tested at the level of **recognition** (the word is understood) or of **production** (the student can provide the word).

### Multiple-choice vocabulary test

This format again offers the quickest and easiest way to evaluate recognition of vocabulary. The test paper should carry up to a hundred items to diminish the chance syndrome and to spread out the scores. It is quickly produced and looks like this:

```
                Vocabulary Test
A glade is              a) a meadow
                        b) a cabin or hut
                        c) a clearing
                        d) a small stream

A steeple is sometimes seen on:
                        a) a mosque
                        b) a church
                        c) a sky scraper
                        d) an apartment block
```

## Multiple-choice grammar test

Again the format assesses recognition of correct forms, rather than production. Some teachers dislike this format for grammar items, because it offers incorrect combinations, as can be seen in the following example. Still, it is better than the *'put the verb into the correct form'* type of test.

```
He was tired, so he      a) lay down
                         b) lie down
                         c) lain down
                         d) lying down

They enjoyed it ... that they stayed to the end.
                  a) that much
                  b) so much
                  c) this much
                  d) how much
```

## Modified cloze

Instead of having a regular deletion rate, you make the deletions selectively. The format is excellent for testing vocabulary (by deleting nouns or adjectives) or awareness of grammar (prepositions, certain verb forms, the auxiliaries, etc). This time the students have to produce the words, not just recognise them. It is a better way to test grammar than the way seen just above; the passages can be interesting and they also have all the features of discourse.

## C-test

This is yet another adaptation of the gapped passage procedure. It is objectively marked and the learners have to produce the needed words. Like any other cloze passage, it evaluates comprehension as well as vocabulary and grammatical sensitivity. To ensure that the exact word is provided, the students get *half* of each deleted word as a cue. Two letters of a four or five letter word are shown, three of a six or seven letter word, and so on. Every second word is deleted (with the exception of the word *a*, the indefinite article). A test passage looks like this short sample:

---

Mary g–– up ea––– that d––. She h–– a lo–– journey bef––– her a–– she wan––– to ch––– in a– the air–––– well i– advance o– the stipu––––– time i– order t– get a win––– seat i– the non-sm––––– section o– the aero–––––.

---

*Word recognition*

In this example the mother tongue (here English, for British students of French) is used to test vocabulary recognition at a very elementary level. The **rubric** (instructions) is also in the mother tongue. Instead of offering a multiple-choice format for each of the six vocabulary items, the guesswork factor has been reduced to about ten percent by scrambling all the options and offering extra words as distractors. The learner simply writes one letter against each mother tongue stimulus, so the marking takes only a few seconds. Remember that this is a French test for anglophones.

---

HOTEL

You are looking for the six places below. Which sign would you look for? Mark the letter of the matching sign next to the English place name.

1. The pool               2. The lift
3. The office             4. The cash desk
5. The information desk   6. The exit


a) RENSEIGNEMENTS         b) CUISINE
c) ASCENSEUR              d) PISCINE
e) TOIT                   f) JARDIN
g) MAGASINS               h) CAISSE
i) CONCIERGE              j) SORTIE
k) BUREAUX                l) ESCALIER

---

# Writing tests

The tests can range from the writing of one word to the writing of an essay length passage. Unless you regard writing as a valuable performance objective, you should not overemphasise written tests.

*Sentence completion*

The students are given some incomplete sentences and have to provide an appropriate start or a finish. Marks are awarded for what is written and how well it is written. Reading comprehension is also involved, though it goes unrewarded. The sentences can be independent, as in the first example, or in the form of a paragraph, as in the second:

---

The man got into his car and . . .

. . ., but she said she'd already seen the film.

---

COMPLETE THE SENTENCES, MAKING A STORY

I returned early that evening, as I had agreed to meet my friend later. First I . . . . . . . . . . . ., then I took a long shower. Next, . . . . . . . . . . . . and switched on the television. I . . . . . . . . . . . so I switched it off again. I had a half an hour to kill so I . . . . . . . . . . . At seven p.m. I kissed my mother and left the house. I . . . . . . . . . . . but my friend was not yet there. The idea of waiting alone in the street was not appealing, especially as . . . . . . . . . . . So, I . . . . . . . . . . .

---

*Guided essay*

It is better to give lots of short written tests over the year than to set one long essay at the end. To mark long essays is onerous, and it is difficult to be consistent in awarding marks. Also, it is easier to make short tasks realistic. Below are three examples of practical written tests. Each is designed to get a class of students of English as a foreign language writing a short letter in English. They are all simulations of real life writing tasks. The first and third are mixed skill tests because the student can only demonstrate an ability to write if the English of the rubric and of the stimulus are fully understood. Only the second (for francophone students) is a pure test of writing. The use of the mother tongue in rubrics and in scene setting can be an advantage, but it is resisted in some circles.

---

APPLY FOR THE JOB ADVERTISED. SAY WHY YOU THINK YOU WOULD BE ABLE TO DO THE JOB WELL.

Young person required for 6 weeks, to help in the kitchens of large London hotel. French speaker preferred, but good English essential.

---

CHEZ UN AMI ANGLAIS, VOUS CASSEZ LA THEIERE. IL EST ABSENT ET VOUS PARTEZ DEMAIN A BONNE HEURE. VOUS NE POUVEZ DONC PAS LA REMPLACER. ECRIVEZ UN PETIT MOT POUR VOUS EXCUSER, EN LAISSANT DE L'ARGENT POUR L'ACHAT D'UNE AUTRE.

---

REPLY TO THIS LETTER

Dear friend,
Did you not get my last letter? I have never received a reply. I was quite worried. I am sure you would have answered. Do you still intend to come to New York this summer, or have your plans changed? How was your Christmas? What gifts did you receive? Please write as soon as possible. Your American friend,
Ashley.

## Speaking tests

If your aim is to develop speaking competence, then you *must* include speaking tests in your on-going evaluation. Even with large classes, there are communicative tests that can be applied.

### Traditional role play

The usual procedure is quite satisfactory for teachers of small classes of up to 30 students. You design a series of situations and play one role while a student plays the second. Each little scene takes only a minute or so to act out. The student has a *talk card* as a prompt. There will be eight or so different short situations, and the situations, though not the details, are leaked to the class a few days before the oral test so that they can prepare.[2]

The talk cards are put face down on the teacher's desk. The student takes one, at random, and looks through it and prepares while the teacher is role playing with the previous student. As each student is called for interview, the next one comes forward for a card, and so on. Each role play takes only a minute or so. Grades are awarded (fail, pass, pass with merit) as the test is conducted. If a numerical mark must be assigned, a marking grid of the sort shown later will help you to remain consistent.[5]

### Free role play

Teachers of large or small classes can use role play in a less prescribed way. You yourself are not involved, except as a marker. This leaves you free to concentrate on the speech. You just describe the half a dozen situations that you will be testing and leave the learners to decide what parts to adopt and how to play out their scenes. The situations are outlined several days beforehand, and are of the following sort:

– A visitor wants to know what there is to do in the town and surrounding district.

– Two people are eating in a restaurant, but they are not familiar with the local dishes so they have difficulty in choosing. The waiter is very patient.

Having been assigned six or so situations, the students pair off or make small groups, depending on how they intend to play the scenes. They prepare in their free time. Knowing that they will have to act out any two of the situations, drawn at random, on the day of the test, they do a lot of work beforehand. Marks are awarded on an individual basis. This prevents one of them becoming a monosyllabic waiter, for example. In fact, they usually rise to the occasion and become imaginative and amusing in the situations they contrive.

They come up group by group and draw the name of their situation (eg a family checking into a camp site) from the face-down slips on your table. They begin play acting at once, with no further preparation. If the test takes place in regular teaching time, the other students can watch. This in itself is wonderful exposure for the audience. Each scene takes only a minute or so. You use a marking grid (described later) to award marks as you monitor the playlet.

When all the groups have been seen once, they begin a second scene. The new situations are again assigned at random, though of course no group may do the same situation a second time. A class of seventy or so students will be in 25 – 30 groups or pairs. They can all be seen in not much more than an hour, once teachers and students become used to this style of teaching and testing. So it is necessary to allow about three hours for all of them to carry out their two assignments under test conditions.

*Group topic discussion*
An excellent way to conduct oral tests with a large class is through assigned topics. This approach is communicative in that all members of the group interact in a discussion mode and have to respond to what others say. Topics should relate to the interests of the class and to the syllabus (feminism, the rural exodus, the Olympic Games, third world debt problems, American pop music, etc). Again, the five or six topics are announced some time beforehand. This ensures that the students do a great deal of preparation, individually and in their own time.

This way of testing takes a little longer than those above, but not excessively so. It is for advanced classes, for whom the test is seen to be a serious evaluation of their communicative and interactional skills.

On the day of the tests the students are called into the room in groups of three or four. These groups are made up entirely at random *at the moment of testing*. The teacher spreads the six or so topics, on slips of paper, face down on the table. The first candidate takes one and immediately makes a short presentation on that topic. This may last for a couple of minutes. Afterwards the others ask questions or contribute to a short discussion. Because they have all prepared all of the topics, their contributions will be worth listening to. Once the discussion has finished, the next person draws a topic, and so on until all four have given a little talk on a different topic and have responded to the questions from the others in the group.

The group's four presentations and the discussions will take about fifteen minutes. You mark as you listen, using a marking grid (described later). You assign one mark (perhaps out of ten) for the quality of each student presentation. You award a second mark for each student's involvement in the debates. This could again be out of ten, making a nice round total of 20 possible marks. Then the next group of four students come in, and so on.

## ■ MARKING SCHEMES FOR SPEAKING AND WRITING TESTS

Where the students have opportunities to be creative in their writing or speaking, your marking will be subjective. This does not matter too much if you remain consistent. The degree of subjectivity can be reduced, almost eliminated if you use a simple marking scheme.

### Marking written tests

Look back at the three essay type tests. All three of those texts specify what has to be accomplished by the writer, so you know roughly what ought to be said in the three letters. It is simple enough to check this by means of a list.

#### Task check lists for guided essays

A check list could be drawn up for each of the three answers to the three tests above. These are on a *yes-no* basis so that you can check for successful or practical task fulfilment. The first test will have a checklist of the following kind:

Is the letter begun in a businesslike way?
Does the student state name, age, etc.?
Are arguments put forward to support the application?
Does the student specify French as mother tongue, with working competence in English?
Is the application closed appropriately?
Is it readily comprehensible?

#### Marking grids for essays

Marking grids are often used with essay type answers. Normally the grids are designed to give a round maximum total. This example takes account of the appropriateness of the content, the choice and spelling of words, sentence structure and the overall coherence and feel. Each factor has a maximum of five marks. One student may write ungrammatically, but succeed quite well in getting the message across. Another may write a series of short and accurate sentences which lack cohesion, and so on.

| Marks: | 1 | 2 | 3 | 4 | 5 |
|---|---|---|---|---|---|
| Vocab/spelling | | | | | |
| Sentence structures | | | | | |
| Cohesion | | | | | |
| Task fulfilment | | | | | |

### Weighting

The problem with that grid is that only 25 percent of the marks are awarded for task completion, with 75 percent for linguistic competence. If you want to reward communicative competence, then you can apply what is known as *weighting*. For example, the mark gained for task fulfilment could be doubled, giving a final maximum mark of 25 instead of 20. In this way, message content factor gets 40 percent of the total marks.

### Impressionistic marking of essays

Unless you are required to assign a numerical mark, there is really no need to be so analytical and precise. An indication of the students' ability to use the medium functionally is sufficient. It is enough to record a pass grade (most of the content was effectively transmitted), or a fail grade by means of an **impressionistic**, or **global mark**. If you wish, you can reward the best writers by means of a *credit* level. You could even add a fourth *distinction* grade if you really need to spread the results over a greater range.

Impressionistic marking is fast and efficient. Once teachers are used to it, they show a remarkable measure of agreement in the grades they award. To apply this method, you skim each passage to see if the task has been accomplished. You skim it a second time, to see how easy it is to read and roughly how many errors there are.

Any outstanding pieces of work, well written and with communicative quality, are put into a *pass with credit* stack. Most papers will have some errors of vocabulary or structure, but will be satisfactory in terms of putting the ideas across. These go into a central *pass level* stack. Those which are so full of errors that it is difficult to understand them, or which fail to fulfil the specified tasks, go into the third stack, as *failures*. Naturally, most of the class ought to pass. High failure rates indicate poor teaching or an inappropriate test.[3]

## Marking grids for speech

Markers often use grids similar to those used for written work. You refer to them as you monitor the candidate's speech.

### Class grids

A one-page marking grid like the one below will hold the scores of twenty or more students rather than the seven shown. Instead of letters, the students' names would be on the card. Marks are based on how much they said of relevance, how well it was said, how they reacted to what others said, how enjoyable it was, and so on.

It is best to give a mark out of five for each category assessed. A mark of 3 in a factor indicates *satisfactory*, 5 is *excellent* while 1 is *extremely poor*. Some students speak readily and accurately, but with an awful accent. Others say little, but say it well. The individual scores can be entered straight onto a card like this:

| Candidate | A | B | C | D | E | F | G |
|-----------|---|---|---|---|---|---|---|
| Message   |   |   |   |   |   |   |   |
| Accuracy  |   |   |   |   |   |   |   |
| Fluency   |   |   |   |   |   |   |   |
| Compr'n   |   |   |   |   |   |   |   |
| Total/20  |   |   |   |   |   |   |   |

### Marking guide

A simpler guide could have just two categories, giving a maximum of ten. You simply look at the guide as you listen, making a separate record of the individual scores.

| Mark: | 0 | 1 | 2 | 3 | 4 | 5 |
|-------|---|---|---|---|---|---|
| Comprehensibility |   |   |   |   |   |   |
| Accuracy |   |   |   |   |   |   |

## ■ ANALYSING RESULTS

We are concerned here with class testing for the teacher's own feedback, not with inter-class comparisons. There is no need to enter the world of statistics. There are some simple ways of getting the information needed with little or no mathematics. In any case, if you are using a criterion-referenced scheme, no calculations at all are involved, individuals will either pass or fail.[4]

## Central scores

There are several different types of score which teachers can take as a central one, against which to evaluate the members of a class. We shall look at them now. All are easy to identify or to calculate.

### The class average

The true name for this score is the **arithmetic mean score**. This score, more commonly referred to as the **average score**, gives lots of information. First, it tells you about your teaching. A low class average shows that the teaching was not effective, or that the test failed to measure what you taught. To obtain the class average, total all the scores and divide by the number of students. An average of fifteen or more out of twenty is reassuring. Ten is not.

The second item of information you can get from the average score is how well individual students are faring. To do this you need only to compare each student's score with the class average for that test. This helps you with your reporting, and each student learns where extra effort and help are needed. The student will be close to the average (*doing quite well*), above average (*doing very well*), or below (*needs to make greater efforts to . . .*).

### The median

Another way to get a score against which to compare students is to rank all the scores and then take the middle one. In a class of forty, score number 20 becomes your yardstick. Nineteen students are seen to be above average, and twenty are below.

### The mode

This is another **central score** with no calculations at all. What is more, the **mode** offers certain advantages for reporting purposes because it embraces a **range** of scores. In this way, more students obtain a *doing quite well* score and fewer are seen to fall below the central range. To obtain the mode you just enter all the scores on a sort of graph. The score that is *most frequently attained* by candidates becomes your central reference. Usually the mode is very close to the centre of the range of scores and to the mean average score, but it does not really matter if it is not.

The graph that results from the plotting of the scores provides a vivid visual representation of the ability of a class and the range of abilities. The greater the range of scores (highest to lowest) the more difficult the class is to teach. Scores bunched closely together indicate good teaching and a homogeneous class.

An example will make this clear. Each cross represents the score of one student. For reasons of space only 25 student scores are shown. The highest score, obtained by one student, is 19. The lowest (two students) is 11. The score most frequently recorded is 14. This score, the mode, becomes the *doing quite well* score and has been attained by six of the twenty five learners. Against that score, the other students are seen as above or below average.[5]

```
                        Student Scores: Listening
   20
   19   X
   18
   17   X X
   16   X X X
   15   X X X X
   14   X X X X X X
   13   X X X
   12   X X X X
   11   X X
   10
```

# ■ CONCLUSION

Through regular, informal tests, teachers obtain feedback for themselves and the students on the efficiency of the teaching and learning process. Teachers should try to evaluate all the skills, in isolation and by means of mixed skill tests. Where teachers face pressures of time, it helps if listening and reading tests are in the multiple-choice format, with a preprinted answer paper. Marking then takes only moments, by means of a transparent overlay showing the answer pattern.

Written and oral tests have to be marked by impression if creativity is not to be stifled. There can be a pass-fail criterion or the teacher can design a simple marking grid to reduce subjectivity. Oral tests can be conducted more communicatively as well as more quickly if they are done in small groups. It is vital that teachers be seen to test and reward speech and interaction if the students are to perceive communicative competence as important.

Even short tests can be informative, and a series of these will permit the teacher to make a profile of each student for reporting purposes. Usually, teachers will be able to identify some area of competence in which even a weak student is at, or little above, the class average. The results can be plotted and kept in graph form, giving an instant representation of the ability range and the frequency of the different scores.

## Notes

[1] This anecdote shows the dangerous nature of multiple-choice tests. I produced multiple-choice reading and listening comprehension tests in Korean and gave them to a group of trainers attending the Ohio University Summer Program. The range of marks obtained by the international group, not one of whom understood a single word, ranged from 15 percent to well over 40 percent. We were able to rank the students from first to last!

[2] You may have taught well but have designed a test that does not sample what you have taught. In this case, the test has **low content validity**. However, if the test is based on what was taught and a class does badly as a whole, then you must look for reasons in your materials or approach.

[3] The deliberate leaking of information about a test is known as **transparency**, and it is helpful in many ways. Most important, the students prepare carefully, learning what you want them to know. Second, tension is reduced. Third, the actual interview goes quickly. Because students cannot predict which situation they will be assigned, they have to prepare all of them. The specific tasks are on a talk card and are only seen by the student during the very short preparation time.

[4] Criterion-referenced tests are a *can you or can't you?* mode of assessment. Driving tests are of this sort, as are certificate tests for musical instruments. Although it seems unscientific, it is far more valid to assess communicative competence skills (ie not just *linguistic* knowledge) in such subjective ways. When you ask for directions in another language, the person either understands and responds or shrugs and walks away. Good teachers know whether or not a sympathetic native speaker would understand what was written or said.

One thing we cannot do with the results of criterion-referenced tests is rank the students, from first to last. This is not a bad thing. When students are ranked, everyone except the first feels a degree of failure. What is more, a mark or grade tells us nothing concrete about a performance. To say that a candidate achieved a B + or a score of 65 percent in an examination tells us nothing about his or her ability to perform authentic tasks in English.

5 The good thing about comparing individuals with the central scores in a range of tests, assessing *all* skills, is that almost everyone will be above average in some aspect. This allows you to begin a report in a positive way, and this in turn has a good effect on attitudes.

# 16 Improving pronunciation: sounds and spellings

## ■ PHONETICS FOR TEACHERS

A knowledge of phonology and phonetics enables teachers to check the pronunciation of words in dictionaries, to anticipate difficulties and to help students overcome them. A book on the pronunciation of the target language is a necessary part of the teacher's *tools of the trade*. This holds true even for native speakers, who are often unaware of the sound system and the articulation of the phonemes of their own language. Teachers also need to be familiar with the **phonology** of the students' mother tongue.

In this chapter we look at the range of sounds that make up the English language (a similar treatment is possible for any other language), and at their representation in regular writing and phonetic script. We also examine ways of helping students to improve their pronunciation. Language teachers should insist on proper pronunciation from the very beginning. Bad speech habits are difficult to eradicate later.

For readers who are not familiar with phonetic script, the first few pages of this chapter are essential reading and learning. Those who have made a study of phonetics can move straight to the section that describes techniques of practising pronunciation on pp. 214–221 of this volume.

### The spoken model

The pronunciation modelled here is the educated British one, commonly referred to as *RP*, or **Received Pronunciation**. RP is represented, together with IPA script[1], in most grammar and linguistics books, dictionaries and books on phonology. This is not to suggest that other varieties of English are inferior. You should adopt the model that meets your own needs, depending on the availability of materials, native speaker consultants, opportunities for study in an anglophone country, and so on. Differences between British and other educated varieties, including American English, are relatively unimportant as far as individual sounds are concerned.

### Phonetics and the classroom

Phonetic symbols should not be used in schools. To introduce a second orthography risks confusion. The letters of the regular alphabet can show the sound of words if necessary. For example *cough* can be shown as *koff*, *through* as *throo*, *dough* as *doe*, and so on.

210

Let us look at the IPA symbols now. We start with the vowel sounds and the range of spellings that are used to represent these sounds. We do the same with the consonants before looking at ways of practising pronunciation in class.

# ■ THE VOWELS OF ENGLISH

English vowels fall into two main groups, the **pure vowels** and the **diphthongs**. Pure vowels have a single sound quality. Dipthongs are composed of two vowel sounds, with one vowel sliding into another, weaker, vowel. In RP there are twelve pure vowels which can be subdivided into short vowels and long ones. The eight diphthongs can be subdivided into three groups, by virtue of their final vowel sound. This gives a total of twenty different vowel sounds in standard English speech.

With only five written symbols to represent twenty vowel sounds, spellings can give problems. Great use is made of the letters *e* and *r* to show changed vowels sounds. For example, the addition of a letter *e* turns a short vowel into a long one or into a diphthong (hat, hate; bit, bite; met, meet; dot, dote; cut, cute). The addition of letter *r* changes the vowel quality (cat, cart; bee, beer; hut, hurt; bid, bird; pot, port).[2]

In phonetic script one symbol must represent one sound. So, with twenty vowel sounds, some of the symbols look strange to the inexperienced eye. However, they can be learned in a few hours and the results are well worth the investment of time.

Commonly used spellings that represent each vowel sound are given in the tables that follow, but you may think of less common ones that are also used (eg the long ee-sound of qu*ay* and rece*i*pt, the short /e/ of b*u*ry, the long aw-sound of p*our* and d*oor*).

The left hand column in each table gives the phonetic symbol. Different spellings of that sound are to the right. Where a word has two syllables, the symbol-spelling relationship is underlined. Where there are only one or two examples, this indicates that other spellings do not occur or are unusual. Phonetic symbols are shown between **slashes** (oblique strokes) to distinguish them from regular spelling (eg egg /eg /, you /yu: /).

## Pure Vowels

| IPA Symbol | Common spellings | | | | |
|---|---|---|---|---|---|
| **a) Short vowels** | | | | | |
| /ɪ/ | pit | build | pr<u>e</u>tty | s<u>y</u>stem | Mond<u>ay</u> |
| /e/ | egg | head | said | m<u>a</u>ny | friend |
| /æ/ | am | (always letter <u>a</u>) | | | |
| /ɑ/ | log | want | cough | bec<u>au</u>se | |
| /ʊ/ | good | could | full | wolf | |
| /ʌ/ | cup | some | blood | rough | br<u>o</u>ther |
| /ə/* | the | <u>a</u>lone | bitt<u>er</u> | f<u>a</u>tigue | doct<u>or</u> |

211

| b) Long vowels (length is indicated by the colon) | | | | | |
|---|---|---|---|---|---|
| /iː/ | see | sea | feel | thief | people |
| /ɑː/ | arm | heart | calm | laugh | rather |
| /ɔː/ | port | bought | taught | law | ward |
| /uː/ | cool | tune | who | blue | you |
| /ɜː/ | her | fur | stir | heard | word |

Some IPA users have abandoned the use of the colon lengthening sign. They see it as superfluous, as the long vowel symbols cannot, anyway, be confused with the short ones.

## Diphthongs

| a) Those moving into an ee sound /ɪ/ | | | | | |
|---|---|---|---|---|---|
| /eɪ/ | hate | rain | play | they | weight |
| /aɪ/ | bite | high | climb | lie | eye |
| /ɔɪ/ | toy | join | | | |
| **b) Those moving into a oo sound /ʊ/** | | | | | |
| /ɑʊ/ | goat | note | low | toe | sew |
| /aʊ/ | mouth | now | plough | | |
| **c) Those moving into the eh sound (schwa) /ə/** | | | | | |
| /ɪə/ | near | beer | pier | | |
| /eə/ | there | their | hair | stare | pear |
| /ʊə/ | cure | fewer | tour | | |

## Some specific vowel features

A few points merit special attention. First, the short vowel /ə/ (**schwa**) is the most common vowel in English. The second most common vowel is the short /ɪ/ sound. Their high frequency is a result of *vowel reduction*. Most vowels in unstressed syllables are weakened in speech. Here are some examples of both vowels in unstressed positions in phrases or polysyllabic words.

> I can do it /kən/
> Some more? /səm/
> He was a photographer (here the schwa sound occurs 5 times)
> I'll be there /bɪ/
> We waited /ɪd/
> Friday night / 'fraɪdɪ/

The little mark before the first syllable of the phonetic representation of *Friday* indicates that this first syllable is stressed. The mark always precedes the stressed syllable in words with more than one syllable.

Finally, there are a few three-vowel combinations. These **triphthongs** are best viewed as a diphthong followed by schwa:

<u>tyre</u> /taɪə/      <u>power</u> /paʊə/

## ■ THE CONSONANTS OF ENGLISH

Many consonants have the same phonetic symbol as the normal written alphabet and we begin with these. Then we look at sounds with an unfamiliar symbol. In each case the phonetic symbol is in the first column. The second column shows the sound in an **initial** position, the third column gives a word with the sound in a **medial** (central) position and the last column has the sound in a **final** position. It is not possible to give the consonants in alphabetical order, as some letters of the alphabet represent more than one sound (eg letters *c, g, s, th*).

The first ten sounds of this first set are related by pairs – the **articulation** (the position of the speech organs) of both sounds is exactly the same but the first of each pair is **voiceless** while the second is **voiced** (the vocal chords are used).

### Familiar IPA symbols for consonant sounds

| Symbol | Initial | Medial | Final |
|--------|---------|--------|-------|
| /p/ | pie | happy | stop |
| /b/ | buy | rubber | rob |
| /t/ | two | utter | hit |
| /d/ | dog | sudden | could |
| /k/ | cut | liquor | back |
| /g/ | go | bigger | rug |
| /s/ | sit | nicely | rice |
| /z/ | zoo | easy | lose |
| /f/ | fin | laughing | if |
| /v/ | view | loving | move |
| /m/ | more | summer | dumb |
| /n/ | nice | running | soon |
| /l/ | like | silly | ball |
| /r/ | rude | courage | – |
| /h/ | heat | perhaps | – |
| /w/ | wet | nowhere | – |

## New consonant symbols

A voiced-unvoiced contrast between related sounds is found again in the first three pairs of this list.[3]

| /θ/ | thick | author | lath |
|-----|-------|--------|------|
| /ð/ | these | mother | lathe |
| /ʃ/ | she | nation | wish |
| /ʒ/ | – | leisure | beige |
| /tʃ/ | cheese | richer | beach |
| /dʒ/ | jaw | major | edge |
| /ŋ/ | – | singer | ring |
| /j/* | you | beyond | – |

* The **symbol** /j/ (as in *yes*) should not be confused with the **letter** *j*.

## Consonant clusters

Combinations of consonants are called **consonant clusters**. They are common in the basic forms of words (spring /spr/, play /pl/, etc), but we also create them by the use of grammatical markers. This gives us clusters such as desks /sks/, jumped /mpt/, reads /dz/, and so on. Consonants also form clusters when words run together in connected speech (back slang /ksl/). Where the learners' mother tongue only has single consonants, separated by vowels, problems of articulation must be anticipated and special measures taken to help the learners produce these clusters.

## ■ IMPROVING THE PERCEPTION AND PRONUNCIATION OF SOUNDS

Most of these techniques are enjoyable, but like any form of practice they should not be over-used. Apart from a few simple flashcards or blackboard drawings, the main requirement is planning.

Sometimes you will have to focus on a single problem sound or cluster of sounds. At other times a vital distinction between two or more related sounds will need practice. Learners of different nationalities experience different difficulties. This is because they tend to hear and speak English via their mother tongue set of sounds. Sometimes they are unable even to perceive the difference between a target sound and a related sound in their mother tongue. In this case their *aural discrimination* is poor. At other times they can hear a difference but cannot reproduce the foreign sound. Here they have poor **articulation**. Sometimes they can neither hear a difference between distinctive features nor articulate the foreign sounds.

214

## Teaching techniques

There are two approaches. One way is to explain how the sound is made (**manner of articulation**). Once the learners can *make* the sound they will more easily perceive it aurally. The other way is to contrast two related sounds until such time as they begin to hear the difference, after which they should be able to reproduce the sounds. No one way is better than the other, learners vary in their preferred mode.

Naturally, teachers themselves must know how each sound is articulated if they are to explain the positioning of the lips and tongue to the students. You can do this by making the target sounds in isolation in front of a mirror, but reference books on the phonology of the language explain how each consonant and vowel is made by the organs of speech. Let us now look at some exercises.

### Mother tongue or English?

This exercise in aural discrimination helps beginners perceive vital distinctions between the set of sounds of their mother tongue and the phonemes of English. The example is for an EFL class of francophone students (or even anglophones learning French), but the exercise can even be done when languages are totally unrelated.[4] You simply contrast English words with similar ones in the mother tongue. Meaning is *not* important. There is no need for the class to recognise the words. Sometimes the two words chosen will have very different meanings, as in the examples below, but some words may be similar in meaning and form in both languages (**cognates**). The class has only to say if the teacher is pronouncing the English word or one from their own language.

| | |
|---|---|
| TEACHER: Key | STUDENTS: English |
| TEACHER: Qui | STUDENTS: French |
| | |
| TEACHER: Côte | STUDENTS: French |
| TEACHER: Coat | STUDENTS: English |

And so on, with pire/pier, coq/cock, père/pair, bol/bowl, venir/veneer, tu/two, l'eau/low, pipe/peep, long/long, etc.

### Minimal pairs

This is another exercise in aural discrimination, but it leads into pronunciation practice. **Minimal pairs** are pairs of words that differ in only one feature (eg *ring/rang, sun/some, peer/beer, fit/feet,* etc). You begin by giving a clear model and, if necessary, an explanation of the position of the organs of speech. Later, the exercise becomes one of pronunciation. The word pairs are chosen because of a crucial phonological distinction. This may be a vowel (*by/boy, ship/sheep, walk/work, nurse/nice*) or a consonant (*fan/van, lip/rip, path/pass, dare/there*).

The procedure is simple. The two words are written on the board (or flash card pictures are put there) and numbered, 1 and 2. You say one of the words and the class has to identify it, calling out the number:

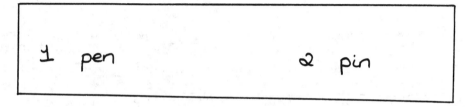

TEACHER: Pen      STUDENTS: One
TEACHER: Pin      STUDENTS: Two
TEACHER: Pin etc.

Once the students can discriminate between the sounds you get individuals or the whole class to pronounce the words. This is done by calling out the number of the word to be pronounced.

*Triplets*
This time, three sounds are contrasted instead of two. To the words above, *pan* has been added and pictures have been sketched on the blackboard, instead of the written words:

Another way to conduct this exercise is to get the learners to draw the items on separate slips of paper. They hold up the appropriate picture as the word is pronounced.

*Two phoneme contrasts*
Many different words can be put on the blackboard at the same time, to contrast the two sounds which are the focus of listening and speaking practice. This increases the level of challenge, so the activity becomes more like a game. The procedure is the same as with just two or three words. You pronounce any one of the words and the learners identify it by number. Later, you call numbers, and designated students pronounce the words. Here, the contrast is between two vowels, with the different consonants acting as distractors:

216

```
1 cut     2 cot     3 cub     4 cob
5 lung    6 long    7 bus     8 boss
```

Here, two consonants are contrasted in the same way.

```
1 Sue      2 zoo      3 zing     4 sing
5 his      6 hiss     7 peace    8 peas
9 course   10 cause   11 sip     12 zip
```

## Multiple contrasts

It is easy to contrive similar word sets, in which only one vowel or consonant is different. Begin with two or three words and add new sounds as the students increase their ability to discriminate between them:

a) 1 fill      2 full      3 feel      4 file
   5 fail      6 foal      7 foul      8 foil
   9 fool      10 fell     11 furl

b) 1 books     2 box       3 bikes     4 beaks
   5 barks     6 bakes

c) 1 noise     2 knees     3 news      4 nose
   5 gnaws     6 nears

d) 1 thought   2 sought    3 short     4 fort
   5 taught    6 caught    7 port      8 sought

e) 1 choose    2 Jews      3 shoes     4 Sue's
   5 zoos      6 whose     7 lose

## Same or different?

This is the simplest of the several varieties of contrast exercises that develop the students' ability to perceive distinctive features. Nothing is written on the board at all. You just pronounce two words and the class has to call out *same* or *different*. In this example, the class is learning to discriminate between the consonants /r/ and /1/.

TEACHER: Royal (pause) Royal.
STUDENTS: Same.
TEACHER: Loyal (pause) Royal.
STUDENTS: Different.
TEACHER: Rain (pause) Lane.
STUDENTS: Different.

More advanced classes can be asked to hear the difference between phrases rather than single words:

TEACHER: A loyal person (pause) A royal person.
STUDENTS: Different.
TEACHER: A walk in the lane (pause) A walk in the lane.
STUDENTS: Same.
TEACHER: A walk in the rain/lane . . .

## Rhyming words

This is an enjoyable way of practising aural discrimination and pronunciation while at the same time conducting a review of recently taught lexical items. Choose a few stimulus words which contain sounds which give difficulties of pronunciation.

It is a good idea to use visuals in conjunction with the stimulus words. In this way you can use new, unknown words as the stimuli. This makes the learners pay great attention to the sound as well as adding interest. Imagine that you want the class to produce the word *cloth*. With a picture of the insect, you could use *moth*, even though the class has never met the word before. The aim is to practise the pronunciation of the /θ/ sound, not to teach the word *moth*, but often children will pick up new words in such casual ways. The activity sounds like this:

TEACHER:/tʃ/: Thatch (*picture to show meaning*).
STUDENTS: Match, hatch, . . .
TEACHER/aɪ/: Tie (*pointing*),
STUDENTS: My, eye, why, cry, . . .
TEACHER/u/: Chew (*demonstrating*)
STUDENTS: Blue, you, two, . . .

## Identifying the vowel sound

The aim of this activity is to develop the ability to identify specified vowels, but again you are revising vocabulary at the same time. The sounds to be identified can be represented by head-words that the class already knows or by pictures. As you pronounce other words, the class decides which group each word belongs to. They call out *one*, *four*, and so on. As a word is correctly identified, it is added to the lists on the blackboard.

In the example just below, the teacher is practising all eight diphthongs simultaneously, but would probably have begun by treating each of the three sets of diphthongs separately, perhaps over several lessons. To practise, the head-words or pictures are put on the board and the students practise saying them for a short while, with special attention to the articulation. Then new words are called out, identified by sound group and assigned to their groups. The pictures or head-words alone can suffice, but a graphic representation of the diphthongs, as in the example, can be helpful to learners because it indicates the articulation:

| | | |
|---|---|---|
| **1** | **2** | **3** |
| e to ee | ah to ee | or to ee |
| play | eye | boy |
| **4** | **5** | **6** |
| ee to er | e to er | oo to er |
| ear | hair | cure |
| | **7** | **8** | |
| | er to oo | ah to oo | |
| | go | cow | |

You go on to call out any monosyllabic word with a diphthong, for example, *train* (set 1), *here* (4), *child* (2), *coin* (3), *brewer* (6), *chairs* (5), *rose* (7), *loud* (8), and so on. The features and parts of the body are a rich source of words with diphthongs (nose, eye, mouth, toe, waist, thigh, etc). After a few minutes, there may be four or five words in each of the nine lists on the board. At this point you can offer practice in saying the words. As each word is indicated, the students either say it in isolation or construct a simple phrase which incorporates the word. Students and teachers alike monitor the pronunciation of the diphthong, listening for the shift into the second weak vowel.

*Word bank improvisation*
This exercise is based on a word bank, composed of words the students know but which have difficult sounds. The words should really be written on a poster to save class time. If the blackboard is used the words are added one at a time and chorused and practised as they are introduced. The activity is enjoyable and creative. The students are asked to improvise phrases which incorporate as

many of the designated words as possible. Of course, they may include any other words they need, but credit is gained for including and correctly pronouncing words from the bank. The exercise is best done as a written pair work task, followed by an oral check.

Because of the unpredictability, follow-up is interesting and funny at times. Although there may not be time to check all the pairs, the students will already have spoken their own phrases to each other while composing and in readiness for a public check. After some random nominations, you can identify and reward the pair which used the most prescribed words in a single grammatical utterance. Below is an example of a word bank and some sample sentences. The pronunciation focus here is on diphthongs, but there is no need to limit the bank to specified sounds. It can contain any words that have been mispronounced in past lessons.

| | | | |
|---|---|---|---|
| where | everywhere | joy | liar |
| my | around | town | now |
| clear | rose | high | brown |
| goat | rice | low | dawn |
| wide | narrow | old | ate |
| plane | today | near | pure |
| road | bike | field | sewer |

The old goat went into the town and ate the rice.
The liar said the brown rice we ate was pure.
Roads in the old town are so narrow that we go down by bike.
Planes today are wide and high, not narrow and low.

## Definitions

This activity is like a crossword puzzle. The students have to guess words and pronounce them carefully. They get excellent listening practice at the same time. The words to be guessed contain sounds that tend to be mispronounced. You give the clue and then designate the students who is to answer. The rest of the class decides if the word is correct and if it has been pronounced properly. If not, they make the corrections. The activity sounds like this:

TEACHER:    This is a male child.
STUDENT 1:  Boy /ɔɪ/.

TEACHER:     A religious building, for christians.
STUDENT 2:   Church /tʃ/.
TEACHER:     We go there to see a show.
STUDENT 3:   Cinema.
TEACHER:     Well, yes. But I want another word.
STUDENTS:    Miss! Theatre! /θ/, etc.

## Buzz words

Again, attention is on listening for meaning, as well as on the production of the specified sounds. You read out phrases, but leave out the word that contains the sound to be practised. The gap is indicated by the word *buzz*. The students call the missing words. Let us look at an exercise to contrast and practise the sounds /θ/ and /s/. It sounds like this:

TEACHER:     The other day I took my son to the doctors. He was *buzz*.
STUDENT 1:   Was he sick, sir?
TEACHER:     Correct. Class, repeat. He was *sick*.
TEACHER:     My friend's wife doesn't eat much. She's *buzz*, not fat.
STUDENT 2:   Thin?
TEACHER:     Right. She's *thin*. Repeat. She's thin.
TEACHER:     Last night I woke up feeling *buzz*. I went to the kitchen for a drink. I felt *buzz*.
STUDENT 3:   Thirsty?
TEACHER:     That's it! Class, repeat. I was thirsty.
TEACHER:     My daughter gave me a surprise gift yesterday. I was pleased. Of course I said *buzz*.
STUDENTS:    Thanks! Thank you.

## ■ DIAGNOSING PROBLEMS OF AURAL DISCRIMINATION

If you are to remedy the problems, you need a systematic way of identifying the sounds that are difficult to perceive. The next procedure is really a test, it enables you to locate problem areas in a matter of minutes. The test is conducted informally and marked by a show of hands, so it can be done quite frequently to help you keep abreast of each class's progress. To do this, you use a 'same or different' test.

### The procedure

The procedure is simple, but you need to plan the activity and draw up the list of related words, in sets of three, like those shown in the example that follows. The idea is to contrast the words, with a short pause between each one. Each set is heard twice only. Do not limit yourself to words that the students know. You get a more accurate diagnosis if there are plenty of strange words, as it is the difficult *sounds* that you want to pin-point for subsequent practice.

Because five different response patterns are possible for each set, guesswork plays a limited part. Nothing is written on the blackboard at any time, nor do the students repeat anything. This is purely an exercise in aural discrimination.

The students need a sheet of paper on which to write their single letter responses as the exercise is conducted (S = same, D = different). Sometimes all three words are the same, sometimes they are all different and sometimes just one of the three words is different from the two others – in which case the odd one out has to be identified by its position, first, second or third. The example that follows will make this clear. Each set of three words is spoken twice and the students write their response pattern after the second listening. Allow about ten seconds for this, then say the next set of three words, and so on. In a normal test, the class might hear twenty or so sets.

When you have finished you can identify the difficult phonemes by going through the sequence again and getting a show of hands to indicate the student choices. If you wish you can then confirm the correct answer pattern, but this is not really necessary as this is a diagnostic test. You make a note of the sounds which gave problems to a large number of individuals. The whole procedure, with public check and corrections, takes about fifteen minutes.[5]

## Worked example

Teacher: Number 1.   Pear (pause) Pear (pause) Bear

(The students should write   S   S   D, as the first two words were the same and the third was different)

Teacher: Number 2.   chair     share     chair

(The students ought to write  S   D   S, as the first and third were the same but the middle one was odd)

Teacher: Number 3.   revel     level     reveal

(The students should have written three D's)

Teacher: Number 4.   glow     glow     glow

(This time they should have written S   S   S)

Teacher: Number 5.   jumps     jumped     jumped

(D   S   S. The first word was different from the two others).

### Remedial treatment of difficult phonemes

The phonemes that you identify as troublesome can be made the subject of one or more of the intensive practices that have already been described. This can be done in any later lesson, with the exercise appearing in your lesson plan as a review, as a reserve activity or even as a game. The techniques you use should be varied in order to avoid boredom. Remedial treatment can be repeated for as long as is necessary; you will know when the difficulty has become less problematic by the results in the ongoing *same or different* tests.

# ■ CONCLUSION

To eradicate poor pronunciation is a difficult task. For this reason it is advisable to include aural discrimination and pronunciation exercises from the start. If a teacher is in too much of a hurry to teach new classes to say something, pronunciation may be overlooked. This can lead to difficulties in listening comprehension, because distinctive sounds that cannot be produced may not be perceived either. Good language teachers should be aware of the sounds and articulation of the target language and of the learners' mother tongue.

There is no need to limit practice to mechanical exercises. There are enough aural discrimination and pronunciation activities for teachers to ring the changes with learners of all ages. The approach can even be made to seem like a game, by encouraging creative language use and an awareness of the content as well as of the phonology.

## Notes

[1] IPA script is that of the **International Phonetics Association**. It has greater world-wide currency than any other phonetic script. **Received Pronunciation** (RP) is the accent that was favoured in royal circles (it was received by the court). It is often called **BBC English** or the **King's/Queen's English**.

[2] RP speakers do not differentiate between *court* and *caught*, but the distinction is made in the USA, where the /r/ is always pronounced. However, RP speakers do pronounce a final /r/ for linking purposes (eg car-oner).

[3] Looking at the consonant lists, it is evident that some consonants do not occur in certain positions in English. For example, no words begin with the sound /ʒ/ and none end with the sound /j/.

[4] Speakers of Egyptian Arabic have words which closely resemble these (though the meanings are totally unrelated); Anna, fee, fill, bait, lay, inter, fill, guy, bill, inter, fain, etc. These Arabic words can be contrasted with the similar English ones, in the way shown.

[5] If you are worried about your own ability to model the spoken language correctly, get hold of some specialist pronunciation publications and work through them carefully. Some come complete with an audio cassette. These specialist works also deal with features of natural educated speech such as elision (nex' time, p'liceman, mos'ly) and assimilation (goob morning, thap big one, I haf to go). Make use of a tape player in the classroom, too, when you use aural discrimination or pronunciation exercises. Get a colleague or friendly native speaker to record some classroom exercises for you. Ask them to record some of the passages in your textbook, too. As well as offering a better model, the cassettes will bring other voices into the classroom and this can add to the interest and motivation.

# 17 Improving pronunciation: the music of English

## ■ THE SUPRASEGMENTALS

Varieties of educated English have different pronunciation. However, most native speaker communities share the features of rhythm, stress and intonation. They tend to stress the same syllables in words and phrases and adopt similar changes of pitch to express surprise, disgust, a questioning attitude, and so on. It is lack of mastery of these **suprasegmental features**, even more than the pronunciation of the separate phonemes, that marks a foreign accent and some language educators see control of these musical features as the most important element for learners to achieve if they are to be readily intelligible.[1]

In this chapter we examine ways to practise these **prosodic features**, making classroom speech more like normal speech and equipping the students to understand spoken English more easily. It is important that the prosodies be a focus of language use, practice and correction from the very beginning of a course. Bad speech habits quickly take root and students may, for instance, begin to speak in an even pitch, giving equal weight to each syllable. By using and eliciting natural sound patterns in class, you can demonstrate that the objective of teaching is, indeed, the correct use of the spoken language.

## ■ STRESS

Stress is the articulation of a syllable with greater emphasis, or more force, than others. Stressed syllables are slightly lengthened and are usually given a higher pitch (**intonation level**). English words of two or more syllables have one syllable which has the major emphasis, in terms of loudness and length. Rules to predict where word stress will come are not very helpful. In most cases the pattern has to be learned with each new word as part of the pronunciation. In some cases, stress acts to distinguish words semantically, for example, a *pre*sent/ to pre*sent*, a *black*bird / a *black bird*, an *ex*port / to ex*port*.

In a dictionary, the stressed syllable of a polysyllabic word is indicated in the phonetic script by a mark immediately above and before the stressed syllable. Any secondary stress is shown by a mark before but below that syllable. Frequently, the vowels in the other, unstressed, positions are weakened, and we shall look at **vowel reduction** now, as it is an important feature for learners to control if they are to produce rhythmic speech.

## Vowel reduction

It might be best to begin by considering the syllables and words which are unlikely to be affected by vowel reduction.

### Content words

In speech, the **key** words (or *content* words) are the words which carry message content and so receive emphasis, though not all of them will be stressed. These content words are normally nouns, adjectives, verbs or adverbs. The vowel in the stressed syllable of any emphasised word keeps its full vowel quality, but vowels elsewhere in the word and in the utterance are usually **weakened** (or **reduced**). The most common reduction is to schwa, but some vowels reduce to the /ɪ/ sound (usually from a long /i:/). Diphthongs often lose the second vowel sound when weakened.

### Function words

Short **grammatical** words (known as **function words**), such as auxiliaries, pronouns, modals, determiners and prepositions, are almost always weakened. Below is a sample of such words, all of which are pronounced with a weak schwa sound unless they are stressed for some special reason.[2]

| | | | | |
|------|------|--------|-------|-------|
| to | and | but | so | for |
| at | then | than | of | some |
| us | you | your | them | her |
| an | have | has | were | was |
| am | are | do | does | would |
| shall | must | should | could | can |

Function words that have the long vowel /i:/ (we, she, me, he) are simply shortened to /ɪ/.

### Grammar words that do not weaken

It might be helpful to list the few grammar words whose vowel sounds are *never* reduced. Perhaps obviously, some words already have a short weak sound that cannot be reduced further (a, the, in, if, is, its, his). Then we have what are known, as **lexical prepositions** (on, off, up, over, under, down, out, by, near). The fact that they carry an important message element may be the reason for their retention of full vowel quality even when they are not stressed. Finally, full vowel value is given to any grammar word ending with a vowel (so, to, do, you) which is followed by another word beginning with a vowel, for example:

| | |
|-------------------------|----------|
| I gave it *to a* beggar | /tu:/ |
| Why don't *you* ask | /ju:/ |
| *So am* I | /səʊ/ |

## Teaching stress and rhythm patterns

You can draw attention to the stress patterns of words and phrases simply by exaggerating the loudness and length of the main syllable when a new word is modelled, but stress patterns can also be shown and practised in other ways:

### Highlighting

The easiest way to draw attention to the sound pattern is to underline empha-sised syllables when words or phrases are written on the board. Alternatively the stressed syllables (shown here in *italics*) can be written with coloured chalk:

    *off*icer                briga*dier*

    See you to*night.*         How's it *go*ing?

### Capital letters

This is easy for individual words, but it is difficult to do for full length utterances because TEACHers have to think aHEAD as they WRITE and THIS isn't EAsy.

    aTTRIBute (verb)    ATtribute (noun)    diploMAtic    exPIRE

### Dots and dashes

This morse code way of representing patterns is fast and easy, for both words and phrases (skyscraper = dash dot dot). Slashes or dashes show the leng-thened syllable. A major advantage is that the words themselves need not be written on the blackboard, so even long utterances can be represented in seconds.

    international  . . / .       establishment  . / . .
    pronunciation  . . . / .    What time is it?  . / . .
    Could you please give him a message?  . . / / . . . / .

### Percentages and secondary stress

We shall look at this type of indicator again, when we deal with the rhythms of continuous speech. By using this system you can indicate the approximate length of the syllables as well as the force with which they are uttered. The number of syllables is divided into one hundred percent, and the stressed syllable gets the lion's share of the time. The system also shows **secondary stress** in those polysyllabic words which have have such a pattern:

    archbishop     30%  50%  20%

The syllable *arch* is longer than *shop* but *bish* gets the main emphasis.

    moneychanger    40%  15%  30%  15%

The two reduced vowels receive less value than the third syllable, which retains its full vowel value but is shorter than the first syllable.

It's a nice one.   20%   20%   40%   20%

There are four syllables. The third is emphasised and the others are about equal in length.

*Conducting*
Stress patterns can be shown by conducting the rhythm like a musician as the class choruses polysyllabic words or phrases.

*Clapping*
It is often quickest just to clap the stress pattern of a word or the rhythm of a short phrase, with the stressed syllables receiving a louder clap and slight pause;

Pass the salt, please. CLAP clap CLAP (pause) CLAP

*Denial drill*
This offers practice in shifting the stress. You change one item at a time in the sentence and the students contradict you. They do this by shifting the stress and changing the intonation and the rhythm of the phrase. A typical example could be based on the following sentence, written on the blackboard:

Mr Jones was late this morning.

TEACHER:    Mr *Smith* was late this morning.
STUDENTS:  No. Mr *Jones* was late this morning.
TEACHER:    Mr Jones was late *yesterday*.
STUDENTS:  No. Mr Jones was late this *morning*.
TEACHER:    Mr Jones was *on time* this morning.
STUDENTS:  No. Mr Jones was *late* this morning.
TEACHER:    *Mrs* Jones was late this morning.
STUDENTS:  No, *Mr* . . .

*Decoding telegrams*
A good way to get students thinking about the words that are to be stressed in speech is to get them decoding telegrams. The class is given a telegram stimulus of this sort, on the blackboard:

Delayed. Arriving late. Meet Waterloo Station, exit platform.

From that the learners construct a message as it might be spoken on the telephone, providing all the unstressed words:

We've been de*layed*. We'll ar*rive* a bit *late*. We'll *meet* you at the *exit* from the *plat*form, at *Water*loo *Sta*tion.

### Writing telegrams

An alternative procedure to that above is for you to write a full message on the board and have the students work in pairs to write out a telegram. After a public check an agreed version can be put on the board. The words of this telegram are then underlined in the original full version. When the sentence is read out, with the underlined words receiving stress, the sentence ought to sound authentic.

### Key word dictation

This technique is similar in some respects. It helps the learners realise that key words are signalled in speech and that there is no need to catch every word to understand the message. You simply speak a couple of phrases at natural speed and the class writes down just the stressed words. The spelling is not the focal point here, so the check is oral:

TEACHER: Take the THIRD on the LEFT (students write *third* and *left*).
TEACHER: CROSS the LIGHTS and GO to the T-JUNCTION (*cross, lights, go, T-junction*).

### WH- question

You give a fixed sentence a shifting stress treatment and the learners have to say what WH- question is being answered and suggest why that particular word might have been stressed:

TEACHER:   I saw Mrs *Jones* in the butchers this morning.
STUDENTS: Who! Perhaps she is supposed to be sick/out of town ...
TEACHER:   I saw Mrs Jones in the *butcher's* this morning.
STUDENTS: Where! Perhaps she is a vegetarian/ ought to be at work/ is in love with the butcher ...

## ■ PULSE AND RHYTHM

Each part of a longer utterance can be split into groups, with each **segment** containing one stressed syllable (or **pulse**). In speech the pulses come at *roughly* equal intervals one from the other, regardless of the number of syllables between them.[3] A single unstressed syllable has to fill the time between two stressed ones. **Ghosting** pauses help fill intervals. If there are several unstressed syllables they are packed into the segment, the interval between two pulses. This is why native speakers of English are often accused of mumbling or of swallowing their words.[4]

The phrases below all take the same amount of time to say. Only one stressed syllable gets 100% of the pulse time available before the next stressed syllable is spoken (the monosyllabic word *good*). In the other examples, the stressed syllable is followed by one, two or three unstressed syllables, all of which must be packed into the same short time interval between the pulses. The percentage indicators need not be exact, but they do give the learners an idea of the decreasing time value given to each stressed syllable as more unstressed ones are packed between two pulses.

| A | good<br>100% | /set (of books) |
| A | lovely<br>70/30% | set |
| A | wonderful<br>60/20/20% | set |
| The | loveliest of the<br>40/20/20/20% | sets |

# ■ INTONATION

Intonation is the musical sound of the language. The voice goes up and down in pitch, though not necessarily in volume. Through intonation we express emotions, attitudes and reactions. The same words can take on different meanings, depending on the tone of voice (harsh, soft, sweet, etc) and the intonation pattern. Learners will acquire correct intonation patterns only if teachers always use them appropriately themselves and insist on natural language use in the classroom. One of the greatest obstacles to the use of meaningful intonation patterns in class is an insistence on display language. Composition style answers cause thoughtful, slowed down speech, unlike natural snappy answers which automatically attribute message stress and the falling intonation pattern that accompanies the giving of information.

## Intonation moves

Intonation **moves** are essentially of two types, those that fall and those that rise though there are also rise-fall or fall-rise patterns which are too complex to describe in a chapter of this length and which are often peculiar to the user and to regional varieties of English. To describe such changing patterns as though they were fixed grammar patterns, right or wrong, would not make much sense. Speakers are fairly free to vary pitch in their own way, making what they say sound interesting by means of pitch level. However, there are a few major patterns that most native speakers use and which you ought to respect in the classroom.[5]

Falling intonation usually accompanies positive statements. Key words are often signalled (in addition to stress) by a slightly higher level of pitch with a slight fall. A falling tone has a stamp of confidence and authority. We use it to gain attention, to make statements, in answers, in commands and in certain sorts of question.

## Questions with falling intonation

In questions, an intonation fall signals that the enquirer expects an explanation or agreement with an attitude. Because questions are used so much in language teaching it is vital that you offer correct models. Try saying the questions below with a falling tone at the end of each.

### WH- questions
The words themselves, spoken in isolation, almost always have a distinct fall if the user is genuinely seeking information:

> – Hey, the boss wants to see you!
> – Why ⌐ ?   Where ⌐ ?   When ⌐ ?

### Sentence length WH- questions
The questions themselves almost invariably carry a falling pattern, all through the utterance:

> – What time's the next train?
> – How late will it be?
> – Why's it always late?

### Tag questions
A rising tone with a tag question shows that the questioner is genuinely seeking information (seen later). Frequently, though, a tag question (which is in the form of a statement rather than a query) is used when the speaker is seeking agreement. In this case, a falling tone for the tag is needed:

> – That was nice, wasn't it?
> – She's a good teacher, isn't she?
> – You didn't like that, did you?

### Choice questions
These always carry a falling tone at the end. The pitch goes up for the first key word and falls for the ending:

> – Is it late or on time?
> – Shall we wait or take a taxi?
> – Is there a seat or must we stand?

## Questions with rising intonation

A rising tone indicates uncertainty, sometimes deference or politeness. As well as in polite requests (Would you mind closing the window?) a rising tone is used in **information seeking** questions of this sort:

### Yes-no questions

These are almost invariably genuine questions and the rising tone signals this fact:

- Is the train on time?
- Can I telephone from here?
- Is the phone working?

### Echo questions

These are requests for a repeat of what was said, where the listener is not certain of having understood. The echo can be in the form of a statement (as in the first two phrases). Sometimes the echo is in the form of a WH- question, but the rising tone signals that the person is asking for *repetition*, not for new information:

- Ten minutes late?
- It stops at every station?
- Why is it late (say again, I didn't hear properly)?
- What did he say?

### Informational tag questions

Here the speaker genuinely seeks information or reassurance and cannot predict the *yes* or *no* of the answer. The rise is on the tag.

- It stops at Woodside, doesn't it?
- There'll be plenty of taxis at the other end, won't there?
- Buses run up to midnight, don't they?

## Techniques for focusing on intonation

You can draw attention to intonation patterns visually or aurally and orally.

### Signalling contours by hand

This is the easiest way of all. The up and down movement of your hand shows a rise or a fall as you give a model for repetition:

- That's lovely (with the hand rising and falling on the last word).
- Really? (the hand is raised from one level to the next).
- Really! (the hand is lowered). etc.

### Signalling contours by chalk lines

Another way is to draw lines to show the contours. You can do this without writing the phrase on the blackboard, or you can show the words as well, as in this example:

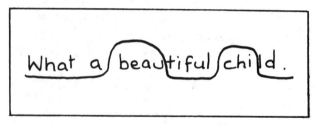

### Echo questions

This oral exercise practises a useful life skill. Often when we are surprised by a statement, or think we may not have fully understood something, we repeat it (or part of it) with a rising intonation in order to get confirmation of what we think we heard. If you wish you can include some transformations, too, as in the last two examples. Such transformations are authentic when they are practised in this real life way:

| | |
|---|---|
| TEACHER: | The headmistress is ill! (falling tone) |
| STUDENTS: | The headmistress is ill? (rising tone) |
| TEACHER: | The electricity's off! |
| STUDENTS: | The electricity's off? |
| TEACHER: | I've forgotten my book! |
| STUDENTS: | You've forgotten your book? |
| TEACHER: | Your father wrote to me! |
| STUDENTS: | My father wrote to you? |

### Echo statements

This is the opposite of the exercise above. You use rising intonation in a questioning way and the students repeat the stimulus as confirmation:

| | |
|---|---|
| TEACHER: | It's an eight o'clock start? (rising intonation) |
| STUDENTS: | It's an eight o'clock start! (falling intonation) |
| TEACHER: | She'll be here on time? |

etc.

## ■ CONCLUSION

It is vital that learners be made aware of the parasegmental features of speech from the early stages of learning. These important features are sometimes overlooked as teachers rush to get students stringing words together. Learners may well benefit from an early explanation, in their mother tongue, of the differences between the patterns of their own language and those of English. Stress is at the heart of the matter, affecting both rhythm and the intonation patterns. There are many ways to focus on stress, to practise it and even play with it. Time spent on the prosodics is time well spent.

## Notes

[1] Stress, tone, pitch, length, rhythm and so on are referred to as **suprasegmental** or **prosodic** features. They are superimposed on *sequences of sounds*. In the chapter *Songs and Rhymes*, it was pointed out that when learners sing they seem to have a much better command of the foreign language. That is because the tunes and rhythms impose control of the prosodies on the singer.

[2] Exceptionally, speakers will deliberately emphasise a grammatical word (I said give him *some* paper, not all of it!). In such cases there is no vowel weakening.

[3] The claim that there are equal time intervals between the pulses should not be taken as absolute. Speech is marked by hesitancies, drawls, pauses for effect, syllable lengthening, and so on. However, English *can*, very easily, be spoken in strict tempo, as in rhymes where this feature is exaggerated. A form of entertainment, which started in the ghetto areas of the USA, is **rapping**. Young people chant rhythmically and fast, composing accounts of their daily life, political incidents and so on. They make little or no use of intonation, but they exaggerate the normal stress patterns. The accompaniment is jazz-like percussion and hand clapping.

[4] At the very end of Chapter Thirteen, a nursery rhyme is laid out in a way that clearly portrays the spoken structure. The layout shows the **feet** (each beginning with a stressed syllable) and the **ghosting** pauses that are needed if the rhythm is to be maintained. These same features are evident in everyday speech.

[5] Whenever I read a book on phonology I find something I disagree with, especially in prosodics. Saying the phrases with the prescribed intonation contours, I rarely feel that I myself would ever speak in that way – though the author clearly would. For this reason, what is written here about intonation should be viewed as a guide only. If it serves to enhance teachers' awareness of the features, so that they begin to monitor speakers on the radio, their own speech and that of their students, this chapter will have been of value. A specialist book on phonetics and pronunciation is an excellent investment.

# Part Four

# DEVELOPING RECEPTIVE AND COMMUNICATIVE SKILLS

# 18 Encouraging creative language use

## ■ GENUINE SPEECH

A major objective of most language programmes is to prepare the learners for meaningful interaction, making them able to use and understand natural speech forms. In this chapter we examine ways in which classroom language can be made more representative of real life speech. We are concerned only with opportunities which are independent of pre-planned activities. Ideas for encouraging freer, natural expression during the course of instruction are developed in subsequent chapters.

Genuine interactional speech differs from classroom discourse in many ways. With the exception of the teacher, no-one in the classroom is a fluent speaker. And of course, the general expectation is that language classes should provide opportunities for learning and practice, as well as for discussion and interactive activities. Inevitably then, classroom language often differs from that of the street. Even so, teachers must not allow themselves to be restricted to the language of the textbooks. Students must learn to cope with utterances containing language they have not previously met, and they need opportunities to acquire forms and vocabulary from outside the syllabus. Most teachers have little difficulty in talking spontaneously, making themselves understood even though their speech contains expressions that have not been formally presented.[1] We begin, though, by looking at some features of natural speech.

## Features of natural communication

### 1 Purpose
We greet people, apologise, criticise, enquire, inform and so on. Speech is purposeful.

### 2 Unpredictability
We cannot guess the nature of most speech acts, let alone the exact words. If this were not the case, there would be no point in our talking at all.

### 3 Slips and hesitations
We cannot monitor our speech, as we do written work. Longer utterances, especially, are liable to violate the grammar norms of written language.

Moreover, speakers pause, repeat themselves, rephrase, and use *ums* and *ers* as they organise their thoughts.

### 4 Creativity
Fluent speakers create and understand novel utterances. Even children produce unmodelled language forms. We are rarely conscious of this wonderful gift. We can all string familiar words into new and quite novel sequences.

### 5 Spontaneity
We do not normally plan what we say. We compose as we talk.

### 6 Economy
Words are not wasted. We take into account what others know about a situation, avoiding redundancies.

### 7 Intonation and stress
Through the music of language, we express attitudes and feelings. We can even make changes of meaning evident by the tone of voice.

### 8 Comprehension checks
We look at people with whom we talk, checking if they have understood. Often there is a verbal check (Right?, Y' know? Know what I mean? Yeah?). The listener may nod or make monosyllabic responses.

### 9 Turn taking
Speakers interact, signalling when they want to take over the speech act or to surrender it. Often the hand over is non-verbal, by facial expression or gesture. Sometimes it is by intonation.

You may think of features of natural interaction not mentioned above; the list is not definitive. The intention is to think about real life speech acts and our obligation to prepare students for entry to the world outside. We can do a lot through interactional activities, but there are many other chances for us to use and elicit language which is close to the imperfect norms of day-to-day speech.

## Language for socialising

School is a society in itself. You should use the foreign language in school on every possible occasion. Use a wide range of greetings, thanks, and so on. These small talk initiatives will get the students accustomed to the different forms, even if they themselves stick to a narrower range of formulaic utterances. Why not try some less used phrases for a change?

### 1 Greetings and farewells
*Hello there, hi!, nice to see you, what terrible weather, nice day, lovely morning, evening all, bye, bye bye, must be off, cheerio, see you soon/tomorrow.*

### 2 Enquiring about health
*How are you this lovely day? everyone OK? feeling alright/fit? all on form? are you well? in good shape this afternoon?*

### 3 Responding
When greeted with *How are you?* there is no need to reply with *Fine, thanks.* There are alternative expressions, such as *very well, pretty good, feeling good, terrific, quite well, not too bad/good, a bit tired, not very well, terrible, awful, I've got a bit of a headache/a bad leg.* Gestures and intonation will make the meaning clear, even to beginners.

### 4 Thanking
To acknowledge a small service say *Thanks a lot, thank you very much, very nice, nice of you, most kind, good of you, that was kind,* etc.

### 5 Praising
As well as *good,* we have *well done, excellent, fine, jolly good, nice work, lovely, terrific, excellent, that's nice, I like that.*

### 6 Chatting
Snatch opportunities for a personal word with a few students. Ask about activities and events of the previous evening, about the journey to school, breakfast, the last lesson, future plans ... This helps them relax and creates an English atmosphere. Talk about yourself, your family, weekend activities and so on. Recount any little anecdotes that come to mind during the lesson: *Oh, that reminds me! I remember once ...*

## Management language

The managerial role gives countless opportunities for meaningful language use. To resort to the mother tongue at such moments gives the impression that the foreign language is for practice alone. Most instructions are used lesson after lesson, and soon become familiar to the class.

### 1 Simple commands
In the language classroom things are going on all the time: books are being distributed, collected in, opened or closed. The blackboard is being cleaned, something is being copied, and so on. All of this should be done through the medium of the target language. With a gesture and a figure written on the board, even absolute beginners will open books at the correct page. If you use

the imperative form rather than a polite request formula, it is important that *please* and *thanks* be used lavishly if you are not to sound rude.

### 2 Discipline

Children sometimes talk, fidget, slump in their seats, read comics, lose concentration or eat a clandestine sweet. Problems of that sort should be handled in the target language, with gestures to show the meaning.

### 3 Organising pair work

Sometimes you can turn alternate rows to face the back of the class, creating small groups. A lone student has to be moved to another bench to create a pair. Gestures will enable you to set up these working arrangements in the foreign language, though it may be necessary to **gloss** in the mother tongue the first time or two.

### 4 Phase marking

Lessons normally have two or three distinct stages, each with several steps. Teachers tend to over use *Right, Alright,* and *OK* as phase markers. It is not easy to find alternative expressions, but you can say *now, now then* or *good* in the same way, perhaps with a clap of the hands at the same time. Phrases like the following are useful, too:

> Let's begin ... (the presentation of new vocabulary) ... now.
> Why don't we ... (check the homework) ... now?
> I'd like you to ... (look now at ...).
> I want you to ... (stop the pair-work now and ...).
> We'll stop/leave (the grammar practice) now and go on to ...
> Let's move on to ...
> Stop (the pair-work) now, please.
> That will do.
> Would you all ... (turn to page 27) ... now, please?
> It's time to begin (the copying).

### 5 Routines

The date is written on the board, homework is checked or set and written work is marked in class. The register, especially, offers a chance for comments:

> Any idea where/how Olive is today?
> Anyone seen Imogen?
> That's three days she's been away, she must have malaria.
> Could anyone find out why Cynthia is still absent?

### 6 Backboard work

As you write or draw, keep up a running commentary, involving the students as much as possible. This is known as the **chalk 'n talk** technique. Be self-critical and invite criticism. Building up a sketch, you might say:

Hey, what about that? Isn't that good? His legs are too long? You think so? OK, I'll shorten them. Better? No? Could you do better? You want to try?

The same two-way talk can be carried on when writing:

Now, let's write that illustrative sentence on the board. How does it go? What was the next word? Who can finish it? How do we spell that word?

### 7 Interruptions

An administrator with a message or announcement can be greeted, introduced and thanked in English. Some will join in and try to make their announcement in English. Lateness can be turned to advantage. Even if the student is unable to explain clearly the reason for lateness, the class will have no difficulty in understanding your admonishment:

This is *not* good enough.
I *won't* accept lateness.
There's *no* excuse for lateness.

Advanced learners can explain lateness or absence, but even comparative beginners can be made to appear to make meaningful contributions to the situation. This is done by firing a few yes-no questions at the culprit:

Is this the first time you've been late?
You're often late, aren't you?
Did you wake up late?
Did you miss the bus?
Did you go to bed late last night?
Weren't you late last week, too?

### 8 Misunderstandings

The students should learn a few set phrases to use when seeking help. The following expressions will be useful for them:

Please Miss/Sir.              Excuse me Miss/Sir.
May I ....?                    Do you mind if I ...?
I don't understand ...        What does ... mean?
How do you say ... in English?

## Natural language forms

Students' responses should respect the norms of natural speech if the aim is to prepare them for genuine interaction, and, as we saw earlier, a characteristic of natural speech is its economy. Most WH- questions elicit an answer of one or two words: (What did he eat? where did he go? how did he travel? who repaired the car? etc).[2] The questions and prompts that make longer answers unavoidable are of this sort:

What did Carew do after she . . .?
Why, in your opinion, did Colin . . .?
What would you have done if . . .?
What makes you think that . . .?
Describe . . . !
Tell me about . . . !

## ■ READING ALOUD IN A SPEECH-LIKE WAY

Textbook passages were never intended to be spoken. They are often quite unrepresentative of authentic speech. An exception may be the dialogue, though even this sounds unauthentic when read aloud, as opposed to being spoken. Most language teaching experts agree that it is harmful for students to listen to each others' imperfect reading. In any case, there is no need for this to happen, as the words and phrases in the text can be elicited in more natural ways.

On the other hand, teachers often read aloud as a model and for listening practice. If you do decide to use a passage in this way, then you should deliver it in a way that resembles normal speech. This is not difficult; guidelines were given in Chapter Seven. The following is a worked example:

First the short text is seen, as it looks in the book. This is followed by its *interpretation*, showing how it is *spoken* by the teacher. Remember that the students' books are closed. They only get to see the passage afterwards, by which time they should have little difficulty in understanding it. You have to imagine the teacher's use of intonation and the change of voice when adopting the role of Mr Watkins and when making asides (comments and explanations). Imagine, too, the stressing of key words, and the vowel reductions in unstressed words. The teacher's asides are shown in brackets.

### Text

Mr Watkins asked Joe if he would step into his office. He told him that he had got something to discuss with him. Once Joe was seated, Mr Watkins coughed once or twice. Although he had prepared the little speech carefully, he was nervous and hesitant.

'Joe,' he said, 'I am now sixty-five years old. The time has come when I must choose a successor to manage the company. I have been watching you carefully over the last year or two and I think that you may be the person we need in this office.'

### Teacher's spoken version (with asides and comments in brackets)

Mr Watkins (He's the boss!) asked Joe (Joe's the sales assistant, remember?) . . . asked Joe if he'd step into his office (Hey, Joe! Would you mind stepping in here for a moment?). He told him (Mr Watkins told Joe, that is) that he'd got something to discuss with him. Once Joe was seated (sitting down, in a chair), Mr Watkins coughed once or twice (He coughed . . . hmm, hmm). Although he'd prepared the little speech carefully, he was nervous and hesitant (Mr Watkins is nervous, and he's the boss! I expect Joe's nervous too, don't you?).

Joe, he said. . . . er . . . I'm now sixty-five years old (Sixty-five? That's not really old, is it?). The time's come when I must . . . er . . . choose a successor (That's someone to follow him as boss. For example the eldest son of a king is his successor. Understood?) . . . I must choose a successor to manage the company. I've been watching you carefully over the last year'r two, 'n I think that you may be the person we need in this office (That is to say, the boss's office. Well well, it looks as though Joe's about to get a promotion! Lucky Joe!).

Comparing the two versions, it is clear that the teacher has put on quite a performance. Remember that the asides and comments were quite unscripted, so they would have sounded more genuine than they will when you simply read the spoken version aloud. The reading passage was converted into something reasonably representative of natural speech and the learners would have enjoyed listening to the story.

## ■ THE TEACHER'S SPEECH ROLE AT DIFFERENT STAGES OF THE LESSON

### Presentation and practice

Extensive listening and reading probably enable students to assimilate a language and gain an implicit command of the basic features. So teachers need not feel guilty about talking. The fact that a teacher does eighty percent of the talking in a lesson is not necessarily a bad thing. Nor is it necessarily good. It depends on the aims of the programme and of the lesson itself.

As with all pedagogy, it is probably best to avoid total allegiance to any one theory, new or old. Be flexible, neither constrained nor wholly emancipated by any one view of learning or teaching. Without dominating all the talking time, snatch opportunities to talk about a point of interest during presentation and practice, ensuring comprehension by gesture, drawings and the like. In this way, a rich linguistic environment is created, which fosters natural acquisition.

Surprisingly, perhaps, dealing with grammar points offers an excellent opportunity to talk in natural ways. Although some theoreticians question the value of grammar teaching, few question the value of the talk that accompanies it, provided it is in the target language. Vocabulary teaching offers even greater chances for natural speech. This is especially true of words and concepts like *to ski*, *bagpipes*, or *free press*, which may be alien to the learners' world.

As far as possible, teachers should permit some element of improvisation in what the students say during practice, too. Clearly the level of unpredictability will be lower than during the production stage, but it is possible to leave the students a measure of freedom. When a new word has been presented, they can compose sentences or questions that incorporate the word. When a structure is shown on the board, it can be in skeleton form, to permit the class to be adventurous in composing utterances from the model. Students should also be required to use natural speech forms, with elisions and vowel reductions, in the practice exchanges and when the text is being exploited.

## The production stage

Whatever the lesson type and skill focus, there should be ample opportunities for creative language use. During the production stage, there is a focus on *what* is said, rather than on the language itself. Students are asked to say what they know or think about a topic. They imagine their own reactions or those of their parents to a controversial situation. They hypothesise about what will happen in the future, or what might have happened at some earlier time. They engage in meaningful activities. During this stage, teachers usually abandon the centre floor, but they are still busy. At the side or the back of the class, they are ready to adopt any of several roles:

### 1 Managerial

The teacher is a manager, ready to introduce a new aspect or raise a question to keep interaction going. The planned questions will not be used unless they are needed. There is no need to intrude if discussion is continuing, even if it is moving away from what was expected. The teacher is also identifying students who are not making a contribution, and can gently elicit remarks from the shy or less extrovert students, ensuring that everyone is involved.

### 2 Informant

The teacher is attentive, ready to supply a needed word or expression. Because the flow of ideas is unpredictable, students will sometimes turn for help or pause, obliging the teacher to offer the needed expression.

### 3 Censor

The teacher must ensure that intolerance and prejudicial statements are not allowed to go unchallenged. Unhealthy attitudes to minority groups, the deformed, beggars, other cultures and so on, should be challenged.

### 4 Educator

The teacher will find opportunities to bring in information about current affairs, the target civilisation, historical events, geographical titbits, etc. Such input is valuable in broad educational terms, as well as in enriching the linguistic environment.

### 5 Monitor

The students are combining words and expressions in novel ways, to transmit their thoughts. Inevitably they will exceed their level of competence and make errors by analogy or mistakes because of lack of thinking time. They will also make the slips which are so characteristic of native speaker speech. The teacher monitors the exchanges, helping where necessary and noting persistent errors and obvious linguistic needs. In a subsequent lesson there can be revision of a tricky grammar point, or the presentation of a new but needed structure.

# ■ CONCLUSION

Classroom language should not be limited to the language of the textbook or to a few set instructions. This is not an appropriate linguistic diet for learners. It is vital that teachers widen such impoverished input and offer samples of natural usage if the students are to develop an ability to listen and respond to other speakers outside the school. Teachers should therefore use words and grammar structures that the students have not met formally, ensuring comprehension by rough tuning. The richer linguistic environment gives learners the chance to acquire words and expressions beyond the language of the book and syllabus. English is not just another academic subject. It is a real language which is used to communicate real ideas, things of importance. The students must perceive that this is so.

English should be used for running the class, for social as well as managerial purposes. Teachers should sometimes just chat, informally. Students should learn to initiate and respond naturally, with an economy of words, even in practice. Full phrase utterances can be elicited by the use of appropriate cues. A passage can be transformed into what is almost authentic spoken English, by reading it theatrically and adding sensitive commentary and explanation.

In every lesson there should be opportunities for fluency practice. During any performance phase, the teacher will vacate the floor, but will adopt a range of equally demanding roles off stage. Given freedom of expression, the students will learn the strategies of interaction and are more likely to adopt the features of natural speech. The content will be unpredictable and student talk will be spontaneous and creative. Inevitably there will be the slips and mistakes that are characteristic of the everyday speech of native speakers. The teacher's attitude to errors at this time will be quite unlike that of the practice stage.

## Notes

[1] The term **rough tuning** is used to describe the process of talking to students so that they understand. Like a parent, a good teacher has an instinct for expressing things in ways that are comprehensible, even though this includes using a proportion of lexical items that are unfamiliar to the class.

[2] Some teachers may argue that practice is practice, and that they should force sentence-length utterances to get the students used to composing them. These teachers insist on *proper* answers to their questions. Their procedure is indicative of inadequate training. With properly contrived questions it is easy to prompt full utterances, but in a natural way. Readers who are uncertain how this can be done should refer to Chapter Six.

# 19 Developing listening skills

## ■ LISTENING AND LANGUAGE ACQUISITION

In this chapter we examine ways of enhancing listening competence. Many language teachers regard this as the most important skill of all. Through active listening, it is thought, students acquire vocabulary and syntax, as well as better pronunciation. Some contemporary approaches even incorporate a lengthy **silent period**, during which the students enjoy intensive exposure to the spoken language but are not required to produce it. Fluent speech, it is argued, is a product not of practice in speaking but of participation in receptive activities. The primacy of listening competence in interaction is evident; to engage in any form of communication, we have to understand and react to what has been said. Consequently, learners need to practise listening, as well as engaging in interactional activities.

Seize every chance to offer plenty of natural input in your talk. Provided meaning is evident, through context, pictures or by any other means, you should feel free to use any tenses, grammar or words that you feel you need. This free input can be offered throughout the lesson, as described in our previous chapter. The more the students hear naturally spoken English, the better. The games and activities described here make few demands in terms of preparation or class time, but they will play a valuable role in developing listening competence.

## ■ LISTENING ACTIVITIES

There is no need to contrive an entire lesson based on listening. Active listening can be included in any type of lesson.[1] The warm-up phase offers a ready slot and is especially suitable, as the listening serves to attune the students to the language. Even though some activities require the class to speak or write, this production is limited and the focus is always on listening. The listening games can also be planned as a reserve activity. They are presented here in a rough order of appropriacy by level. The early ones are for beginner classes and the later ones can be used with more advanced learners.

### Listening games

*Simon Says*

This is perhaps the best known listening game of all. The class is given a series of instructions, but they obey only if the command is prefaced by *Simon says . . .*

– Stand up (*no response*)
– Simon says, stand up (*they stand*)
– Simon says clap twice (*they clap*)
– Clap three times (*silence*)
– Sit down (*they remain standing*)
– Simon says touch your neighbour's shoulder (*they do so*)
– Pick up your pen (*no response*)
– Simon says write your name on . . .

*Telephone numbers*
You read out a few telephone numbers and the students write them down. They are immediately checked at the blackboard. International codes and area codes can be included, to make the task more difficult. Dates can also be called out, the twelfth of March 1947 would be written 12/3/47 (or 3/12/47 if you use American notation).

*Clock faces*
The students draw small circles on a scrap of paper. As you call the times, they draw the hands in the correct positions. There is no need for them to write the figures 1 to 12 around the dial. Alternatively, you can sketch a few clock faces on the blackboard and number them. The times shown should have some relation-ship (5 past 10, 10 to 5, 5 to 10, 10 past 5, 5 to 5, 10 past 10, etc.) The class just has to identify the clock by number as the times are rapidly called and recalled in random order. A third way of playing with clock faces is to draw one dial on the blackboard. Hands are added to show a time. You then use the true-false tech-nique, sometimes giving one or two wrong times before the correct one. The hands are erased after each game, to be drawn in again in new positions.

*Bingo and prices*
These two games are excellent for practising numbers and prices. They require the students to have box grids. Both activities are described in Chapter Twelve (see pp. 153–155).

*Which picture?*
If the textbook has lots of pictures you can describe one of them, chosen at random, giving less important details first. The students flip through the book trying to identify the picture as you talk. It need not be one that they have already seen. Alternatively, you can bring in several pictures which have lots of details in common, put them on the board and work with these. The same set of pictures can be used more than once. Students can also be asked to raise their hands if statements made about a picture are true.

*True or false*
This can be quite independent of visual aids. Almost any tense or grammar point can be brought into play:

245

– Yesterday there was no school.
– We'll all be here again the day after tomorrow.
– You've been learning English for 3 years.
– Next year, you'll have been in this school for 5 years.
– Carrie came top in the last English test.
– Most of you used to go to X primary school.
– If I looked in a mirror I'd see myself.
– From this window we can see the President's palace.

### Following directions

If possible, the students should all have a simplified town map, but this can be on a poster or even the board. Instead of place names (pharmacy, cinema, etc) the letters of the alphabet or numbers can be used to identify buildings, as in the example in Chapter Ten (see pp. 132–133). You just read out a route and the class decides where they have ended up. They trace the route as they listen, for example:

> TEACHER: You are at point B. You go straight ahead, across the first street. Take the second on the right and go to the end. Where are you?

### Which way?

The city dwelling teacher can describe the route followed to school that morning. Places, streets and shops are not named, of course. From the description, the students have to identify the streets the teacher followed:

> TEACHER: Which streets did I walk along coming to school? Write down their names. Ready?
>
> I bought my newspaper at the kiosk near the big hotel that the Europeans all go to. I was early, so I went a long way round. In the first street there are two shops that sell medicines. I went as far as an open space, where I turned left. I walked in front of the place where we go to collect our letters, but I didn't look in my box. I took the next road on the right, the one with all the eating places, and stayed on it until I got to the school.

### Guess who

Describe a famous personality, leaving any outstanding characteristics until towards the end.

### Which weekend?

Describe a weekend just spent or to be spent, but giving three versions, only one of which is true. The learners then have to guess which it is. Knowing something of your personality and way of life, the students enjoy guessing and finding out more about your interests and family.

### Name the product

Take the labels from a tin of food or a package. The cooking instructions, ingredients, or any other sorts of information are read out and the class has to identify the product (chicken soup, soap powder, bleach, instant coffee, etc). If you cannot get labels, you can translate the details from a local product. The same thing can be done with a cookery book. A recipe is read aloud and the students identify the dish, which involves a lot of listening, for example:

> Gently fry two chopped onions and four tomatoes in olive oil. Chop in three cloves of garlic, add a bouquet garni and seasoning. Add 5 pints of water. Bring to the boil. Add a sole or other flat-fish and a crab, . . . (fish soup).

### Listen and respond

This listening activity has been left until last, not because it is difficult but because it has become an influential method of teaching beginner classes, called **Total Physical Response**, but more usually known by its initials, **TPR**. It incorporates a **silent period**, to which we referred at the start of the chapter.

TPR is easy to implement and your own beginners might well be given a few hours of intensive listening of this kind. They themselves say *nothing*. They just *listen and do*, internalising the new sound system and becoming familiar with some of the words. You use the imperative form of verbs. Commands and vocabulary are mixed to keep the class alert. New vocabulary is introduced ostensively, with no form of explanation. You simply demonstrate the first time, and again if necessary. Often one pupil at a time obeys an instruction (or chain of instructions) while the rest watch to check if it is carried out correctly. You can include a whole-class commands of the sort seen above in the game *Simon says*, as well as individual ones like this:

> – Ashley, go and stand outside the door.
> – Lorraine. please put your bag on my table.
> – George, go and get Ashley.
> – Lisa, go to the blackboard and draw a table with a bottle on it. Sign the picture.

Gradually, familiar imperative forms and words are strung together in new ways. After perhaps 20–30 hours of exposure in this way, students have an enormous recognition vocabulary and can perform extremely complex strings of commands, as can be seen in this example:

> – Go to the items on the table, pick up the smaller packet of tea and show it to the class. Check the price tag, then go and write that price on the blackboard.

## Passage length listening activities

There are several ways to approach a passage which is one or more paragraphs in length. Such passages have the advantage of linguistic cohesion, with referents, conjunctions and other markers of continuous speech. Also, a phrase is often understood because of the context or something that was said before. These activities are all simple to do in class.

### Spot the words

This is really an aural scanning activity. The class copies a short list of words that may or may not be in the passage they will hear (most, of course, will in fact be heard). The key words are dictated, but out of sequence, and written in the students' rough books. All they have to do then is tick off the words if they hear them. Sometimes a word is used more than once; if so, they have to note how many times it occurs.

### List the items

The passage should include a variety of topic vocabulary (eg vehicles, fruit, clothing, shops). Afterwards the learners try to recall the exact items mentioned. As an extension, they could be asked to suggest items that might have been included but were not, turning the listening practice into vocabulary revision.

### Jigsaw listening

You work with a paragraph, perhaps four or five sentences long. The class listens intently as the sentences are read, but out of sequence and with a short pause after each one. Then the students think for a moment and write down the order in which they think the sentences should have been spoken, using only figures to show the sequence. It may be necessary for the jumbled sentences to be read out more than once, but this suits your aim – to offer listening practice.

### Cloze listening

The **cloze** (gapped text) procedure (see Chapter Fifteen, pp. 194–195) can also be used for listening, if the passage is not too difficult. You can compose your own passages if you prefer. You just read out a passage or dialogue, deleting some content words. Normally one deletion in each sentence is enough. The students have to suggest words that are appropriate for the gaps. Sometimes more than one word is possible, creating added interest. Two alternative procedures are possible.

**1 The memory cloze** The text is heard once in its entirety. Then it is read again, but with pauses for the class to try to recall the next word. With this procedure quite long passages can be used.

**2 The buzzed cloze** The text is read straight through, but you say *buzz* in place of each deleted word. The *buzz* can be marked grammatically, as in the example. Having buzzed the passage once, you read it a second time. This time you pause after each buzz phrase for the students to write or call out the words they want to provide. It sounds like this:

> When I leave school this weekend I'll go straight to the bus station. There, I'll buy my buzz and catch the bus to Xville, where my family buzzes. My mother will be buzzed to see me because I haven't been buzz for several months. I expect she will have arranged a buzz for me ...

(The deleted words are ticket, lives, pleased/delighted, home, party/dinner/meal)

## Spot the differences

The class looks at a passage as you read it, but with changes of fact. As they listen they try to remember the discrepancies. They may not make written notes. You carry on with your normal lesson for a while and then come back to the reading passage, asking the students to recall the different facts. Alternatively you take a passage that is not in their textbook, speaking it twice but with a slightly different second version. Now the students have to rely solely on listening and memory to identify the differences.

## Dictation

A good old fashioned way to get students listening carefully, this exercise needs no description. You should not worry unduly about precise written accuracy, the aim is to get the class listening and demonstrating comprehension. The normal procedure is a first rapid reading, followed by a steady dictation. It is important that you dictate in **sense groups** of words.

The class must know the rules. Each dictated clause is repeated once only (ie spoken twice). If not, there can be chaos as students request third and fourth hearings. There is a final rapid reading before the public check at the board (students can exchange papers and mark each other's). This gives a total of four listenings and a chance for them to see what they might have failed to understand aurally.

## 7 Dictogloss

This is also referred to as **dictocomp**, and it offers an interesting variation on word-for-word dictation. As the name suggests, the exercise is a mixed skill one. It is a good pair work activity. A step by step description of the procedure will be helpful:

**1 Key word identification**. The text is read aloud at a normal speed. The students can note any key words. They compare their words with those of their partners.

**2 Second listening**. The text is read a second time, still at normal speed. The students compare key word notes again, perhaps with those of neighbouring pairs, as well.

**3 Reconstruction**. The pairs try to reconstruct the original text, recycling the key words they have noted. You circulate and monitor.

**4 Pairs exchange their written versions with one or two nearby pairs**. They read these versions, indicating any errors that they notice. Then they make changes or additions to their own version, if they wish.

**5 Public check**. You check by random nomination to ensure full involvement. This is best done key point by key point. Only after hearing two or three student versions do you re-read the original version for a comparison.

## Word focus dictation

You write a list of basic word forms on the board, explaining that these words will be heard in the passage, but not necessarily in that order or that form. The passage is read out at normal speaking speed. The students have to identify each word and write the form in which it was spoken. An adjective may be heard as an adverb, a verb in a past form, a noun in the plural, and so on, as in these examples:

fish (fishing)    catch (caught)    net (netted)
sell (sold)    freeze (frozen)    ship (shipped)

## ■ EXTERNAL AIDS

It is important the learners become accustomed to voices and accents other than your own. Knowing the classes you teach, you automatically monitor your speech and use words they already know – something no stranger will ever do in the real world. They need to hear **natural**, unplanned speech at times. This can be done, even under the most difficult circumstances.

### Class visitors

It is quite easy to find someone who will come and talk to the class for a few minutes about a given subject. Colleagues will drop in, if asked. In the community there are often native speakers or fluent speakers of the language. The visitor will need a prior briefing, rather like the guidance given when they are making a cassette recording (below). You can suggest questions that the speaker could put to the class during the talk, so that the students are not passive. Speakers will need, also, a *rough* idea of the students' ability to follow speech so that they can pitch their talk at a comprehensible level.

Visitors who have no training in pedagogy will need advice on their presentation. They cannot simply talk *at* the class for five minutes. You should provide them with supporting visuals or advise them on ones that they can bring in themselves. Pictures of their home or family, a tourist poster, a newspaper or other realia are most interesting to a class. Visitors need to be told how to use the blackboard to support their talk with a title and sub-titles. Even an occasional key word on the board offers a change of focus and helps students follow.

### Types of recorded materials

Even if you personally have no wish or opportunity to use a tape player, please read on, as some of the underlying principles in respect of materials are important and may help you improve your own treatment of spoken texts. Thanks to batteries, tape players can be used anywhere, provided they are big enough to be heard clearly. Through recordings, the class can be offered the chance to hear naturally spoken English, with elisions, linked consonants, weakened vowels and all the hesitations, false starts and imperfections of unplanned speech. Equally important, you can introduce new voices into the classroom.

The content of recorded material you use will depend on the age of the learners, the nature of the course followed, the availability of speakers to make recordings and the clarity with which anglophone broadcasts can be picked up. Where professional recordings of textbook materials are not available, you can contrive home-made ones to support the course. The investment of time is not great, and the tapes can be used year after year. The types of text recorded will fall into three main categories:

### Authentic texts

These are recordings made from the radio, live recordings made in the street or market place, unedited and unscripted talks or discussions by native speakers, and so on. They are suitable for advanced classes for the most part, as you can exercise no control over the content.[2]

### Scripted texts

These are recordings of fluent speakers reading exactly what is on a page, but trying to sound spontaneous. Published textbook support materials are of this sort. They are not at all representative of the ways in which people really speak to each other, but they can be very useful, even so. They are certainly better than no listening at all.

### Semi-scripted texts

These are a useful compromise for teachers who want to exercise some control but who, even so, want a class to hear more or less authentic forms. The speakers are given guidelines but are free to express these ideas in their own ways. An example is seen later.

## Guidelines for making recordings

Below are some ideas for recording authentic, scripted and semi-scripted texts for teaching purposes.

### Textbook passages

Passages from the textbook can be recorded so they can be heard as well as (or instead of) being seen. Native speaker informants will often be prepared to record textbook passages and dialogues. It is easy and takes very little time. If you do not need the exact words in the passage, you can turn it into something more representative of a good listening passage in this way.

Ask the native speaker (or fluent colleague) to read the passage a couple of times. Then put it to one side and get him or her to **retell** the passage. The speaker should not make a conscious attempt to use the exact words or expressions of the original version.

### Dialogues

Dialogues are an obvious target for recording. Males can speak male parts, girls can take girls' roles, and so on. Naturally, the dialogue ought to sound spontaneous. As with a reading passage, it often sounds better if the actors work from memory. Slight deviations from the original are more helpful than harmful. Any hesitations, *ums* and *ahs* are typical of true speech. Sometimes, the speakers can be asked to improvise – changing the setting, embellishing and personalising. Dialogues can be purpose-produced by giving the speakers cryptic guidelines:

A. Introduce yourself politely at a party.
B. Respond, friend of host. What about A?
A. Reply. Foreigner working in country. Job? B's job?
B. Job details. Find out how long A has been/will be here.
A. Respond.

And so on.

### Semi-scripted topics

For topic listening, semi-scripted speech is best. The speakers are told roughly what to say, and the level at which the talk should be pitched, but are left to their own devices as far as expression is concerned. This allows you to control the content to a great extent. For example, the speaker could be given a list of points in abbreviated form, like this:

FAMINE IN AFRICA

a) Regions worst affected: Horn of Africa, Sub-Sahara, etc.
b) Causes; Population growth, increased demands on scarce resources, deforestation. Inept or corrupt government, inter-ethnic conflicts, etc.
c) Role of international aid agencies, the World Bank, IMF, charities (e.g. OXFAM, BAND AID). Attempts at bottom up intervention in economies via the village etc.
d) Long term solutions?

### Radio broadcasts

The radio provides native speakers 24 hours a day. Texts taken from the radio are truly authentic, even though a lot of material is read aloud by announcers, not improvised. There are problems in getting appropriate recordings, but many teachers overcome them. Some leave a cassette recorder going throughout a news broadcast or talk show, in the hope of catching two or three minutes of appropriate materials. It can take hours of listening to find that short text you need. Difficulties for students (and teachers) are not always a result of linguistic complexity. Often problems arise from a lack of the shared knowledge that the radio audience brings to a programme. As a consequence the prelistening phase is often longer than the actual exploitation.

News headlines are eminently suitable for gist listening. In fact, that is what they were intended for in the first place. They normally total only four or five sentences, and are of real interest and relevance. Students will sometimes antici-pate an item through their own knowledge of current affairs, so comprehension is made easier.

The weather forecast is also comprehensible, once the class has been taught the phrases and vocabulary that native speakers actually use (textbook treatment of the weather rarely includes *scattered showers*, *overnight frost*, and the like). The headlines and the weather can be used frequently, even at fairly early levels, as a change of activity or as the basis of an entire listening lesson. In such a case you would add the recording of the expanded follow up to one or more of the headlines.[3]

### Exchanges

School-to-school exchange tapes always attract a lot of interest from students. Audio cassettes are easily posted, and teachers can, if they want to be helpful, include a transcript of what is on the tape. The same applies to video tapes, if you are lucky enough to have such equipment. Where both schools are in a foreign language situation (eg British children learning French and corresponding with a French school) it is best if the students speak and write their mother tongue rather than the target language. This gives a good model to both sets of students and genuinely authentic language. Where both schools are in an EFL situation, it must be accepted that the English spoken and heard will be inferior. Nevertheless, such tapes are motivating and interesting because of their unpredictability. A school to school link can have enormous benefits in terms of motivation, language improvement and general education.[4]

## ■ CONCLUSION

If interaction with other speakers is an objective; if students are to learn to cope with spoken language that contains words and structures they have never been taught; if they are to be offered the rich input so necessary for the acquisition process; then they must be exposed to authentic speech. Listening skills must be given the major emphasis from the start of a language programme. Learners may well benefit from an initial silent period, during which they internalise the phonology of the new language while demonstrating comprehension in non-verbal ways. From then on, listening game and activities ought to be a regular part of their diet.

Native speakers can often be persuaded to take part in lessons. If this is to be successful, their contribution needs planning and advice from the teacher. They cannot simply become a target for questions. Nor can they just be told to talk about something that interests the class. They need clear guidelines. To have a native speaker talking in an incomprehensible way would be disastrous in its effects on motivation.

Recordings offer a good, more easily controlled alternative to the live speaker. Sometimes teachers will be fortunate enough to capture off-air texts that are at a suitable level. Semi-scripted texts, made by fluent speakers, offer near authentic models of everyday speech.

### Notes

[1] See Chapter Eight (pp. 84–87) for the steps of a model listening lesson based upon a passage from a textbook. The plan of that same lesson is given in Chapter Eleven (pp. 143–144).

[2] Authentic listening material comprises anything that was really intended to be heard in real life; such as announcements, records, broadcasts, and the like. Copyright restrictions on the recording and use of broadcast materials are really intended to stop unauthorised commercialisation. In practice broadcasting companies seem unconcerned by a classroom teacher's use of the day's news or an extract from a discussion.

[3] As a teacher of French I began every lesson, from the second year of study, with a fast exploitation of that same day's news. All I had to do was get up early, record the French news headlines and decide which words would need prior presentation. Where an item was of real interest, the detailed report of that incident was added. The pre-listening phase was one of elicitation and anticipation, during which the class discussed the items that they might expect to hear. The listening was of a skimming variety as the class checked which of their anticipated items were, indeed, included. In follow-up, the students would ask questions about current affairs or give their opinions. I am convinced that the activity was educational in the best sense of the word.

[4] Where your classes correspond with a foreign school, you may be able to persuade their local Embassy to forward and receive small school-to-school packages through diplomatic channels. Embassies have a Cultural Section whose role is to provide information about their country. The administrators of these sections are usually delighted to help language teachers establish and maintain educational links.

# 20 Developing reading skills

## ■ READING AND LANGUAGE TEACHING

Reading offers language input, as listening does. However, because it is fast and silent, the efficient reader is exposed to much more accurate linguistic content in a short space of time than when listening or engaging in interactive activities. Good readers become autonomous, able to read outside the classroom and to stay in touch with English through periodicals and books when they leave school. Through the rich language environment, readers can acquire a large vocabulary and an implicit command of the limitless language forms, pleasurably and almost effortlessly. Good writing is probably the product of reading, too. We learned to write our mother tongue largely as a consequence of reading, not by practising spelling and writing.

Clearly, reading in the foreign language deserves attention, and reading passages should not be viewed merely as a springboard for speaking or writing activities. An aim of most language teaching programmes should be to develop the students' reading competence. In Chapter Seven we looked at a three-stage procedure for a reading lesson. Now, we look at other ways of introducing reading activities and improving reading skills. Some of the activities are based on texts that you will be able to find or contrive yourself, others can be carried out with typical textbook passages.

## Attributes of real reading

First, we should consider the attributes of reading in our mother tongue. Our pedagogy ought to be influenced by the uses that our students may make of reading skills as language users.

### Choice

We read selectively, when we want or need to, not at prescribed times. We do not read everything that happens to come our way, we choose our texts. We may buy a newspaper but omit whole sections or articles because of their lack of personal appeal.

### Purpose

We read for a reason; for pleasure (a novel), information (a railway schedule, a newspaper), knowledge (a scholarly journal or book), curiosity (a guide book), to satisfy a need (instructions for a new machine), and so on. Our purpose in real reading is not to scrutinise every word or analyse the syntax.

### Strategies

We adopt different strategies depending on the purpose and the text. We get information from that railway schedule as well as the newspaper, but our approach to each is quite different. We do not read a novel in the same way as we do a memorandum from a superior. We might read a difficult document several times in order to understand every nuance. Sometimes we rush through a long article or chapter in a book by just scanning the first and last lines of each paragraph until we get to an especially interesting part, which we read more carefully.

### Quantity

We read a great deal each day. Advertisements, road signs, shop names and posters vie for our attention in the street. Only in a country whose language we cannot speak or read, do we realise just how much casual reading of that sort we do all the time.

### Silence

We read silently in literate societies. Except for TV and radio announcers, people read visually, not out loud. Our interaction with the writer is private.

### Speed

We read swiftly. We can read a passage far more quickly than it could be spoken. Slow readers are often the product of schools where reading aloud was the norm. They often continue to mouth the words as they read privately. An efficient reader can enjoy a thick newspaper, reading selectively, in less than an hour.

### Context

We read through difficulties, coping with complex syntax and strange lexical items and getting the general meaning from the linguistic context. We do not read with a dictionary at our side.

## Classroom approximations to real reading

The list above is not definitive, nor are the features in any special order. What is apparent though, is that standard reading procedures in language teaching classes often have little relationship with real purposeful reading. It is vitally important to bear in mind the attributes of real reading and to vary the texts and the approach to each sort of text. Let us look at each point above in the light of the classroom and see what can be done to improve matters.

### Choice

It is very difficult to allow students to read selectively, as they do in their mother tongue. Typically, the students have only the textbook passage or any passage brought in by the teacher. What is more, language students usually read when told to, not from choice. The lesson times are fixed, as is the homework schedule. You can, of course, increase the students' desire to read a passage by arousing interest in the topic and the interest level of the texts you select is a key factor in enhancing their wish to read. If at all possible, a selection of books should be provided as a class or school library, so that students can choose a book to read at home. This is a point we shall return to later.

## Purpose
You can make class reading purposeful by setting appropriate focus tasks for the while-reading phase and any follow-up that might be valid. The nature of the text should suggest an appropriate approach.

## Strategies
You should cultivate the subskills of reading, and the associated reading strategies. This implies the provision of a range of texts. For scanning you need a page from an encyclopaedia, a page of newspaper advertisements or a text with statistics. For practice in skimming you need a historical passage, a story, a report or something similar. For extensive reading you should provide long and interesting texts that can be read without undue problems.

## Quantity
The more students read, the better. Reading need not always be of passages. Shop signs, headlines, labels, slogans and advertisements offer examples of authentic texts that native speakers and travellers encounter every day.

## Silence
Silent reading should be the norm. Reading aloud by students is at best unnecessary, at worst harmful.

## Speed
It is misguided to allow too much time for reading. You should constantly urge students towards greater reading speeds, but bearing in mind the nature of the text and the task.

## Context
Resist the temptation to explain every new word. Let the students learn to cope with passages which include lexical items and grammar structures that they have not met. Students must realise that they can enjoy a text without the help of a dictionary or teacher. If they persist in reading a lot, and in reading through any difficulties, the students' reading will gradually become more fluent and the difficulties will diminish of their own accord.

## ■ USING AUTHENTIC TEXTS

Authentic texts are those produced for the genuine reader, not for teaching. There is an increasing tendency for language teachers to use these texts, rather than contrived ones. At the same time, these teachers try to ensure that the tasks they set are also authentic.[1] The trend is a good one, not least because most pedagogic texts are impoverished sources of language input. They were constructed to promote oral practice, so they do not develop the sort of reading skills that will be useful to students later in life.

### Availability and sources

Authentic texts are obtainable without difficulty in most countries. Newspapers or magazines are excellent sources for cuttings and offer constant variety.[2] Short stories and novels can be read in their entirety at advanced levels, but selected paragraphs or pages are often usable lower down the school. Recipes, books, labels, poems, instructions, songs, letters to newspapers, airline schedules, advertisements, rhymes, menus, the leaflet from a medicine pack and so on, all offer short reading possibilities. Anything that was written for a native speaker community is the possible basis of a short reading activity or even a full lesson.

*Visual impact*
Authentic texts should be duplicated in their original form if possible, they look more genuine than retyped versions. An editor spent time planning the visual presentation, so it is a pity to lose this. It is enormously satisfying for a class to see that they are working with *real English* materials.

It is a good idea to number every fifth line on any long text *before* you photocopy it. This facilitates the identification of any words or phrases that you or students want to talk about.

### Copying texts economically

Copying can be a problem. Most schools have a spirit copier or a stencil duplicator, and the masters for these can be typed or neatly handwritten. Photocopies are expensive but if you are lucky enough to have access to one, economies of valuable time and of cash can be effected, for example, in the following ways:

*Size reduction*
Two full pages can be reduced on the copier, making them into a single master page (albeit with small print).

*Cramming* cut + paste
Use every bit of available space, do not reproduce blank areas of paper. Two or three short texts can be stuck onto a single sheet of paper and photocopied, to be scissored apart afterwards. Sometimes you can cut a small advertisement from a newspaper and stick that in an empty corner of the master copy, or even along the side. Cuttings from free brochures (airlines, tourist folders, etc) are printed

in very small type so you get a lot of words for your money. If you are creating your own texts, remember that typed scripts take up less space than hand written ones and that two typed pages can be reduced to A-4 size by a good photocopier.

### Non-disposable texts

Ensure that the students handle worksheets carefully and that they never write on them. In this way the copies can be used again and again.

### Pair work

If students develop the habit of working in pairs, only one text is needed for each desk. In this way twenty non-disposable copies will suffice for 50 or more students, seated two and three to a bench.

## Contriving semi-authentic texts

Semi-authentic texts are an alternative to rejecting a text that is too long or too complex. Production is easy. In some cases you need only scissors and glue, for others you need access to a typewriter and duplicating facilities. There are several ways to produce a semi-authentic text.

### Abbreviation

Shorten the original text by cutting out unnecessary words or phrases, but do not change the language of what is retained. With newspaper articles, whole paragraphs can often be scissored out and no retyping is needed.

### Sentence shortening

Reduce sentence length, by removing conjunctions and other cohesive devices. A structurally complex sentence may become several short sentences. Students often have trouble in understanding quite simple language, because it is strung together in a complicated syntactic fashion. The further away subject nouns are from verbs, the more difficult comprehension becomes. If you wish, the original text can be read afterwards, when it will give no problems.

### Simplification

Simplify the text, lexically and grammatically, leaving as much as is possible of the original. Use simple words in place of less common ones. Use an active construction instead of a passive one, direct speech instead of indirect, and so on. Again, the authentic version will be understood with ease after the simplified version has been exploited.

### Recreation

Have the story or account retold by a native speaker informant. Once the original has been read a couple of times, it is taken away and the informant rewrites it in as simple a way as is possible. This creates a new authentic text.

## Composition

Have native speakers or fluent colleagues write letters, advertisements, diary accounts, telegrams and similar texts to order. Ask them to use natural but not too difficult English, using short sentences, but do not restrict them to a prescribed list of words, tenses or grammar points.

## Using textbook passages

Not everything needs to be authentic or even semi-authentic. You will often have to make do with the passages in the book. Do not think that such texts must be treated in a formal way, though. Most of the reading tasks suggested below are valid for textbook passages as well.

## ■ CLASS READING TASKS

Having aroused interest in a text, elicited ideas and presented any needed lexical items (pre-reading stage), the class should be given a purpose in reading. The task, like the follow-up activity, will depend on the linguistic complexity, the level of the class and the interest level. Difficult texts can be used with one or more of the simple tasks suggested below, whereas simple texts can be assigned a difficult task. The ideas put forward at various points in Chapter Seven are still valid, but here are some alternative activities.

## Scanning tasks

Remember that when we scan we do *not* read the entire text. In fact, it would be wrong to do so in the majority of cases. The texts chosen for scanning practice are used for scanning alone. There would normally be no presentation and no follow-up. The aim (to practise scanning) is achieved quickly. After one or two scanning tasks have been carried out the text is discarded so that the class can get on with another activity. All of these tasks are given orally. For example you can tell the class to:

### Find new words for old

This is a good way to focus upon a new word or useful phrase. You can do this with any type of text, authentic or not. Tell the students to find synonyms or antonyms, giving the clues in words that they already know. For example you can ask them to find a word which means *dirty* (*filthy*), to find a phrase which has the opposite meaning of *she was interested* (*she was bored*).

### Locate grammar features

Make a list of specified grammar features, such as all the irregular past tense verbs (*fought, broken*), the prepositions of place, the conjunctions, verb forms ending in -*ing*.

### Find a specified advertisement

Find an item specified on a whole page of advertisements, or the time of a specific radio programme or TV show in the entertainments page of a newspaper or programme guide.

### Compare details
Check a set of brochure cuttings to find which airlines offer midweek flights from, eg, London to Rome.

### Check dates
Using a short biography or obituary notice, ask the class to identify a person's date and place of birth. Alternatively, they can calculate their age at entry to a profession, or their age today (if still alive) or at death.

### Shopping lists
List all the vegetables available in the different parts of a menu or find the cheapest dry white wine in the brochure of a wine merchant. With a long shopping list, note all the products that would be bought in a specified shop.

### Make word sets
List specified sets of words (those beginning with a prefix, adjectives, collective nouns, topic vocabulary, etc).

### Newspaper headlines
Cram a selection of newspaper headlines onto a worksheet and ask the learners to find the one (or more) that treats a specified topic.

## Skimming tasks

Unlike scanning, this involves reading, but done at a fast speed. Most of these tasks can usually be given orally. Ask the class to do any of the following:

### Compare values
Find the best value saucepan, washing machine, divan bed, or whatever you like to choose, from a set of similar advertisements for the product.

### Find and compare events
From an obituary or biography, decide the major achievement of a person's life.

### Select a title
Choose the most appropriate title for a passage from a multiple-choice array on the same page or on a separate worksheet or poster.

### Draw inferences
Draw inferences about the writer's attitude to a situation or topic.

### Decide the question
Decide what question the author set out to answer.

### Create a title
Compose an alternative title or subtitle for the text or for each paragraph.

## Intensive reading tasks

This involves the class in the close reading of a passage, normally a fairly short one. Ask the students to:

### Match nouns and verbs
Circle all the subject nouns or noun phrases and indicate the verb that goes with each one.

### Split sentences
Put a slash between the two or more parts of a longer sentence to show where it could be broken down into shorter sentences. List the words that would be removed in the process.

### Combine sentences
Indicate where shorter sentences could be combined, suggesting the connecting words (link words) that might be used.

### Make summaries
Produce a summarising sentence for each paragraph.

### Reorder sentences
Read a jigsaw sentence paragraph and decide the order of the sentences in the original.

### Reorder paragraphs
Read a longer passage where the paragraphs have been jumbled and reorder them.

### Fill the gaps
Read a gapped passage and provide suitable words for each gap.

### Complete tables and graphs
Read an article and list the events. Complete a table or a graph to present any data visually.

### Take sides
List arguments for and against a proposition, those that are given in the passage and those that the students themselves might like to make.

### Read and choose
Choose among multiple-choice stimuli. These can be at the level of vocabulary, comprehension of detail or inference.

### Select a summary
Choose the best of several summaries of a passage, all written by the teacher, but with slightly different emphases.

### Compare versions
Compare two newspaper reports of the same incident. The students should

make lists of points that are reported in both articles and those that are listed in only one, identifying any factual differences.

### Identify facts
Read an article or report and separate facts from opinions.

### Focus on form and style
List all examples of specified grammar points in the text, such as use of the passive voice, indirect speech, the past perfect simple tense, etc.[3]

## Extensive reading tasks

This implies a supply of long reading passages or books that students can take away to read in their leisure time.[4] It also implies a measure of freedom and non-interference from you, the teacher, so there should be little follow-up. The aim is to get the learners reading for enjoyment. Even so, you have to show interest and allow the students to offer some form of feedback. You can ask them to do some of the following, each time they borrow a publication to read at home:

### Keep records
Just the routine of keeping records of what they have read is motivating and encourages students to read more, especially if you commend avid readers from time to time. Let them keep a little booklet, with the names of the authors, the titles and the date on which they read each book. An alternative procedure is for you to keep a class record, checking the student's reaction when a book is returned.

### Wall chart
Some teachers put a poster on the wall, listing the books available. The students are allowed to initial the titles of the books they have read and award a mark out of ten for each one. This mark is for its interest. A succession of high marks encourages other students to take the book home.

### Make summaries
The readers can be asked to write a short written summary of each chapter or of the book as a whole. This report can be done in their record books or their exercise books.

### Indicate the difficulty
Stick a slip of paper in the front of each book. Ask the students to award a **grade** (A, B, C or D) for the level of difficulty and to initial their award. An A grade indicates that they found it easy, a D shows that it was difficult. Again, a succession of A's and B's encourages others to borrow the book (although you must ensure that it is not too simple for this class). A succession of D's tells you that this book really belongs in the book box for the class above.

# ■ CONDUCTING READING LESSONS WITH AUTHENTIC MATERIALS

Dozens of different types of reading activity are possible, as is evident looking at the activities above. Below, as an example, is the description of a lesson I taught recently, using authentic materials. Several articles in an *Environment Supplement* of the *Guardian* dealt with the problem of population growth. What is more, there was a map with projected population growth for many different regions and countries of the world which formed the basis of a follow-up writing assignment which is described in the next chapter. I used the introductory article, with a worksheet, in the following way.

## Preparing the text

The article (*Simply Dying to be Counted*) was stuck onto a sheet of A-4 and photocopied. It was about twelve paragraphs long and happened to fit a sheet of typing paper perfectly, making it easy to run off photocopies. Sometimes an article needs scissoring and reshaping in order to fit onto the page. When this is done, though, unnecessary paragraphs can be removed to shorten the piece.

*Designing a worksheet*
Next I produced an accompanying worksheet (shown on p. 266):

1 All the headlines from all the articles from this special issue were typed at the top of the page. These provided a pre-reading stage, as will be seen.
2 Below the headlines, I listed the names of people whose views, often contradictory, were explained in the article.
3 The readers were asked to summarise the arguments of each person (for and against population control), writing as briefly as possible.
4 Finally, there were some questions to be answered from the text. The idea was to add an additional task for those who finished the summaries quickly. It was not expected that everyone would do these questions.

## Conducting the lesson

The students were told to use their exercise books for their limited writing. In this way, the whole package can be used again in the future. The lesson was in three stages, in which reading led into a communicative discussion stage.

*Stage one: anticipation*
The worksheet was given out but without the article. The students looked at all the reproduced headlines. In pairs, then in public, they anticipated the topic, the countries, ideas and vocabulary that might be met in the article that they were soon to read. There was no formal presentation of lexis or grammar during this

pre-reading stage as the aim of the reading lesson was to get the students scanning and skimming, using an authentic piece of journalism.

### Stage two: reading

The article was distributed. The students read it, in pairs, summarising the main arguments. Those who finished went on to do the questions. When most had completed the summaries neighbouring pairs compared their findings. As the summaries were literally a few words long, this took only a few moments, but there was a useful buzz of interaction and it certainly served to deepen comprehension for some of the students.

### Stage three: follow-up

Randomly chosen students presented their summary of a viewpoint. These were challenged or improved upon by the others. After checking the new titles that they had composed, we moved into class discussion and students volunteered their own reactions to the piece, which touched upon their own lives. Finally, the answers to the written questions were rapidly checked.

The worksheet is given on page 266. The passage itself is not reproduced, as the content is easily imagined.

## Possible extension activities

I had no wish to exhaust every possibility of exploitation, my reading aims had been achieved. If I had wanted, I could have added a second worksheet, which might have looked something like this:

*Supplementary worksheet*

---

True or False?
Thomas Mann probably died in the: 17th
               18th
               19th century

The European population is:  stable
             increasing
             decreasing

Summary
Fill each gap with one word from the text: Over-population brings about _____ _, which leads to the _____ of the world's life support _____. A recent suggestion is that there should be a _____ for voluntary sterilisation and the withdrawal of financial _____ for families if they give _____ to a second child. Proposals to_____ the growth of population receive accusations of _____ from those who quote the Declaration of Human _____. Others pin their hopes on the _____ of poverty, the emancipation of women and the _____ of birth control and of education. However . . .

---

---

### WORKSHEET: READING PASSAGE

Look at these headlines, from a special issue of a British newspaper. Discuss them with your partner and decide the topic. What sort of statistics might we find? What sort of proposals may we expect to meet? Which countries may be mentioned?

### HEADLINES

Simply Dying to be counted.
Chairman Mao's bleak bequest.
The population bomb about to explode.
India.
The day of doom has been postponed.
World's fastest growing nation.

### READING TASKS

1. Read through the article quickly. Stop each time you get to one of the names below. Read that person's opinion or suggestions carefully. Summarise each reaction or recommendation in a few words, writing in your note book:

| | |
|---|---|
| Thomas Malthus | Paul Erlich |
| Irvin & Ponton | Lappe & Shurman |
| David Icke | Your own viewpoint? |

2. Of the many suggestions for solving this problem, which has the greatest chance of success, in your opinion?

3. Compose a new title for the article.

### FOLLOW-UP QUESTIONS (refer to the text)

What is 'the Green Movement'?
What do the Greens say about Britain?
What is meant by 'the earth's life support systems'?
What is one principle of the UN Declaration of Human Rights?
What is meant by 'stick and carrot payments'?
What is the trend in Europe?
Can you think of any reason why Ireland is unlike the other European countries in this trend?

---

# ■ CONCLUSION

Through reading, students meet and become familiar with new grammar structures. At the same time, they widen their vocabulary. The meaning of unfamiliar lexis is deduced from context. Students who are taught to read the foreign language efficiently and independently can remain in touch with it for the rest of their lives. Their ability to write well and accurately will improve in direct relationship to the amount of reading they do.

There is no need to exhaust every aspect and every word of every passage. The aim is to practise the subskills of reading, not to make an analysis of the text. You should attempt to provide a range of authentic or semi-authentic texts with a variety of follow-up activities, as a welcome change from textbook passages and practise exercises. The tasks should be designed to develop the real life skills of scanning, skimming and extensive reading, as well as the more usual intensive form of reading.

## Notes

[1] Authentic tasks are those that a native speaker would perform in reading those materials. For example, a recipe is read most carefully, but nobody actually reads a page of the telephone directory. Today, teachers attempt to match texts with tasks that approximate to authenticity. It would be unwise to get too worried about this point.

[2] Permission to copy articles for classroom purposes is readily given by publishers in the majority of cases but ought not to be taken for granted.

[3] Although reading lessons are not grammar lessons, this is not to imply that grammar should be neglected. One of the great things about a longish passage is the fact that it is grammar in context and in action. It is quite possible that teachers can speed up the language assimilation process by drawing attention to the formal features and making learners think about, and even account for, the use.

[4] Simplified readers are written by professional native speaker authors, using vocabulary of high frequency and short syntactically simple sentences. They are authentic texts, despite their simplicity. Some are classic novels, retold more simply. Others are original stories. Some work at the *500 word level* and can be read by near beginners (this means a **lexis** of 500 different words, the books are usually about 30–60 pages in length). Others work at a vocabulary level of **1000 words** and so on up to **3000** or more words. This means that you can build up a **book box** for each class you teach. There is a huge range of simplified readers, very modestly priced. With determined fund raising, most teachers can build up a collection of titles.

# 21 Developing writing skills

## ■ WRITING AND LANGUAGE TEACHING

In this chapter we consider the role of writing and the problems of using this medium. We also consider ways of marking written work done by large classes. We look first at examples of controlled writing, then move to guided tasks and freer types of writing. Truly free, creative writing is not dealt with, as it is inappropriate for most general learners.

There have been radical changes of attitudes towards the role of writing in language teaching programmes in schools. A hundred years ago modern languages were taught in the same way as the classics, through the written translation of texts. Then came the direct method of the 1930s and writing was virtually outlawed. Since then, through the audiolingual method and most subsequent innovative approaches, little written work has been included in language teaching. Linguists have tended to view the written language as a secondary, and often quite different, form of expression. It is rare to find accurate writing as an official objective of a language programme today, although it still holds an important place in examinations in many countries.

It is obviously quite true that writing is the least used of the four skills for the average foreign language user. Few school leavers will ever again write the language. In terms of needs and of preparing learners to enter the real world, writing is more difficult to justify than the other skills. However, the school is a micro-world of its own, in which writing holds a most important role. And, despite the research which has been conducted, we still know precious little about language learning in the classroom. If research has taught us anything, it is that no one method suits everyone and that there are many different learning styles in each group.

Whatever our own teaching preferences, it is probable that many students can and do internalise vocabulary and structures through writing. For some, especially the introvert and the cognitive learner, writing may even be the most effective learning mode of all. It would be wrong to exaggerate its importance, but for the eclectic teacher, it offers a useful change of focus and activity and a respite from intensive oral work. The wise teacher will regard writing as a skill which is to be neither overvalued nor ignored.

Moreover, we should not overlook the relationship between reading and writing. The more students read, the more fluently they will write. Some sort of written response is often a natural follow-up to what has been read. Unlike oral work, writing can be done outside the classroom, increasing exposure time but without encroaching on precious teaching time.

## Ways of correcting written work

It is impossible for teachers of large classes to correct all written work, since that would be too time consuming. Moreover, if writing is viewed as a learning and communicative medium, rather than a testing one, it becomes largely unnecessary anyway. This is not to say that you should never check, correct or mark what students write. There are times when this needs to be done, for purposes of feedback or in order to reassure students that their written work is taken seriously. Teacher correction is needed, too, when the assignment has allowed free expression. In general, though, it is better that students check their own work, finding and correcting mistakes and requesting explanation for difficulties. This process has the additional advantage of offering an opportunity for the real use of language, as well. The correcting and marking procedures described below will serve for most of the activities described in this chapter.

### Spot check
Circulate when students are writing, making spot checks. Tick the exercise books that you look at, so that there is evidence of interest. Underline errors for self-correction, if necessary; tell the student how to make the correction. Write *good* in the margin next to a neat piece of work, so that students and parents can see evidence of an interest in the quality of their work.

### Peer marking
Have students mark each other's work whenever possible, under your direction. Checks can be oral for most written work; an occasional uncorrected spelling error does no harm. Alternatively, one student can write the model version on the board.

### Pair work
Have some written tasks done as a pair task, thus reducing errors as well as cutting down the number of books to be checked. Get neighbouring pairs to monitor and correct each other's work.

### Group secretaries
Where a writing activity is comparatively free, have alternate pairs (or threes in large classes) turn around and consult with those on the bench behind, creating small groups. This reduces the number of pieces of work you have to check to a fifth or so of the full number of students. The creative work is done on rough paper. One person from each group acts as the secretary, coming to you for advice and corrections every two or three sentences. As each part is corrected, the group members make a fair copy in their exercise books before going on to produce the next chunk.

## Global marking

Mark free writing by **impression**. With a little practice, you will be able to assign a mark to a hundred full page scripts in less than an hour. This is not a correction scheme, as nothing is written on the papers. Nevertheless, it is an excellent way to assign a grade for your own records.

### The procedure
Despite an apparent casualness, the method works very well.[1] The procedure for marking by impression is as follows:

### Step 1: Skim through each essay
Try not to be influenced by neatness and handwriting. Is it absolutely full of language errors? Is it safe, but boring? Is the spelling more or less correct? To skim a page takes only seconds. It is the impression that is important. Put the paper on the left of the table if it is *extremely good*. Put it on the right if it is *terrible*. A *reasonable* piece of writing goes into the centre. *Above average* (but not excellent) goes to the left of centre. The *below average* (but not terrible) pile of work is built up to the right of centre. This gives five stacks, ranging from A (on the left) to E (on the right) in terms of grades.

### Step 2: Sort stack A
Skim all the stack A essays again, but this time shuffle the best to the top and the least good (of this excellent group) to the bottom.

### Step 3: Sort stack B
Do the same with the stack B essays. Look at the best papers of this group to see if they merit promotion to the bottom of group A. Check whether any of the weaker papers in stack A deserve to be shifted down to the top of stack B. Should any of the weaker papers in the B set be demoted to set C? Again you finish up with the best of the B's at the top, and the weakest at the bottom.

### Step 4: Sort the remaining stacks
Do the same with the remaining three stacks, putting them into a rough order of merit and promoting or demoting a paper as you do so. You now have five stacks, each with their best papers at the top.

### Spreading the range of grades
The five piles of papers represent grades A to E, but this narrow range can easily be stretched if you wish. Each pile has a top section of best papers. A few of these can be awarded a **plus mark** (A+, B+, C+, D+, E+). The central papers in each pile keep the **standard** grade. The bottom papers in each pile get a **minus**

grade (A−, B−, etc.). This gives you a total of *fifteen* categories of grade (from A plus down to E minus).

### Assigning numerical scores

If necessary, a numerical score can be assigned to each of the 15 categories. You choose the range of scores that you want, for example A+ = 20, A = 19, A− = 18, and so on down to a score of 5 out of twenty for E minus.

Alternatively, each of the 15 grades can be given a percentage score. You decide the lowest score you will award (for the E minus papers) and deduct this from the maximum score you will give (for the A plus papers). You then divide the 15 scores into the resulting percentage difference. For example, with an E minus score of 25 percent, the other grades would increase by 5 percent for each step to an A plus score of 95–100 percent.

## ■ CONTROLLED WRITING

Writing is controlled when the outcome is wholly predictable. It is the graphic equivalent of much of the rather boring oral work that is conducted in some classrooms during practice and during the exploitation of the text. One good thing about such written work is that it is either right or wrong, so it can be corrected quickly by the students themselves, in class. Another good point is that everyone is involved and an occasional written task offers a change of pace. The bad thing is the predictability and lack of original expression. The classroom is not the place for too much time-consuming practice of this sort though. The longer mechanical tasks found in some textbooks can be done for homework.

## Examples of controlled writing tasks

Below are some controlled writing tasks that take up very little classroom time (though any of them might well be done for homework anyway) and which are quite enjoyable.

### Jigsaw sentences

This is straight copying, but done thoughtfully. The students must match the halves of several sentences and write them out. The exercise is simple, but the sentences are not always easy to contrive. You have to ensure that all the endings can go with all of the starters grammatically, leaving semantic distinctions alone to make some sentences unlikely. It does learners no harm to copy well-structured absurdities, but it would be harmful if they were to write and internalise incorrect structures. The activity, which needs to be on a worksheet, looks like this:

| A | B |
|---|---|
| Teachers and lecturers | get to visit many countries |
| Ski enthusiasts | profit from long holidays |
| Animal lovers | often go to beach resorts |
| Bird watchers | enjoy game park safaris |
| Tourists | enjoy the countryside |
| Hotel owners | prefer winter holidays |
| Air crews | work through holiday periods |

## Copying with corrections

The class rewrites a paragraph, changing incorrect details. These can be made nonsensical to add some amusement to the exercise, as in the next example:

> British Airways is one of the smallest airlines in the world. Their buses fly all over the country. It is best to check in two or three days before the advertised arrival time. Travellers in economy class are restricted to 22 tons of luggage, in addition to any foot baggage. This should be small enough to fit inside the cockpit.

### Gapped passages

Gapped passages are often used as reading tests, but they are also a good teaching tool. For writing, the passages will be two or three paragraphs long at most. The writing is usually too time consuming to be done in class (except during a lesson where the teacher needs to be free for a while – perhaps to conduct oral interviews at the front of the class), but cloze passages provide worthwhile additional exposure and writing practice if done for homework. The check is rapid, with the words accepted being written on the blackboard for self correction. Any of the different types of gapped passage can be used:

### Pure cloze passages

These have a regular deletion rate (usually every seventh word). They are quickly produced by blanking out every Nth word and making photocopies. The students copy the passage, supplying one appropriate word for each gap. If a grammar word has been deleted there will be a limited choice or none at all, but if the deleted word is a content one many possibilities may be appropriate.

### Modified cloze passages

Instead of making regular deletions, you select the words to be removed. This has some advantages as a teaching instrument, allowing you to focus on a specific area of vocabulary or grammar. The average rate of deletion will be one or two words in a sentence.

## Multiple-choice cloze passages

If you can produce worksheets, a paragraph can be broken down into a series of short phrases or sentences. Each sentence is then provided with two or more options at various points. Some teachers offer **grammatical** choices, others offer **discourse features** or even **content** options. The worksheet might look like this:

---

Switching on the light (he/she/Mr Cossey/Mrs Cossey) looked at the (bedside clock/newspaper/table lamp). It was only (5 am/5 pm). In another hour he/she would be able to(watch the breakfast show/go back to bed/telephone the doctor). (Still/Yet/Now), there was no reason why (he/she) (wouldn't/shouldn't/won't) make a nice cup of tea. (Sitting up/Getting up/Getting out of bed), the old lady . . ., etc.

---

### Find and copy

This is an excellent vocabulary expanding exercise. As well as allowing you to bring in new words and expressions, it gets the students focusing on the parts of the text that merit special attention. The writing can be of words, phrases or of whole sentences. The assignments can be given orally, as in these examples:

- Write out the words in the passage that give an impression of steaminess, of vapour (*humid* and *damp*).
- Write out the sentence that tell us that these people were walking in long grass (*They walked through the meadow*).
- List all the past forms of verbs in the passage and try to give their basic forms.

### Gapped illustrative sentences

When teachers present new vocabulary they often write the new words in an exemplifying sentence to give them a meaningful context. At the end of the lesson, all of this is copied. But there is no reason why the illustrative sentences should not be gapped. After all, the students will all have heard the full sentences more than once during the lesson. When the time comes for copying, you just erase a few words in each sentence. In this way the mechanical task of copying becomes more challenging.

## Dictation

Dictation is enjoying new popularity. A good way to do dictation is in pairs or groups, with students taking it in turns to dictate lines from a passage that they have studied. In this way, students work at their own pace, correcting after each sentence. You remain free to monitor the activity.

### Sentence combining

The class is given a passage written in short sentences. They combine these sentences, using appropriate connectives which are scrambled on the black-board, with extra ones as distractors.

### Reducing

The class copies a passage, taking out all unnecessary words and phrases. The students are permitted to make only minor necessary cosmetic changes to the original structures. This is best done in pairs, with permission to compare work with neighbours.

### Dictogloss

This is essentially a note taking exercise. It is described in Chapter Nineteen (see p. 249).

### Telegrams

The aim is to transmit a message as concisely as possible, because every word costs money. The message or situation can usually be given orally:

> You have been given a few days off work to recover from a badly sprained ankle. Telegraph a relative in another town to say you want to spend a few days with him or her. State the time and place of arrival so that you can be met.

The exercise can be done in reverse, with a letter being written on the basis of a dictated telegram like this:

> FEW DAYS SICK LEAVE STOP MEET BUS STATION 4.15 P.M.
> FRIDAY 15TH STOP ANOUSHKA

However, this last activity could equally be sited in the realm of guided writing, so it acts here as a convenient bridge to our next section.

## ■ GUIDED WRITING

The following exercises are roughly graded, with the later ones leaving more scope for creativity.

## Examples of guided writing tasks

With any form of free writing, it is important to prepare the ground carefully. Ensure the task is understood and that the stimulus materials are clear. Brain-storm the task at the blackboard, jotting down any useful words or expressions that the students feel may be useful to them. This will offer support to weaker students.

### Picture description

The picture to be used can be taken from a magazine or drawn on a poster or portable roller board. The subject could be a famous person, a domestic scene, an event, a shop, a well known building or place, and so on. A good way to begin is by having the students compose a few questions about the picture. These can then be answered in writing in the form of a description. Any needed vocabulary can be introduced at this time.

### Picture sequence essay

The class is shown a series of four to six pictures which indicate a story line. The picture may well be jumbled, if the aim is also to get pairs or groups into discussion. The students then write the story in their own words.

At the checking stage, the pictures are talked about one by one. Three or four nominated students read out the sentence or sentences they have written to accompany a given picture and the other students suggest any necessary corrections. Then the next picture is treated in the same way, and so on.

### Formal practice

A grammar point can become the basis of a guided paragraph, but the practice need not be just a written version of a mechanical drill. To practise the passive voice, for example, the class can be asked to suggest items which are grown or produced in their own country. Then they can be asked to name other consumer products. All the suggestions are written on the board, in two groups. Afterwards the class is asked to say why you have separated them (countable-uncountable).

Next you elicit the origins of the products, together with their destinations and processing. The passive forms of the verbs are written on the board as they are elicited or provided. By the end of the oral work, the blackboard will look like the example shown, on p. 276, and the students should be able to write a paragraph or two about crops, imports and exports, with little likelihood of error.

### Summary

After a passage has been read intensively it can be rewritten in summary form. Clear instructions of this sort should be given:

> Summarise the passage in one paragraph, drawing attention to the five main points.

In this way, the check relates to the major points of content, rather than to the use of language itself.

### Making connections

This is related to the sentence-combining activity seen earlier. This time the class

Cotton Rice Maize Oil Rubber Coffee etc.
IS
(grown, produced, harvested, sold, bought, processed, packed, cleaned, shipped, etc.)

Bananas Mangoes Pineapples Radios etc.
ARE
(canned, frozen, assembled, made, exported, imported, produced, distributed, etc.)

works with an essay length text, but one which is made up of a series of short sentences. The task is to produce an elegant piece of prose, providing appropriate connectors. Because of the length, the model should go onto a worksheet. The text will look something like this:

Mr Purt is an accountant. He is married. He has two children. The girl's name is Emma and the boy is called Alistair. His wife is called Gail. Mrs Purt is a teacher. She works at the Grove school. The school is in ...

*Note writing*

Cues for a note can be given verbally. The cue can be a situation, as in the first example below, or a message taken over the phone, as in the second:

- You call to see an acquaintance only to find him absent. Leave a note to say you called. Explain when and where you can be contacted.

- Hello. 41 44 72? This is a friend of Daryl's. Would you tell him I called? My name's Hans – Hans Heisterkamp. Just say that Hans called. Would you tell him that there's a picnic at the Sporting Club this Saturday and that I'd like him to come along? Tell him just to bring a bottle, would you? Thanks.

*Key word essay*

This technique is often found in examinations. Key ideas are put on the blackboard and the students take these as the basis of their story. The problem is that without visual stimuli (as used in the picture sequence essay, above), there can be little or no pre-writing discussion, so errors are more likely. The cues will look like this:

---

Yesterday, birthday

Susan, 12 years old

Postman, cards

Family, greetings and gifts

Celebration dinner, restaurant

---

*Replying to letters*

The students reply to a stimulus letter. This is written in a natural way, but contains a certain number of requests for information to shape the response. This has to be given in worksheet form as it is too wordy for a poster. It will look rather like this:

---

Dear Friend,
You will be surprised to hear from me after all this time. We are now in Nicosia, in Cyprus, where my dad will be working for another two or three years. How are things with you? Is the family OK? I am at the International School here. The curriculum is a US one. It's all very relaxed and friendly and we have nice small classes. I had pretty good exam results this year. My best marks were for maths and physics. I didn't do too well in Greek, though. How about you? Any changes? Still at the same school? What grade are you in? What are your best subjects? Do write back if you have a few minutes,
                    Your pen pal, Leslie

---

*Replying to advertisements*

The class is given an advertisement of some sort, preferably an authentic one from a newspaper or magazine. They have to ask for details of something or send details about themselves. Several advertisements of this sort can be photo-copied on a single sheet of paper, then separated for use when required.

> SUMMER HELP. Monitors wanted for summer camps on ranch in midwest of the USA. Job entails looking after young children. Six weeks. Applicants should offer some of following: riding, horse care, games, sports, swimming, hiking, music and singing, etc. Also, general work around camp kitchen. Generous pocket money and all expenses. Send details and queries to:
> JB, Hocking Valley Ranch, Logan, Ohio.

### Newspaper clippings

Genuine newspaper headlines can be given as a starter, on the blackboard. From this the students have to try to create the full article, as in this example:

> **MAN FALLS FROM ROOF AND LIVES**

Neighbouring groups can compare what they have written. One or two students can be asked to read out their version. After this, you can read the original clipping aloud, stopping to make any necessary explanations as you read it. There is no need to make any analysis of the text as the aim is to get the class writing.

### Half dialogues

One speaker's lines are written onto a worksheet or poster. As the pairs copy them, they compose the speech of the missing speaker. When they have finished, they can compare their version with that of their neighbours, check it with the teacher and try speaking their parts. Afterwards, a few pairs are nominated at random to come out to the front and act out their parts. The worksheet looks something like this:

> **ARRANGING A MEETING**
> A. ?
> B. I'm afraid not, I'm lunching with a client.
> A. ?
> B. No, not tomorrow either. How about Thursday?
> A. ?
> B. Good, Thursday it is. What time and where?
> A.

### Diaries

At the beginning of each week, and immediately before a weekend or holiday, students should describe their own plans and activities. Usually this will follow some public reporting by you and by a sample of students. As they are writing you circulate, checking and acting as an informant. There is little scope for error, even though every person's diary is different from the others, since the verb forms are those that occur frequently.

### Story completion

To allow individuals to write a story from a first given sentence invites errors. Nevertheless, essay-style work can be done if the class works in groups with appointed secretaries who check with you line by line, as described earlier. One good way is to build up a story, with the writers responding to what others have written. Write the first line yourself. Get each group to write their second line and then exchange papers with another group. They read what the others added and then write a third sentence. They all change again, but with a different group. After four or five sentences, they can be instructed to complete the story in one or two sentences. Afterwards the stories can be circulated for amusement or you can read a few aloud.

## ■ WRITING FROM MAPS, GRAPHS AND STATISTICAL DATA

Visuals such as graphs, flow charts and the like make excellent cues for written work, especially if they follow extensive discussion on the topic. We can take as an example some of the materials cited at the end of the last chapter. There we saw how a long newspaper article was used for reading comprehension purposes, after which the class discussed the problem of population growth in the developing world (see pp. 264–266).

Accompanying that article there was a map of the world which showed the present populations of ten major regions of the world. It also gave the annual birth rates, starkly contrasting the difference between the rate in Europe and the USA and those in Africa, India and other developing countries. As well as providing present populations, the map gave the projected population figures – at the same rate of growth – in twenty years' time. The statistics were quite frightening in their implications.

Having just read a long related article and having discussed the topic so profoundly, it seemed appropriate to do some written follow-up. The map was of a suitable size for photocopying. Each group of four or five students received a copy and they collaborated to produce a factual report, prompted by that map. The title, given orally, was *A look into the future*. It was a vague enough title for the groups to have total freedom in what they wrote.

Each group had its secretary who came out at regular intervals to check what was being written. The entire lesson was taken up with the composition and there was no time for groups to read each other's essays, so all the reports were rewritten neatly by one member of each group (in free time) and they were all stuck onto a large poster and displayed on the wall of the classroom. The maps were collected in to be used again at some future date.

A few days later there was an article in the same newspaper about immigrant pupils in British schools. A professor had analysed public examination results and showed how the majority of immigrant groups are now outperforming native British pupils. The article was perfect for rapid reading and discussion, being fairly short and clearly written. Even so, a couple of superfluous paragraphs were cut out before it was photocopied. This article was used as the basis of an oral lesson. It was given out, scanned, and used as a discussion starter.

An accompanying table in the newspaper, in graph form, showed the average examination scores achieved by English, Scots, Irish, and Welsh pupils, together with those achieved by pupils from ten different immigrant groups.[2] It was perfect for the follow-up written work, in which the students were asked to summarise the passage (which they had seen briefly and discussed a few days before). The graph was copied onto a poster and served as a cue for the short summary. The less able did little more than quote the scores, but others used superlative and comparative forms and even ventured hypotheses on the basis of the discussions we had enjoyed.

## Pen friends

Finally a word about **real** writing. A school to school link is excellent, usually more durable than a pupil to pupil exchange of letters. Where postage is expensive, students can compose a class letter. This is cheap, as only one sheet of paper, perhaps with a photograph or two, is sent. The students can also write to famous people. Surprisingly, perhaps, many take the trouble to reply. Tourist offices or major companies in other countries will frequently enclose brochures and maps with their replies.

## ■ CONCLUSION

The ability to write accurately is not the most important skill for the general learner of a foreign language, but this is not to say that it should be neglected as a tool for learning. A written response of some sort can demonstrate comprehension and all the students can write the responses that cannot be made orally by everyone in large classes. Equally important, the methodology of language teaching should not differ drastically from that of other subjects in the curriculum, where literacy is required.

In general it is better that students write at reasonable length, rather than in isolated sentences. Writing of a purely manipulative or mechanical nature can be boring. Written work needs careful preparation to minimise errors. To write and internalise incorrect language forms can be harmful for learners, so errors should be brought to their notice promptly. Writing should not be equated with testing. Where possible self-correction or peer-correction should be effected. In correcting their own mistakes, learners gain valuable feedback and insights.

Any written task that takes more than a few minutes should be done for homework. Through such written assignments the learners can remain in thoughtful contact with the language outside the classroom. Pair work is often preferable to individual work because it allows consultation, especially if neighbouring pairs are encouraged to compare what they have written and to read and criticise each other's work. With large classes it is better if any free writing is done in groups, with group secretaries. In this way, the number of scripts to be controlled is reduced to manageable proportions.

## Notes

[1] This impressionistic way of evaluating essays has been widely tested and found to be reliable. Marking the same set of essays at a later date, a teacher will rank them in a sequence that is very close to the original assessment. What is more, inter-marker agreement is surprisingly high, for such a rapid and subjective approach. Two or three teachers marking the same set of essays will rank them in more or less the same order. It is stressed that this is a classroom grading scheme, not one that would be used for national examination purposes.

[2] The graph mentioned was only about two inches by three inches in size, too small to photocopy economically. However, the data were easily transferred to a poster, making a list of the fourteen nationalities with their average scores (computed from British O-level and A-level examination grades). Local magazines and newspapers often carry tables and graphs that give clear data for written factual reports. They can be converted into English in moments. Editors and writers readily give permission for articles or extracts to be photocopied for teaching purposes, but it should still be sought – unless the information therein is conveyed in a different form, as were the figures from the graph.

# 22 Developing oral skills

## ■ LANGUAGE, COMMUNICATION AND MEANING

Throughout this book, the concern has been to help teachers develop an eclectic pedagogy based on a view of language use in which the meaning of what is being said is more important than the form in which it is conveyed. Most of the activities, exploitation strategies and games already described have a communicative basis. We have continuously emphasised the need for natural patterns of interaction and discourse and the avoidance of unnecessary display language. Readers have been encouraged to use question types that invite unpredictable responses and provoke unplanned discourse, discussion and argument. So, teachers who have followed the advice given are already developing the students' communicative oral skills.[1]

This chapter presents a range of communicative activities to incorporate into everyday teaching. From them, readers should gain fresh insights into the nature of classroom communication and learn how to create materials that will engage the learners in meaningful face-to-face interaction. This offers everyone a welcome change from teacher dominated activities. Teachers can easily spend too much time telling learners what to say and how to say it. All too often, we prevent them from initiating and expressing their own ideas. If our objective is to enable the learners to use the foreign language as a medium of unself-conscious expression, then we need to include activities which offer practice in negotiation and self-expression.[2]

We begin by looking at **discussion provoking** activities that can be fitted into any type of lesson. After this, we examine some **drama techniques** that need no special materials, other than a prompt of some sort. Finally we move on to **information gap** activities. These normally require special conditions and supplementary materials, but you are shown how to adapt them for large, under-resourced classes.

## ■ DISCUSSIONS AND DEBATE

In previous chapters, discussion was used in following up the text. There is absolutely no need, though, to restrict debate to the topics of printed passages. Anything that is worthy of thought and discussion can be the basis of a communicative session. Debate can be introduced at any time and last for just as long as interest persists. Almost daily, there are events in the local or international press which can be taken up for discussion, with neither text nor visual. By broaching provocative issues and current affairs in the classroom we get the full mental involvement that we seek. We want the students to forget, if possible, that they are expressing themselves in a foreign language. The focus must be on what they are thinking and saying.

## Organising discussion groups

It is best if discussion takes place in groups, with a secretary designated to summarise in any public follow-up. In the small group situation, everyone gets an opportunity to offer an opinion and the supralinguistic features of genuine interaction are developed, too. Eye contact and body language are important aspects of real talk. Students also learn turn-taking strategies, how to interrupt and to express agreement or dissent. And they can talk at a normal volume, not loudly and unnaturally clearly as they have to in full class discussion.

## Using discussion cues

A simple blackboard or poster prompt can provide the stimulus for a lengthy discussion or argument. In newspapers, there are frequently interesting statistics in ready-to-copy graph or chart form. Recent examples in newspapers have been attractive tables, histographs, maps and pie charts showing the following data most starkly:

*excellent*

- world-wide population growth,
- the decline of the elephant,
- the decline of the dolphin and the whale populations,
- the acreage of forests that the world is losing annually,
- the encroachment of deserts into once fertile regions,
- average salaries in countries of the Common Market,
- the cost of postage in different countries of the world,
- a comparison of salaries within Europe for the same job,
- salaries in terms of buying power, Eastern and Western European economies,
- the proportion of workers in agriculture, industry and services in the twelve states of the European community,
- increased life expectancy in France over this century.

Such mainly non-linguistic visuals can even be taken from local publications. They are easily transferred to the blackboard or poster. On p. 284 is an example of a discussion starter from a French magazine, prepared by translating the few words into English. There were several similar tables, showing the many changes in French society over 25 years. This particular table led to animated discussion of the changes that had occurred in the students' own society in recent years.

```
ELECTRICAL EQUIPMENT IN FRENCH
         HOMES (%)


                        1963        1988
Telephone                9           92
Refrigerator            43           98
Washing machine         32           87
TV set                  28           94
```

## Project presentations

Project work lets us extend learning time and gets students doing something original and worthwhile in English. Even introvert students enjoy tackling a project. A project is an in-depth study of a topic of interest to the individual students. They collect all the information and data themselves and build up a document of some sort – usually with text, diagrams and pictures, but perhaps supported by a poster, a brochure, realia or even a cassette recording. An entire term could be allowed for completion. All the research and writing is done in free periods or at home. It is best to let students choose their own projects: fashions, sport, recipes, a historical period, a region of a different country, a city, the life of a favourite member of a rock group, etc.

When a project is complete, the student (or pair) is encouraged to make a short presentation to the others. They will make and use any needed visuals for this, acting as teacher for a while. The rest of the class, not having worked on that particular project, will be interested by what is said. Project folders can be taken in and marked, as part of your ongoing assessment. They make ideal display materials for any open evening, when parents are invited into the school to meet subject teachers.

## Topic talks

Topic talks are different in that they involve little or no research. Nor is written work needed, apart from notes. The range of topics should reflect learner interests as well as examination topics. A list of six or more topics can be agreed by the class, after which the students form groups of four to six, depending on seating, and each member of the group chooses a different topic.

They then prepare their short talk over the following week. On the designated day, members each make their brief presentation to their group. The others ask questions and offer opinions. Learners feel less threatened in the security of a small group.

# ■ DRAMA ACTIVITIES

Role play is used a great deal in situations where the students' future use of the language can be defined fairly clearly. It is frequently found in state schools, as well as in LSP situations.[3] As well as being enjoyable, it offers a mental escape from the classroom. It can be tightly controlled, perhaps as a logical development of a dialogue in the textbook, or it can be relatively free, with considerable scope for imagination and creativity.

Special arrangements of furniture are not vital, though it helps if a small area at the front of the room can be used for acting out. Most role play can be done at the desks. Various way of using drama techniques are possible, even in difficult contexts.

## Role adoption

Role adoption is a term to describe a drama-type activity where just one student of a group or pair takes on a new identity, transforming practice and exploitation of the text into real performance.

When students ask each other simple biographical questions, the activity is unexciting and predictable: *What time do you get up?*, *How do you travel to school/ work? What do you like/dislike most about your school/job?*, and so on. The moment that a chosen student becomes someone else, that same practice becomes **simulation**, with potential for the unexpected. Imagine putting those same questions and similar ones to a student who is pretending to be a doctor or a long-distance lorry driver. Role adoption can also be based upon a character in a reading passage in the text book. One of each student pair becomes a major character from the text and the partner is free to ask any questions of that character. Imagination is allowed free rein. There is the buzz of genuine, unpredictable conversation – with occasional laughter, if things are going really well.

### Introducing role adoption

The first time you use role adoption, bring one good student to the front of the class to take the role. The questions asked by the class will probably be factual, confined to the text or very close to it. With prompting, though, the questions will become more liberated and probing (*Ask her if she ever* ..., *Ask him why he* ...). Answers will then become fanciful and the passage will have served as a point of departure for imagination and spontaneity. Once the class realises that questions can be free ranging, the activity can be done in private pairs. Afterwards, certain pairs can go to the front and repeat their performance. Another sort of follow-up might consist of having the students ask their best or funniest questions of you, as you yourself adopt the role.

## Prescribed role play

In any role play there are two or more actors. Prescribed role play is often functional in focus, with a series of tasks to be accomplished in a specific situation. Usually, the class is taught the needed formulaic expressions and related vocabulary beforehand, in a traditional presentation-practice mode. Some teachers, though, prefer to make the students realise the need for a word or expression by letting them play on until they get stuck and ask for help. Where there is a situational dialogue in the textbook, role play can be contrived to make the students apply the same language in a new context. The criterion of success is the effective (even if linguistically faulty) accomplishment of the tasks. The students act out the playlet at their desks in pairs or small groups. If there are more students than roles they take turns as observers.

Some experts argue that prescribed role play is not really communicative, that it is just another practice activity. This may be so, but most students come to us in order to learn how to function in the real world at some distant date. This type of role play offers rehearsal for such later, genuine communication by engaging the students in simulated situations, forcing them to satisfy needs and express meanings by use of their limited linguistic resources.

In well-resourced language schools, role play is easy because of the provision of reusable materials. Usually, each pair gets a **talk card**, like the one below, on which the successive steps of the scene to be played are written or symbolised.

*Talk cards*

---

AT THE HOTEL

A. Check if there are any vacancies.
B. Ask what sort of room the traveller needs.
A. Explain that there are four of you, so you want two rooms.
B. What facilities do they need?
A. Shower, W.C., preferably a nice view.
B. You have one room only with shower. There is another large double with bathroom.
A. Accept. Check on view from each room. Balcony?
B. Describe. Ask how long they will stay.
A. Two days. Price?
B. Give price.
A. Check if tax and extras are included.
B. Reply. Offer breakfast as option.
A. Accept. Does hotel offer main meals?
B. Affirm. Give prices.

---

It is evident that much of the language needed is printed right there on the card. This may not be a bad thing, especially where the language is new or where a student is weak and needs support. For advanced learners, however, it would certainly be a more challenging task if it were all written in the mother tongue. Another way to avoid giving the students too much of the language they will need is to use cryptic language, as in this example:

```
IN THE RESTAURANT

WAITER: Greet. Assign table. Offer menu.
CUSTOMER(s). Order meal (any questions?)
W. Describe dishes. Help choices.
C. Choose. Drinks?
W. Serve. Check all OK.
C. Bill? Check it. Comments? Pay.
W. Thanks and farewells.
```

In under-resourced schools, teachers just have to put the details on the blackboard or a poster. In such cases you can be even more economical with words by using symbols or sketches to represent ideas. In prompting a hotel scene, for example, you might use visuals like those on p. 288, instead of words.

*Role play at the desks*
Once the students have the outline of the playlet, in whatever language or style is appropriate, they play act it, marshalling all their linguistic resources to convey the messages. After sufficient time has elapsed for most learners to have played through both roles, the pair work is stopped. Next, a short public check is made, with two or three randomly nominated pairs performing at the front. This check is important. If it is not always done, you risk having students waste their time.

## Free role play

This is more difficult, but only in that the students have to devise their own scene. Every playlet created is different in several ways from those composed by other pairs. An advantage is that weaker students can restrict themselves to a few simple exchanges, while more able learners profit from the freedom to be creative and take risks. The guidance is oral, with only a context being given:

- You are going to talk to a landlord about an apartment which you may want to rent.
- You are in a post office in the USA and want to send a parcel home.
- You are in a job centre, looking for summer work.

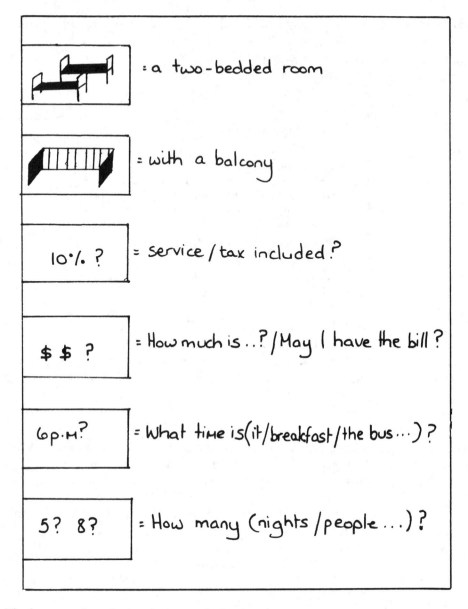

= a two-bedded room

= with a balcony

10% ? = service / tax included?

$ $ ? = How much is ..? / May I have the bill?

6p.m? = What time is (it / breakfast / the bus ⋯)?

5? 8? = How many (nights / people ...)?

The learners then devise their own little play, with two or three roles, depending on the way they want to play out their scene.

*Preparation for role play*
The preparation can be done as a homework assignment, saving valuable class time. Given a week's notice the students can choose their own partners (not necessarily their neighbour) and prepare at home or during recreation periods. As each playlet lasts only a minute to so, a teacher can monitor all or most of the pairs (or threes) in the space of an hour even in a large class.

Free role play quickly becomes a popular event. Even the weaker students enjoy it, as they can devise a part with little speaking and learn their lines by heart. They will even bring in props such as a hat, false moustache, a driver's licence, a credit card and other role supports.

## Free role play from a text

This involves no preparation time at all, for the teacher or for the students, a number of whom go to the front of the class to become the people portrayed in an incident in the day's text. However, they are told that it is one week (a month or a year) later and that they are to act out a follow-up. They can explain why they acted in the way they did, they can accuse others, argue, insult, apologise, say what happened to them afterwards, continue from where the text left off, and so on, depending on the nature of the passage.

The other students enjoy the show, but they can also be substituted into parts as the scene is played out (this will often continue for quite long, enjoyable periods). In addition, other students can join the others at any time having invented a new, related role for themselves: (*Hey, how can you say that? I'm her mother, and she is not at all a wicked girl!*) There is no way to predict ways in which the talk will go; everyone will have fun and there will be genuine interaction and communication.

### Role play activities and continuous assessment

Where there is insufficient time for formal oral testing in the school examinations, you can use these activities regularly and assign scores to students for their participation.[4]

## ■ THE COMMUNICATIVE APPROACH AND THE INFORMATION GAP

**Information gaps** are part of everyday communication. The speaker or writer informant is saying something that the receiver does not already know. The listener or reader is actively decoding and reacting. Then the listener speaks, becoming the informant for a while. The new receiver cannot predict exactly what will be said, and so on.

When a teacher exploits a text with questions, there is no information gap. Everyone in the room can predict the content, perhaps even the exact words, of the response. When a hypothetical question is put, though, no-one can be certain of the responses that will be given. There is an information gap. Everyone listens. People are curious.

Teachers who deliberately exploit the information gap principle are very concerned about **here and now communication**. They attempt to create the *need* to communicate real messages, today. It should not be thought that we have to choose between situational role play and information gap activities. Both fit easily into our repertoire.

## The nature of information gap materials

In schools where information gap activities are in regular use, teachers have access to ready-made materials. Normally, there is a set A and a set B of everything. Students sit in pairs. One looks at worksheet A while the other looks at worksheet B. The two sheets each carry part of the information needed to solve a problem. Sometimes the students are put into conflict situations which must be resolved. This is quite easy to organise if you happen to be teaching small classes, but if you have sixty or more students it is a different matter. By the time you have gone around the class handing out two worksheets to each desk (one A and one B) and have ensured that they are not looking at each other's paper, you have lost several minutes. You may even have lost control of the class.

## Adapting the communicative approach for large classes

Nevertheless, many information gap activities can be conducted in a simple and cheap way in regular classrooms, while still remaining exciting and effective. In its simplest form, the teacher needs only a single blackboard drawing or, far better, a poster.[5] It may seem illogical to have only one visual. Can there be an information gap if everyone can see the same poster? Indeed, there can be, as will be seen. However, when total secrecy is needed, it is quite easy to turn alternate rows of students around, so that half the class is facing the students behind them, just as for group work. In this way, only the front facing rows have access to the information on the blackboard or poster.

More often, the teacher will use the same set-up but with two different posters. One is visible to the front facers, and a different one can be seen by those facing the back of the room. The students talk until they have solved the problem. A third possible set up, even easier, is to have the pupils turn sideways to look squarely at their partner. The two posters are then attached to the two side walls. Each of the pair is now looking at a different stimulus.

## Information gap activities

Let us look at examples of some information gap exercises. Once you have tried a few, you will easily imagine more in the same vein. If you are able to make plenty of photocopies, you may decide to do these same activities in the traditional worksheet way. If so, you draw what is on the posters, below, onto regular sheets of paper and run off as many copies as you need. However, it really is simpler and cheaper to use posters.

### Which face?

This activity is forward facing for everyone. A large poster carries head and shoulders drawings or pictures of about twenty people. There is no need for professional quality drawings. Sketches of the sort shown in Chapter Nine are quite adequate. Make the first outlines in pencil and then go over them with a thick felt-tip pen. Colours can be used, but they enable students to identify a picture more easily. The people depicted should be male and female, old and young, bearded and clean shaven, spectacled and unspectacled, with and without a necklace or a tie. Two women will be alike, except that one wears a blouse and the other a cardigan. Two pipe smokers are distinguishable by the pattern of their ties, and so on. In short, there should be a range of people, each closely related to others in several ways.

Each face is numbered, for identification. To play, one of a pair chooses a face but does not, of course, divulge the choice to the partner, who has to make guesses that will narrow down the field:

> Is the person male or female? Is she old or young?
> Does she wear glasses? Is she wearing a necklace?
> It must be number seven!

And so on

The other way to play is for one student to describe a face in such a way that the other can guess the identity, as in this example:

> I am looking at a man. He is old and bald but he has no beard. He wears glasses. His tie has stripes. Yes, number four! Your turn.

### Who's who?

Photos of people with unusual jobs are stuck onto a poster (or a worksheet if the pictures are small). The students have to decide, in pairs or groups, which person does which job, judging by their faces, dress, age and other visual clues. Collect pictures from newspapers and magazines, they need not be the same size. A set I used recently included a composer, a poet, a jazz singer, a novelist, a BBC executive, a philosopher and a radio announcer. This gets the students talking about the special qualities that are needed to do different types of work, using lots of adjectives. The check-up comprises a show of hands, with randomly chosen pairs justifying a choice, before the true answers are given.

### Describe and draw

This is another single poster activity, but this time half of the class must be turned around or made to face sideways. A simple picture is placed so that only half of the class can see it. Their counterparts have to draw to their descriptions, asking for clarification if they wish. The effectiveness of the communication is seen when the drawers are allowed to compare their work with the original. The same activity can be carried out with two different poster pictures, which is even more fun. Both partners are simultaneously describing, querying, answering questions and drawing.

### Loss of memory

No materials of any kind are needed, so this game is useful for warm-up or to fill the last few minutes of the lesson. It is played in simultaneous pairs, after a demonstration by the teacher. The demonstration is like this – one student writes the name of a well-known personality on the blackboard, but the teacher does not see this name. Then the teacher, who is supposed to be that person but suffering from amnesia, asks yes-no questions to discover his or her character and identity:

> TEACHER: Am I still alive today?
> Am I old or young?
> Am I a man or a woman?
> Do you see me on the TV?

To set up the game for simultaneous pairs is easy. Half of the class turns to face the back momentarily. You write the name of the famous personality on the board, then erase it. The back-facing students can then turn around again and begin to question their partner to find out who they are.

Once the class is familiar with the activity, you can allow them to choose their own personalities, in pairs, with the **knower** writing the name of a chosen character in an exercise book. As soon as the **guesser** has discovered the identity, the knower shows the written name. Then there is a change of roles and the game is played again.

### Which place?

This time there are two posters. The activity offers vocabulary revision with ordinal numbers. It can be played even with beginners. The only structures needed are:

> What's your first/second, etc. object?
> My third object is a ...
> Where is your ...?
> It's in the second row, in fourth place.

On the two posters you portray any objects known to the students; a pen, a watch, a bag, a skirt, and so on. The pictures can be taken from magazine advertisements, but you will need two editions of the same magazine to create the two posters. Each poster carries exactly the same objects, but in a different order. The objects are in rows, perhaps four or five objects across, three or four rows deep. The students have to discover, by negotiation, the two positions occupied by every object (eg the bag is in third place of the first row in one poster, and is in second place of the fourth row in the other). The first pair to finish signals the fact and the teacher stops the activity. At that point, everyone is allowed to look at both posters and check their own work.

### Objects in common

This activity is similar, but much more difficult, since it involves a great deal of largely unpredictable talk. So it can be used with quite advanced classes. This time, the two posters do not picture exactly the same objects; there can even be objects whose names the students do not know, but which they must describe and assign a general name to (eg a *rifle* = a long gun, a *compass* = an instrument to check the direction). As well as noting all the objects that each poster has in common, the students have to list any objects which do not feature on both posters.

To make the task more challenging, traps are set. For example, on one poster there can be a spanner (US *wrench*), while on the other there is a screwdriver; the learners may use a general word like *tool*, and assume that they each have the same one. When they compare the two posters after the activity and check their own lists they realise their error and will also want to know the correct name of the tool that they failed to name. Such traps are easy to set and create great fun – as well as involving the students in a great deal of description, once they know that they need to be wary. For example, a regular wrist watch on one poster can be a digital watch or a pocket watch on the other, a standard lorry can be counterparted with an articulated lorry, a single-decker bus can become a double-decker, and so on.

### Jumbled pictures

This activity is best conducted in groups, with alternate pairs facing backwards. Two posters each carry three or four pictures, out of sequence. Together, the six or eight different pictures on the two posters tell a simple story. Each half of a group can see only half of the pictures, of course. The students try to reconstruct the story. One student begins by describing a picture that might offer a logical start to a story. Then someone identifies a following step, and so on until they have a complete story.

The check is oral. If you want to avoid a long check-up, the students can be asked just to call the sequence of picture numbers. After all, it is the activity itself, the interaction, that is of real value, not the public display afterwards.

### Shared information

Here, each of two posters carries half of the needed information, but with a slight overlap to assist the learners in identifying the matching parts. The completed information will show a railway timetable, a businessman's schedule –in fact anything that can be presented in tabular form. Below is an example of a register of tourists visiting London. There are five items of information to ascertain for each person, but there could well be more (age, accompanied by wife/children) or there could be more people on the register. Poster A, which only one of a pair can see, carries the following information:

Poster A

| NAME | NATIONALITY | HOTEL | REASON FOR VISIT | DURATION |
|------|-------------|-------|------------------|----------|
| Mr Jones | Canadian | | | 3 |
| | French | Savoy | Medical seminar | |
| Ms Parr | | | Consult lawyer | 2 |
| Mrs Abel | | Park | Tourism | |

Poster B has all the missing bits of information. Between them, the two players have just one overlapping item for each person.

Poster B

| NAME | NATIONALITY | HOTEL | REASON FOR VISIT | DURATION |
|---|---|---|---|---|
| | Scottish | Tower | Consult lawyer | |
| Mr Lenoir | | Savoy | | 5 |
| | Israeli | | Tourism | 7 |
| | | Plaza | Consultancy | 3 |

The exchanges will be as follows:

> Have you got a Mr Jones?
> No. Have you a Scottish person?
> No, I haven't. Do you have a Canadian?
> No. Sorry. Have you anyone staying for 3 days?
> Yes. I have. A Mr Jones.
> OK. He's here on a consultancy.
> Thanks. He's a Canadian.

# ■ CONCLUSION

If teachers want their students to become creative in the ways in which they use the foreign language and to develop communication strategies, then they must provide opportunities for interaction in situations where what the students hear and say in reply is relatively unpredictable. Their whole attention must be engaged by the task or topic.

Easiest of all to initiate are discussions, perhaps sparked by a simple visual. Students can also be asked to make short presentations on prepared projects or topics. Afterwards, they are questioned or challenged by their comrades.

Role play techniques range from the semi-scripted, in prescribed situations, to the entirely free. Drama techniques are easy to introduce, they require only a scene setting and a cue of some sort. The necessary language can be presented quite formally, either beforehand or when the students actually feel a need for it. Role play can be done with no change of seating arrangements, though it is motivating if some learners are allowed to act out their playlet afterwards.

To inject unpredictability into face-to-face situations, teachers can devise activities with an information gap, or create conflict of some sort. Proper information gap activities require students to work in pairs, looking at different worksheets. The problem can be overcome in under-resourced situations by turning alternate rows of students around or facing them sideways. They then see only one of two posters, one at each end or side of the classroom. Through questions and volunteered information, they try to complete the task. The achievement or partial achievement indicates the degree of efficiency with which they are using the foreign language.

# Notes

[1] A concern with communication does not have to imply a pedagogy which disregards linguistic accuracy. It would be wrong to permit the class to pidginise the target language in the interests of getting messages across. However, as well as developing accuracy skills, teachers have to offer practice in using language effectively in interactional situations. Our students have to learn to think on their feet; improvising, adapting and simplifying when they lack the needed expressions or lexis, processing and expressing their thoughts under pressure of time. Any major errors will indicate needs for new linguistic items or for remedial teaching.

[2] Some language educators believe that language teaching is most effective when the whole attention of the learners is engaged by the activity, not by the language. Language then becomes an instrument, not an end in itself. The bilingual school, where students are being educated through a language other than their mother tongue, is a perfect example of this philosophy in action.

[3] LSP is the abbreviation for Language for Specific Purposes. Because the language needs of the group are specified, the syllabus is instrumental and targeted narrowly at the participants' future usage (eg English for air hostesses, or commercial representatives). Role play forms a major part of such programmes. It also holds a major role in many European schools, where students can easily travel to the nearby country whose language they are studying. The syllabus is defined from the types of interaction in which the students will be engaged in the near future (buying a ticket in a railway or bus station, sending a postcard at a post office, changing money at the bank), perhaps on a school journey.

The pedagogy is quite traditional, often from the basis of a drilled dialogue. Stage one is a drilled presentation. Stage two is pairwork practice, with substitutions. Stage three is free role play, where the students are encouraged to compose their own playlets, bringing in previously learned language.

[4] It is important that teachers be seen to value oral work, which is often undervalued in formal tests for a variety of practical reasons. Keep a record of each student's participation in oral work of this kind, assigning a subjective grade for effort and fluency. This record can be referred to when reports written. This procedure is known as **continuous assessment**. See, too, the section on oral testing in Chapter Fifteen.

[5] Poster size sheets are freely available in most societies. They can be retrieved from the dustbins of news agents, travel agencies and supermarkets, as well as from notice boards, and so on. Some teachers use sticky tape to make posters from six or more A-sheets.

# Keep reading

This book has no bibliography – not because any of the chapters is considered the definitive work on the subject, but because we believe that teachers who have developed a specific interest will have no great difficulty in finding specialist books to consult or acquire. Those who have British Council offices or American Cultural Centers nearby will be able to make use of their libraries, and in the United Kingdom the Centre for Information on Language Teaching and Research (CILT) in London will be willing to help at all levels. Write to the Director, CILT, Regent's College, Regent's Park, London. Teachers of all languages would do well to look at EFL lists; in general, teachers of English have a much greater choice of books at their disposal, and most of these will be largely relevant also to the teaching of other languages.

Journals are especially valuable, though you should perhaps be careful to choose the more practical ones rather than research journals. Not only will they keep you in touch with the latest news and developments, but they often provide useful material for use in the classroom. If you join one of the language teachers' associations, you will receive its journal on a regular basis. Teachers in developing countries can receive free copies of *Forum* an excellent classroom journal published in the USA. Just ask the editor to add you to the mailing list by writing to The Editor, *Forum*, USIS, Washington, DC, 20547 USA.

Reading such materials will ensure your continued professional development. You will stay in touch with colleagues in other places and learn about their innovations, thus gathering ideas for activities to try out in your own lessons. Be bold! Experiment! And above all, enjoy your teaching. If you do, your students will also enjoy their learning, which is one of the surest ways of guaranteeing success. Good luck!